1995

The Complete Poems of
CHRISTINA ROSSETTI

CHRISTINA ROSSETTI

Oil painting done by her brother, Dante Gabriel Rossetti, in 1848, when Christina was seventeen.

The Complete Poems of CHRISTINA ROSSETTI

A VARIORUM EDITION
VOLUME I

Edited, with Textual Notes
and Introductions, by
R. W. CRUMP

LOUISIANA STATE UNIVERSITY PRESS
BATON ROUGE & LONDON

Copyright © 1979 by Louisiana State University Press
All rights reserved

Manufactured in the United States of America

Design: Dwight Agner
Typeface: VIP Baskerville
Composition: The Composing Room of Michigan, Inc.
Printing: Thomson-Shore, Inc.

1991 printing

LIBRARY OF CONGRESS CATALOGING IN PUBLICATION DATA

Rossetti, Christina Georgina, 1830–1894.
  The complete poems of Christina Rossetti.

  Includes indexes.
  Bibliography: p.
  I. Crump, Rebecca W., 1944–   II. Title
PR5237.A1   1978   821'.8   78–5571
ISBN 0–8071–0358–6

Table of Contents

I *Goblin Market and Other Poems* (1862)

viii   *Table of Contents*

III Poems Added in *Goblin Market, The Prince's Progress and Other Poems* (1875)

Preface and Acknowledgments

In 1898 Mackenzie Bell predicted that "the critic of the far future, of whom we hear so much and think so little, will accord a high place among the great poets of this century to the poet to whom we owe 'Amor Mundi,' 'An Apple Gathering,' 'Maude Clare,' 'The Convent Threshold,' and 'Maiden-Song.'"[1] So far his prediction has proved correct, for today virtually every major anthology of nineteenth-century poetry includes examples of the work which that author, Christina Rossetti, produced during her long literary career. Born in 1830, she began composing verse at the age of eleven and continued to write for the remaining fifty-three years of her life. Her brother Dante Gabriel Rossetti, himself a poet and painter, soon recognized her genius and urged her to publish her poems. By the time of her death in 1894 Christina had written more than eleven hundred poems and had published over nine hundred of them. Although this work has earned her recognition as the greatest woman poet of the Victorian age, there is still no authoritative edition of her poetry. The most inclusive collection to date, published by her brother William Michael Rossetti in 1904, is incomplete, although it is still invaluable for its annotations and memoir. The present edition is designed to bring together all of the known poems of Christina Rossetti.

I have divided the poems into three categories. Christina's published collections, which constitute the first and by far the largest group, include *Goblin Market and Other Poems* (1862), *The Prince's Progress and Other Poems* (1866), *Sing-Song* (1872), *A Pageant and Other Poems* (1881), and *Verses* (1893), as well as the poems with which she expanded those volumes after their initial publication. Her published collections comprise the first two volumes of the

---

1. Mackenzie Bell, *Christina Rossetti: A Biographical and Critical Study* (London: Hurst and Blackett, 1898), 320.

present edition. Within each collection the poems are arranged as they were for the first edition, followed by the poems she later added.

The second category consists of the poems that Christina published individually but never included in one of her collections. In this group are the poems she published in anthologies, on single sheets, in periodicals, or in her own prose works such as *Commonplace, and Other Short Stories*. These poems will be presented in Volume III.

In the third category are the poems that Christina did not publish. This section includes the poems privately printed as well as those not printed at all in her lifetime. Most notable within the group are the poems in the volume entitled *Verses: Dedicated to Her Mother*, which was privately printed by Christina's grandfather, Gaetano Polidori, in 1847 and contains some of her earliest poetry. The unpublished poems will make up the remainder of Volume III. This organization distinguishes the poems that Christina deemed suitable for publication from those which she chose to withhold from the public eye.

I have chosen to do a variorum edition for several reasons. First, it will reveal the poetic process of Christina's compositions, showing her intentions for a poem at a certain time and how they later changed. Tracing these changes will also indicate Christina's painstaking concern for the technical details of her poetic compositions, a concern she believed to be an essential responsibility of the poet. Another reason for doing a variorum edition is that no single authoritative text of Christina's poems is completely satisfactory. The manuscripts, though free of the problem of printer's errors, often do not include the extensive revisions she later made when submitting the poems for publication. The first editions contain most of her revisions but also some printer's errors which, as her letters reveal, Christina did not detect in time to correct.[2] Her

2. With regard to the accuracy of her own first editions, Christina noted a number of times that errors had gone undetected until it was too late to correct them. She wrote to her brother William in 1866: "This morning *Pr. Pr.* [*The Prince's Progress*] actually came to breakfast—blemished, to my sorrow, by perhaps the worst misprint of all left uncorrected. I don't remember where to hunt for some others— and only think of the American edition misprinted entire! However, it can't be helped" (letter of June 4, 1866, in University of British Columbia Library). Her concern for correcting such mistakes in subsequent editions may be seen in a letter to

latest revised editions correct many of the previous printer's errors and sometimes include new authorial changes but are marred by fresh printer's errors. Moreover, it is sometimes impossible to determine whether a variant is an authorial revision or a printer's error.[3] By seeing the variants in the order in which they occurred, the reader who wishes to do so can easily reconstruct the full text of every line. Where there is a suspected printer's error, the reader may come to his own decision as to the correct reading, or at least be aware of the choices open to an editor.[4] I have grouped all of the variant readings at the back of the volume so that the texts of the poems may be presented with as few interruptions as possible.

Following the preface is a list of all Christina's holograph poems that I was able to find and use in preparing the texts and notes.

Frederic Shields in which she discusses the errors in the first edition of *The Face of the Deep: A Devotional Commentary on the Apocalypse:*

> If my book commends itself to you I am truly pleased. All too late I discovered several grave mistakes (some my own, some I think the printer's) which had escaped me in what I endeavoured to make a careful revision. I venture to enclose a list of all of real importance which I have yet observed. Possibly you may like to mark them in your copy. When quite done with, would it trouble you to return the list to me? as I might send it to some one else to whom I gave an early copy. Since those first issued a slip of errata has been prepared and printed, so that I trust the book as now on sale exhibits fewer glaring imperfections (letter of July 15, [1893,] in the Rossetti Collection of Janet Camp Troxell, Princeton University Library).

Christina's printed errata sheet was inserted into the remaining copies of the first edition of *The Face of the Deep,* and the mistakes were corrected in the second and third editions.

3. Some of the errata that Christina found in the first edition of *The Face of the Deep* are obvious printer's errors, such as *there* instead of *their* or *patence* for *patience*. Other errors she lists, however, would be hard for an editor to detect and even more difficult to correct to the intended reading. In the following sentence, for example, Christina asked that the second comma be changed to a colon: "Even natural instinct attests as true the revelation of One Divine, universal Father, the heart's desire of all nations heretofore thirsted for, and now in some measure acknowledges, the revelation of God the Son" (first edition of *The Face of the Deep: A Devotional Commentary on the Apocalypse* [London: S.P.C.K., 1892], 126). *The Face of the Deep* is the only volume for which we have such an errata sheet made by the author.

4. Christina expresses the kind of frustration that an editor or reader may feel when she asks, "Is any book ever absolutely accurate? Kegan Paul says in his Preface that he has added 17 new poets to his re-issue, whereas on careful examination I find (and fail to see any other explanation) 18. I should like to know which is correct" (letter of December 4, 1893, to William Michael Rossetti, in William Michael Rossetti (ed.), *The Family Letters of Christina Georgina Rossetti* [London: Brown and Langham, 1908], 200).

Any new discoveries will be added to the list in subsequent volumes of this edition. The table of editions and reprints (Appendix A) includes second and third editions.

To all of the libraries, institutions, and private collectors named in the list of holograph poems I would like to express my gratitude for their courteous help and kind permission to use their books and manuscripts in the present edition. I am indebted as well to Robert Fraser, curator of rare books, Princeton University Library, for invaluable assistance and advice. My thanks are also due to the following people who kindly aided me in my research: Donald E. Stanford, professor of English, and Dorothy Bankston, instructor of English, Louisiana State University; John S. Mayfield, Bethesda, Maryland; Norman Colbeck, Vancouver, British Columbia; T. A. J. Burnett, assistant keeper, Department of Manuscripts, The British Library; Mrs. Sandra Mooney, assistant librarian, Louisiana State University Library; E. E. Bissell, Ashorne, England; Evelyn Courtney-Boyd, Ayrshire, Scotland. A great many librarians and curators, too numerous to list here, were extremely courteous and prompt in their response to my queries about their libraries' holdings. Without their cooperation this project could not have proceeded. The American Council of Learned Societies and the National Endowment for the Humanities assisted my work with summer stipends, and the Louisiana State University Council for Research and College of Arts and Sciences repeatedly granted money that enabled me to gather and study the necessary materials. I am also indebted to the staff of the Louisiana State University Press, especially to Les Phillabaum, director, and Catherine Barton, manuscript editor, for their help in producing this work. My special thanks go to my husband for his patience in listening to the editorial problems I encountered and for making numerous helpful suggestions concerning the introductory material.

My deepest debt is to the University of Texas libraries, Humanities Research Center, and graduate department of English for their support and encouragement of my project. I would like to dedicate this edition to the University of Texas and acknowledge particular indebtedness to Professors Oscar Maurer, Clarence Cline, David DeLaura, Robert Wilson, William B. Todd, and Gordon Mills, all of the graduate department of English; Kathleen

Blow, head research librarian, University of Texas Library, whose amazing ability to trace elusive references is, to the best of my knowledge, unsurpassed anywhere; F. W. Roberts, director, David Farmer, assistant to the director, and Sally Leach, librarian, Humanities Research Center, University of Texas.

Holograph Poems and Their Locations*

Bodleian Library, Oxford, England
  Nine notebooks of poems, 1845–1856
  Manuscripts of "The Offering of the New Law, the One Oblation
    Once Offered" and "Heaven Overarches"

British Library, London, England
  Seven notebooks of poems, 1842–1845, 1856–1866
  Bound holograph volume of *Sing-Song*
  Bound holograph of *Il Rosseggiar dell' Oriente*
  Manuscripts of "Valentines to My Mother," 1876–1886
  Manuscripts of "Sleeping at Last," "Love's Compass," "A Song of
    Flight," "An Apple-Gathering," "By Way of Remembrance,"
    "Counterblast on Penny Trumpet," "He and She," "Hymn after
    Gabriele Rossetti," "Mirrors of Life and Death," "My Mouse," and
    "To My Mother on Her Birthday"
  Manuscript of "Hear what the mournful linnets say," in Maria Ros-
    setti's handwriting

Brown University Library, Providence, Rhode Island
  Manuscript of "A Year's Windfalls"

Mrs. Geoffrey Dennis, Woodstock, England
  Notebook of poems, 1859–1860
  One of Christina's copies of *Sing-Song* (1872), with her holographs of
    the poems added in the second edition of *Sing-Song* (1893)
  Manuscript of "Michael F. M. Rossetti"

Duke University Library, Durham, North Carolina
  Manuscript of "Methinks the ills of life I fain would shun"

Christopher Erb, Bayonne, New Jersey
  Manuscript of "One Seaside Grave"

Harvard University Library, Cambridge, Massachusetts
  Manuscript of "A Ballad of Boding"

Historical Society of Pennsylvania, Philadelphia
  Letter containing the first stanza of "Passing Away"

  *Any new discoveries will be added to the list in subsequent volumes of this
edition.

Huntington Library, San Marino, California
    Notebook containing *Maude: Prose and Verse*
    Manuscripts of *Later Life: A Double Sonnet of Sonnets*
    Manuscripts of "Behold the Man," "Up-Hill," and part of "At Home"

Iowa State Department of History and Archives, Des Moines
    Two pages from Christina's rough draft of "The Months: A
    Pageant"

Henry W. and Albert A. Berg Collection, New York Public Library, New
York
    Manuscript of "I love very well the first blossoming"

Mrs. Roderic O'Conor, Henley-on-Thames, England
    One of Christina's copies of *Sing-Song* (1872), containing her Italian
    translations of the poems, and the poems added in the second edi-
    tion of *Sing-Song* (1893)

Pierpont Morgan Library, New York
    Manuscript of "A Dirge"
    Manuscript of "Song" ["When I am dead, my dearest"] and part of
    "What Sappho Would Have Said Had Her Leap Cured Instead of
    Killed Her"

Open Collection, Princeton University Library, Princeton, New Jersey
    Manuscripts of "Autumn," "A Coast Nightmare," "A Discovery,"
    "An Escape," "A Hopeless Case," "My Old Friends," "A Prospec-
    tive Meeting," "Reflection," "A Return," "Rivals," "River Thames,"
    "Ruin," "Solitude," "A Study," "Summer," "Sunshine," "Winter. A
    Christmas Carol," and "A Year's Windfalls" (The last poem is not
    in Christina's handwriting.)

Rossetti Collection of Janet Camp Troxell, Princeton University Library
    Rough drafts of eighteen *bouts-rimés* sonnets
    Manuscripts of "A Christmas Carol" ["A Holy Heavenly Chime"],
    "Cor Mio," "De Profundis," "Hadrian's Death-Song Translated,"
    "Heaven Over Arches," "Husband and Wife," "Imitated from the
    Arpa Evangelica: Page 121" ["Hymn after Gabriele Rossetti: Sec-
    ond Version"], "In resurrection is it awfuller" ["By Way of Re-
    membrance"], "L'Uommibatto," "Meeting," "Parted," "Si Rimanda
    la tocca-caldaja," "Time and Opportunity," "Hope in Grief," "O
    Ptimogenita," and "The Succession of Kings"
    Manuscript containing deleted partial stanzas of three poems, in-
    cluding "The Key-Note"
    Manuscript of the first three stanzas of "A Christmas Carol" ["Before
    the paling of the stars"]
    Manuscript of the first stanza of "Up-Hill"
    Manuscript of the short story "Commonplace," containing "In July
    no goodby" and "Love hath a name of death" ["Love's Name"]

Harold F. Rossetti, London, England
  Manuscript of "Sonnets are full of love"

Robert H. Taylor Collection, Princeton University Library
  Letter containing "Mr. and Mrs. Scott and I" (on indefinite deposit at
    the Princeton University Library)

University of British Columbia, Vancouver, Canada
  Letters containing Christina's Italian translations of "Bread and milk
    for breakfast," "Hear what the mournful linnets say," "O sailor
    come ashore," "The horses of the sea," "Oh fair to see," and "If a
    pig wore a wig"
  Letters containing "A roundel seems to fit a round of days," "My first
    is a donkey," "Pity the sorrows of a poor old dog," "The two Ros-
    settis (brothers they)" ["The P.R.B."], "In Progress," and part of
    "A sonnet and a love sonnet from me"

University of Kansas, Lawrence
  Manuscript of "The whole head is sick, and the whole heart faint"
    and the last three lines of "The Trees' Counselling"

University of Texas Library, Austin
  Notebook containing *A Pageant and Other Poems*
  Manuscripts of "Song" ["She sat and sang alway"], "Three Seasons,"
    "An Echo from Willowwood," and "The Way of the World"
  Letter containing the first stanza of "Up-Hill"

Yale University Library, New Haven, Connecticut
  Manuscript of "A Bird Song"
  Fourteen numbered pages containing six poems: "Symbols," "Some-
    thing like Truth" ["Sleep at Sea"], "Easter Even," "The Watchers,"
    "Once," and "Song Enough"

The Complete Poems of
CHRISTINA ROSSETTI

Introduction

The printing history of *Goblin Market* and *The Prince's Progress* dur-
ing Christina's lifetime is critical to the determination of the text of
this volume. The history is illustrated by the diagram on the follow-
ing page. As the diagram indicates, the poems underwent two lines
of development—the English and the American.

In England Macmillan published *Goblin Market* in 1862 and *The
Prince's Progress* in 1866. Christina's extant correspondence shows
that Macmillan allowed her to revise the proofs, although the usual
house practices were imposed upon her spelling and paragraphing.
Subsequent English editions demonstrate continuing authorial re-
vision of the two collections. In the second edition of *Goblin Market*
(1865) Christina sought to correct the typesetting errors that had
occurred in the first edition. In the 1875 volume, which combines
Goblin Market with *The Prince's Progress,* she completely rearranged
the poems, omitting five entirely and incorporating thirty-seven
new ones; she also made some word and punctuation changes and
added some new lines.[1]

The 1875 volume is the last English version of *Goblin Market* and
The Prince's Progress revised by the author herself. When Macmillan
decided to issue a new enlarged edition in 1890, Christina discov-
ered that the first section of the book would merely be a stereotype
of the 1875 text and that she would only be able to make changes in
the second section of the new volume.[2]

---

1. Poems omitted from the 1875 volume are: "A Triad," "Cousin Kate," "Sister
Maude," "Light Love," and "A Ring Posy."
2. In a letter to William Michael Rossetti, Christina wrote, "I find my *Poems*
vol. [*Goblin Market, The Prince's Progress, and Other Poems,* 1875] is stereotyped, but
not the *Pageant* [*A Pageant and Other Poems,* 1881]: so to utilize the former I must
make all additions to what at present forms the latter. Finally of course they will be
numbered in sequence. To achieve a tolerable (?) arrangement I think of keeping
the 2 sets of pieces so far distinct as to style them 'First Series,' 'Second Series,'
respectively" (letter of June 18, 1890, dated by William Michael Rossetti, in the
University of British Columbia Library).

MACMILLAN'S, LONDON

ROBERTS BROTHERS, BOSTON

1862 — *Goblin Market and Other Poems*, 1st edition

1865 — *Goblin Market and Other Poems*, 2nd edition (Some typesetting errors are corrected in this edition.)

1866 — *The Prince's Progress and Other Poems*, 1st edition

1866 — *Poems* (Follows order and wording of the English editions, but contains numerous changes in punctuation and spelling done by an editor at Roberts Brothers)

1872 — *Poems* (Reprint of 1866 *Poems* with only a few changes, all of which were retained in the 1876 edition)

1876 — *Poems* (Revised reprint of the 1872 *Poems*, incorporating the omissions and additions of poems in the 1875 Macmillan edition). Reprinted without change in 1882. Reprinted in 1888 as Volume I of a two-volume edition of three collections

1875 — *Goblin Market, The Prince's Progress, and Other Poems* (Revised by Christina and completely reset, combining and rearranging the 1865 and 1866 collections, and adding 37 new poems). Reprinted without change in 1879, 1882, 1884

1890 (London and New York) — *Poems* (Unrevised stereotype of the 1875 edition, which comprises the "First Series" in the volume). Reprinted without change in 1891, 1892, 1893, 1894

1893 — *Goblin Market* (A separate printing of the title poem)

While Christina appears to have encountered little editorial interference from her publishers in England, she evidently did not have the same good fortune with her American publishers. In 1866 Roberts Brothers in Boston issued a one-volume edition of the two collections, entitled *Poems*.[3] It is apparent from several of Christina's letters that Roberts Brothers received copies of the English editions directly from the Macmillan publishing office and that Christina had no opportunity to make revisions in the texts used as copy for the American edition.[4] The Roberts Brothers edition of 1866 prints the poems from *Goblin Market* first, followed by those from *The Prince's Progress*, maintaining the English arrangement of poems within each collection and following the English wording and paragraphing. There are, however, many changes to American spellings and numerous changes in punctuation which are evidently the work of an editor at Roberts Brothers. In 1872 the American text was reprinted with a small number of changes.

In 1876 Roberts Brothers issued a new edition of *Poems*. Basically a reprint of the 1872 text, it contains extensive alterations. The 1872 arrangement of poems is maintained, but the five poems omitted from the English edition of 1875 are also dropped from the new American edition. Moreover, the thirty-seven new poems added to the 1875 volume have also been included. Seven are inserted in the spaces vacated by the five poems dropped; one is added at the end of the *Goblin Market* section; and the remaining twenty-nine are inserted between "Under the Rose" and "Despised

3. Roberts Brothers of Boston was established in 1833 by Lewis A. Roberts, who was later joined by Thomas Niles. Jean Ingelow, Dante Gabriel Rossetti, and Christina Rossetti were among the English poets whose work was published in America by that firm. In 1898 it was taken over by Little, Brown, and Company.
4. On January 3, 1866, Christina wrote an agent of Roberts Brothers that she would "direct that a copy of *Goblin Market* be forwarded to your London address. ... If I can manage it my forthcoming volume [*The Prince's Progress*, 1866] shall accompany *Goblin Market*" (letter, in the Rossetti Collection of Janet Camp Troxell, Princeton University Library). Christina then asked Alexander Macmillan to "oblige me by ordering a copy of *Goblin Market* to be forwarded to the address Mr. Niles gives in his P.S. I do not know whether you may think it well to let a copy of *Pr. Pr.* [*The Prince's Progress*] accompany *G. M.* [*Goblin Market*]; you approving, I should be well inclined to let him have it at once; but of course the interest of our English edition must be first of all considered" (letter of January 3, 1866, in Lona Mosk Packer (ed.), *The Rossetti-Macmillan Letters* [Berkeley and Los Angeles: University of California Press, 1963], 58). See also the letter quoted in note 2 in the preface herein.

and Rejected." There is no evidence to indicate whether this arrangement was Christina's idea or the work of an editor at Roberts Brothers, but it differs markedly from that of the 1875 English edition.[5] Also added to the 1876 text are some word changes and new lines, all of which correspond to revisions seen in the 1875 edition. Christina's correspondence reveals that the Macmillan office sent her revised proofs of the 1875 edition to Roberts Brothers.[6]

The 1876 edition is the last American version of *Goblin Market* and *The Prince's Progress* revised during Christina's life-time. It was reprinted by Roberts Brothers without change in 1882 and again in 1888.

I chose as the copy-text (or basic text) for this volume the first English editions because they appeared to come closer to the intent of the author than did her manuscripts, which do not contain the numerous changes in punctuation and spelling that she and her brother Dante Gabriel Rossetti made before sending the poems to Macmillan for publication. Christina clearly approved of her brother's editorial assistance with the first two collections of her poetry.[7] Moreover, her correspondence with Alexander Macmillan shows that he permitted her to control the wording, punctuation, much of the paragraphing (that is, line indentations and stanza

5. See Appendix B, herein, for a comparison of the arrangements of poems in her 1875 and 1876 collections.

6. When the new 1875 edition was being planned, Christina wrote to Macmillan about the proof sheets: "I dare say I may count on your obliging me with proof sheets for Messrs. Roberts: may I not? & so excluding any rival edition from the U.S.A. And if so, I am sure you will favour me by letting me have a proof of the 1st sheet for them, tho' this has already passed thro' my hands,—as well as of the others" (letter of March 25, 1875, in *The Rossetti-Macmillan Letters*, 108). Later during her work on the proofs Christina wrote to Macmillan, "One of your name, but I know not whether your son or nephew, sent me the obliging assurance whilst you were away that my proofs should go straight to Boston from your office. This I trust meets with your approval, & I owe thanks both to you & your namesake" (letter, dated "Tuesday 24th" [1875], in Packer (ed.), *The Rossetti-Macmillan Letters*, 113).

7. In an inscribed copy of *Goblin Market* (1893) Christina wrote: "And here I like to acknowledge the general indebtedness of my first and second volumes to his [Dante Gabriel Rossetti's] suggestive wit and revising hand" (inscribed copy, in Iowa State Department of History and Archives, Des Moines). For the complete inscription, see the textual notes herein to "Goblin Market."

breaks), and all of the spelling except for certain common words that followed the house spelling.[8]

I emended the first editions in the following ways: I restored house spellings to manuscript spellings; where the printed paragraphing violated Christina's usual practices, as seen in her manuscripts, I adopted the manuscript paragraphing; I corrected typesetting errors to the manuscript reading; and I incorporated into the text some readings which appear for the first time in the 1875 edition. For that edition, Christina revised the wording of some of the poems; according to the *Complete Catalogue of the Library of John Quinn*, she wrote those revisions in the margins of her own copy of the 1872 Roberts Brothers *Poems*. I have been unable to locate this annotated copy to determine the extent of those marginalia, but all the word revisions described in the *Catalogue* correspond to word changes seen in the 1875 edition.[9] I therefore inserted the 1875 word changes into the text. Occasionally the principles just enumerated were inadequate to determine the reading; deviations from these principles are recorded in the textual notes. The present edition thus furnishes an eclectic text, which, unlike any single authoritative version, is based on a consideration of Christina's extant manuscripts, letters, editions, and individual printings of her poems in journals and anthologies.

---

8. For her correspondence with Macmillan, see *The Rossetti-Macmillan Letters.*
9. *The Complete Catalogue of the Library of John Quinn, Sold by Auction in Five Parts [With Printed Prices]* (2 vols.; New York: Anderson Galleries, 1924), II, 798–99, gives the following description of Christina's own copy of the 1872 Roberts Brothers *Poems*:

> This was the author's own copy, and contains numerous changes in punctuation and spelling in her handwriting throughout the volume. There are also changes by her in the text on pages 23, 34 and 52. A new stanza of five lines has been written on the margin of page 136, to be inserted in "The Prince's Progress," and three new lines have been inserted in "Under the Rose," on page 229.
>
> This revision was for the new edition of 1876, and in this connection there is an A.L.S. [autograph letter signed] from her to the publishers referring to the new edition—decoration on the cover, title-page, etc.

See the variant readings for the "Note" to "In the Round Tower at Jhansi" (for the change noted above as being on p. 23), line 46 of "Noble Sisters" (for the change on p. 34), the title of "Winter: My Secret" (for the change on p. 52), lines 439–44 of "The Prince's Progress," and lines 251–52 and 256 of "The Iniquity of the Fathers Upon the Children" ("Under the Rose").

I Goblin Market
and Other Poems

(1862)

GOBLIN MARKET.

Morning and evening
Maids heard the goblins cry:
"Come buy our orchard fruits,
Come buy, come buy:
5   Apples and quinces,
Lemons and oranges,
Plump unpecked cherries,
Melons and raspberries,
Bloom-down-cheeked peaches,
10   Swart-headed mulberries,
Wild free-born cranberries,
Crab-apples, dewberries,
Pine-apples, blackberries,
Apricots, strawberries;—
15   All ripe together
In summer weather,—
Morns that pass by,
Fair eves that fly;
Come buy, come buy:
20   Our grapes fresh from the vine,
Pomegranates full and fine,
Dates and sharp bullaces,
Rare pears and greengages,
Damsons and bilberries,
25   Taste them and try:
Currants and gooseberries,
Bright-fire-like barberries,
Figs to fill your mouth,
Citrons from the South,

30   Sweet to tongue and sound to eye;
     Come buy, come buy."

     Evening by evening
     Among the brookside rushes,
     Laura bowed her head to hear,
35   Lizzie veiled her blushes:
     Crouching close together
     In the cooling weather,
     With clasping arms and cautioning lips,
     With tingling cheeks and finger tips.
40   "Lie close," Laura said,
     Pricking up her golden head:
     "We must not look at goblin men,
     We must not buy their fruits:
     Who knows upon what soil they fed
45   Their hungry thirsty roots?"
     "Come buy," call the goblins
     Hobbling down the glen.
     "Oh," cried Lizzie, "Laura, Laura,
     You should not peep at goblin men."
50   Lizzie covered up her eyes,
     Covered close lest they should look;
     Laura reared her glossy head,
     And whispered like the restless brook:
     "Look, Lizzie, look, Lizzie,
55   Down the glen tramp little men.
     One hauls a basket,
     One bears a plate,
     One lugs a golden dish
     Of many pounds weight.
60   How fair the vine must grow
     Whose grapes are so luscious;
     How warm the wind must blow
     Thro' those fruit bushes."
     "No," said Lizzie: "No, no, no;
65   Their offers should not charm us,
     Their evil gifts would harm us."
     She thrust a dimpled finger

In each ear, shut eyes and ran:
Curious Laura chose to linger
70   Wondering at each merchant man.
One had a cat's face,
One whisked a tail,
One tramped at a rat's pace,
One crawled like a snail,
75   One like a wombat prowled obtuse and furry,
One like a ratel tumbled hurry skurry.
She heard a voice like voice of doves
Cooing all together:
They sounded kind and full of loves
80   In the pleasant weather.

Laura stretched her gleaming neck
Like a rush-imbedded swan,
Like a lily from the beck,
Like a moonlit poplar branch,
85   Like a vessel at the launch
When its last restraint is gone.

Backwards up the mossy glen
Turned and trooped the goblin men,
With their shrill repeated cry,
90   "Come buy, come buy."
When they reached where Laura was
They stood stock still upon the moss,
Leering at each other,
Brother with queer brother;
95   Signalling each other,
Brother with sly brother.
One set his basket down,
One reared his plate;
One began to weave a crown
100   Of tendrils, leaves and rough nuts brown
(Men sell not such in any town);
One heaved the golden weight
Of dish and fruit to offer her:
"Come buy, come buy," was still their cry.

105 Laura stared but did not stir,
     Longed but had no money:
     The whisk-tailed merchant bade her taste
     In tones as smooth as honey,
     The cat-faced purr'd,
110 The rat-paced spoke a word
     Of welcome, and the snail-paced even was heard;
     One parrot-voiced and jolly
     Cried "Pretty Goblin" still for "Pretty Polly;"—
     One whistled like a bird.

115 But sweet-tooth Laura spoke in haste:
     "Good folk, I have no coin;
     To take were to purloin:
     I have no copper in my purse,
     I have no silver either,
120 And all my gold is on the furze
     That shakes in windy weather
     Above the rusty heather."
     "You have much gold upon your head,"
     They answered all together:
125 "Buy from us with a golden curl."
     She clipped a precious golden lock,
     She dropped a tear more rare than pearl,
     Then sucked their fruit globes fair or red:
     Sweeter than honey from the rock,
130 Stronger than man-rejoicing wine,
     Clearer than water flowed that juice;
     She never tasted such before,
     How should it cloy with length of use?
     She sucked and sucked and sucked the more
135 Fruits which that unknown orchard bore;
     She sucked until her lips were sore;
     Then flung the emptied rinds away
     But gathered up one kernel-stone,
     And knew not was it night or day
140 As she turned home alone.

     Lizzie met her at the gate
     Full of wise upbraidings:

"Dear, you should not stay so late,
Twilight is not good for maidens;
145 Should not loiter in the glen
In the haunts of goblin men.
Do you not remember Jeanie,
How she met them in the moonlight,
Took their gifts both choice and many,
150 Ate their fruits and wore their flowers
Plucked from bowers
Where summer ripens at all hours?
But ever in the noonlight
She pined and pined away;
155 Sought them by night and day,
Found them no more but dwindled and grew grey;
Then fell with the first snow,
While to this day no grass will grow
Where she lies low:
160 I planted daisies there a year ago
That never blow.
You should not loiter so."
"Nay, hush," said Laura:
"Nay, hush, my sister:
165 I ate and ate my fill,
Yet my mouth waters still;
Tomorrow night I will
Buy more:" and kissed her:
"Have done with sorrow;
170 I'll bring you plums tomorrow
Fresh on their mother twigs,
Cherries worth getting;
You cannot think what figs
My teeth have met in,
175 What melons icy-cold
Piled on a dish of gold
Too huge for me to hold,
What peaches with a velvet nap,
Pellucid grapes without one seed:
180 Odorous indeed must be the mead
Whereon they grow, and pure the wave they drink

With lilies at the brink,
And sugar-sweet their sap."

Golden head by golden head,
185   Like two pigeons in one nest
Folded in each other's wings,
They lay down in their curtained bed:
Like two blossoms on one stem,
Like two flakes of new-fall'n snow,
190   Like two wands of ivory
Tipped with gold for awful kings.
Moon and stars gazed in at them,
Wind sang to them lullaby,
Lumbering owls forbore to fly,
195   Not a bat flapped to and fro
Round their rest:
Cheek to cheek and breast to breast
Locked together in one nest.

Early in the morning
200   When the first cock crowed his warning,
Neat like bees, as sweet and busy,
Laura rose with Lizzie:
Fetched in honey, milked the cows,
Aired and set to rights the house,
205   Kneaded cakes of whitest wheat,
Cakes for dainty mouths to eat,
Next churned butter, whipped up cream,
Fed their poultry, sat and sewed;
Talked as modest maidens should:
210   Lizzie with an open heart,
Laura in an absent dream,
One content, one sick in part;
One warbling for the mere bright day's delight,
One longing for the night.

215   At length slow evening came:
They went with pitchers to the reedy brook;
Lizzie most placid in her look,
Laura most like a leaping flame.
They drew the gurgling water from its deep;

220 Lizzie plucked purple and rich golden flags,
Then turning homewards said: "The sunset flushes
Those furthest loftiest crags;
Come, Laura, not another maiden lags,
No wilful squirrel wags,
225 The beasts and birds are fast asleep."
But Laura loitered still among the rushes
And said the bank was steep.

And said the hour was early still,
The dew not fall'n, the wind not chill:
230 Listening ever, but not catching
The customary cry,
"Come buy, come buy,"
With its iterated jingle
Of sugar-baited words:
235 Not for all her watching
Once discerning even one goblin
Racing, whisking, tumbling, hobbling;
Let alone the herds
That used to tramp along the glen,
240 In groups or single,
Of brisk fruit-merchant men.
Till Lizzie urged, "O Laura, come;
I hear the fruit-call but I dare not look:
You should not loiter longer at this brook:
245 Come with me home.
The stars rise, the moon bends her arc,
Each glowworm winks her spark,
Let us get home before the night grows dark:
For clouds may gather
250 Tho' this is summer weather,
Put out the lights and drench us thro';
Then if we lost our way what should we do?"

Laura turned cold as stone
To find her sister heard that cry alone,
255 That goblin cry,
"Come buy our fruits, come buy."
Must she then buy no more such dainty fruit?

Must she no more such succous pasture find,
Gone deaf and blind?
260 Her tree of life drooped from the root:
She said not one word in her heart's sore ache;
But peering thro' the dimness, nought discerning,
Trudged home, her pitcher dripping all the way;
So crept to bed, and lay
265 Silent till Lizzie slept;
Then sat up in a passionate yearning,
And gnashed her teeth for baulked desire, and wept
As if her heart would break.

Day after day, night after night,
270 Laura kept watch in vain
In sullen silence of exceeding pain.
She never caught again the goblin cry:
"Come buy, come buy;"—
She never spied the goblin men
275 Hawking their fruits along the glen:
But when the noon waxed bright
Her hair grew thin and gray;
She dwindled, as the fair full moon doth turn
To swift decay and burn
280 Her fire away.

One day remembering her kernel-stone
She set it by a wall that faced the south;
Dewed it with tears, hoped for a root,
Watched for a waxing shoot,
285 But there came none;
It never saw the sun,
It never felt the trickling moisture run:
While with sunk eyes and faded mouth
She dreamed of melons, as a traveller sees
290 False waves in desert drouth
With shade of leaf-crowned trees,
And burns the thirstier in the sandful breeze.

She no more swept the house,
Tended the fowls or cows,

295 Fetched honey, kneaded cakes of wheat,
Brought water from the brook:
But sat down listless in the chimney-nook
And would not eat.

Tender Lizzie could not bear
300 To watch her sister's cankerous care
Yet not to share.
She night and morning
Caught the goblins' cry:
"Come buy our orchard fruits,
305 Come buy, come buy:"—
Beside the brook, along the glen,
She heard the tramp of goblin men,
The voice and stir
Poor Laura could not hear;
310 Longed to buy fruit to comfort her,
But feared to pay too dear.
She thought of Jeanie in her grave,
Who should have been a bride;
But who for joys brides hope to have
315 Fell sick and died
In her gay prime,
In earliest Winter time,
With the first glazing rime,
With the first snow-fall of crisp Winter time.

320 Till Laura dwindling
Seemed knocking at Death's door:
Then Lizzie weighed no more
Better and worse;
But put a silver penny in her purse,
325 Kissed Laura, crossed the heath with clumps of furze
At twilight, halted by the brook:
And for the first time in her life
Began to listen and look.

Laughed every goblin
330 When they spied her peeping:
Came towards her hobbling,

Flying, running, leaping,
Puffing and blowing,
Chuckling, clapping, crowing,
335 Clucking and gobbling,
Mopping and mowing,
Full of airs and graces,
Pulling wry faces,
Demure grimaces,
340 Cat-like and rat-like,
Ratel- and wombat-like,
Snail-paced in a hurry,
Parrot-voiced and whistler,
Helter skelter, hurry skurry,
345 Chattering like magpies,
Fluttering like pigeons,
Gliding like fishes,—
Hugged her and kissed her,
Squeezed and caressed her:
350 Stretched up their dishes,
Panniers, and plates:
"Look at our apples
Russet and dun,
Bob at our cherries,
355 Bite at our peaches,
Citrons and dates,
Grapes for the asking,
Pears red with basking
Out in the sun,
360 Plums on their twigs;
Pluck them and suck them,
Pomegranates, figs."—

"Good folk," said Lizzie,
Mindful of Jeanie:
365 "Give me much and many:"—
Held out her apron,
Tossed them her penny.
"Nay, take a seat with us,
Honour and eat with us,"

370 They answered grinning:
"Our feast is but beginning.
Night yet is early,
Warm and dew-pearly,
Wakeful and starry:
375 Such fruits as these
No man can carry;
Half their bloom would fly,
Half their dew would dry,
Half their flavour would pass by.
380 Sit down and feast with us,
Be welcome guest with us,
Cheer you and rest with us."—
"Thank you," said Lizzie: "But one waits
At home alone for me:
385 So without further parleying,
If you will not sell me any
Of your fruits tho' much and many,
Give me back my silver penny
I tossed you for a fee."—
390 They began to scratch their pates,
No longer wagging, purring,
But visibly demurring,
Grunting and snarling.
One called her proud,
395 Cross-grained, uncivil;
Their tones waxed loud,
Their looks were evil.
Lashing their tails
They trod and hustled her,
400 Elbowed and jostled her,
Clawed with their nails,
Barking, mewing, hissing, mocking,
Tore her gown and soiled her stocking,
Twitched her hair out by the roots,
405 Stamped upon her tender feet,
Held her hands and squeezed their fruits
Against her mouth to make her eat.

White and golden Lizzie stood,
Like a lily in a flood,—
410 Like a rock of blue-veined stone
Lashed by tides obstreperously,—
Like a beacon left alone
In a hoary roaring sea,
Sending up a golden fire,—
415 Like a fruit-crowned orange-tree
White with blossoms honey-sweet
Sore beset by wasp and bee,—
Like a royal virgin town
Topped with gilded dome and spire
420 Close beleaguered by a fleet
Mad to tug her standard down.

One may lead a horse to water,
Twenty cannot make him drink.
Tho' the goblins cuffed and caught her,
425 Coaxed and fought her,
Bullied and besought her,
Scratched her, pinched her black as ink,
Kicked and knocked her,
Mauled and mocked her,
430 Lizzie uttered not a word;
Would not open lip from lip
Lest they should cram a mouthful in:
But laughed in heart to feel the drip
Of juice that syrupped all her face,
435 And lodged in dimples of her chin,
And streaked her neck which quaked like curd.
At last the evil people
Worn out by her resistance
Flung back her penny, kicked their fruit
440 Along whichever road they took,
Not leaving root or stone or shoot;
Some writhed into the ground,
Some dived into the brook
With ring and ripple,
445 Some scudded on the gale without a sound,
Some vanished in the distance.

In a smart, ache, tingle,
Lizzie went her way;
Knew not was it night or day;
450   Sprang up the bank, tore thro' the furze,
Threaded copse and dingle,
And heard her penny jingle
Bouncing in her purse,
Its bounce was music to her ear.
455   She ran and ran
As if she feared some goblin man
Dogged her with gibe or curse
Or something worse:
But not one goblin skurried after,
460   Nor was she pricked by fear;
The kind heart made her windy-paced
That urged her home quite out of breath with haste
And inward laughter.

She cried "Laura," up the garden,
465   "Did you miss me?
Come and kiss me.
Never mind my bruises,
Hug me, kiss me, suck my juices
Squeezed from goblin fruits for you,
470   Goblin pulp and goblin dew.
Eat me, drink me, love me;
Laura, make much of me:
For your sake I have braved the glen
And had to do with goblin merchant men."

475   Laura started from her chair,
Flung her arms up in the air,
Clutched her hair:
"Lizzie, Lizzie, have you tasted
For my sake the fruit forbidden?
480   Must your light like mine be hidden,
Your young life like mine be wasted,
Undone in mine undoing
And ruined in my ruin,
Thirsty, cankered, goblin-ridden?"—

485 She clung about her sister,
    Kissed and kissed and kissed her:
    Tears once again
    Refreshed her shrunken eyes,
    Dropping like rain
490 After long sultry drouth;
    Shaking with aguish fear, and pain,
    She kissed and kissed her with a hungry mouth.

    Her lips began to scorch,
    That juice was wormwood to her tongue,
495 She loathed the feast:
    Writhing as one possessed she leaped and sung,
    Rent all her robe, and wrung
    Her hands in lamentable haste,
    And beat her breast.
500 Her locks streamed like the torch
    Borne by a racer at full speed,
    Or like the mane of horses in their flight,
    Or like an eagle when she stems the light
    Straight toward the sun,
505 Or like a caged thing freed,
    Or like a flying flag when armies run.

    Swift fire spread thro' her veins, knocked at her heart,
    Met the fire smouldering there
    And overbore its lesser flame;
510 She gorged on bitterness without a name:
    Ah! fool, to choose such part
    Of soul-consuming care!
    Sense failed in the mortal strife:
    Like the watch-tower of a town
515 Which an earthquake shatters down,
    Like a lightning-stricken mast,
    Like a wind-uprooted tree
    Spun about,
    Like a foam-topped waterspout
520 Cast down headlong in the sea,
    She fell at last;

Pleasure past and anguish past,
Is it death or is it life?

Life out of death.
525 That night long Lizzie watched by her,
Counted her pulse's flagging stir,
Felt for her breath,
Held water to her lips, and cooled her face
With tears and fanning leaves:
530 But when the first birds chirped about their eaves,
And early reapers plodded to the place
Of golden sheaves,
And dew-wet grass
Bowed in the morning winds so brisk to pass,
535 And new buds with new day
Opened of cup-like lilies on the stream,
Laura awoke as from a dream,
Laughed in the innocent old way,
Hugged Lizzie but not twice or thrice;
540 Her gleaming locks showed not one thread of grey,
Her breath was sweet as May
And light danced in her eyes.

Days, weeks, months, years
Afterwards, when both were wives
545 With children of their own;
Their mother-hearts beset with fears,
Their lives bound up in tender lives;
Laura would call the little ones
And tell them of her early prime,
550 Those pleasant days long gone
Of not-returning time:
Would talk about the haunted glen,
The wicked, quaint fruit-merchant men,
Their fruits like honey to the throat
555 But poison in the blood;
(Men sell not such in any town:)
Would tell them how her sister stood
In deadly peril to do her good,

And win the fiery antidote:
560 Then joining hands to little hands
Would bid them cling together,
"For there is no friend like a sister
In calm or stormy weather;
To cheer one on the tedious way,
565 To fetch one if one goes astray,
To lift one if one totters down,
To strengthen whilst one stands."

IN THE ROUND TOWER AT JHANSI, JUNE 8, 1857.

A hundred, a thousand to one; even so;
    Not a hope in the world remained:
The swarming howling wretches below
    Gained and gained and gained.

5   Skene looked at his pale young wife:—
    "Is the time come?"—"The time is come!"—
Young, strong, and so full of life:
    The agony struck them dumb.

Close his arm about her now,
10   Close her cheek to his,
Close the pistol to her brow—
    God forgive them this!

"Will it hurt much?"—"No, mine own:
    I wish I could bear the pang for both."
15 "I wish I could bear the pang alone:
    Courage, dear, I am not loth."

Kiss and kiss: "It is not pain
    Thus to kiss and die.
One kiss more."—"And yet one again."—
20   "Good bye."—"Good bye."

***I retain this little poem, not as historically accurate, but as written and
published before I heard the supposed facts of its first verse contradicted.

DREAM-LAND.

Where sunless rivers weep
Their waves into the deep,
She sleeps a charmèd sleep:
    Awake her not.
5   Led by a single star,
She came from very far
To seek where shadows are
    Her pleasant lot.

She left the rosy morn,
10   She left the fields of corn,
For twilight cold and lorn
    And water springs.
Thro' sleep, as thro' a veil,
She sees the sky look pale,
15   And hears the nightingale
    That sadly sings.

Rest, rest, a perfect rest
Shed over brow and breast;
Her face is toward the west,
20   The purple land.
She cannot see the grain
Ripening on hill and plain;
She cannot feel the rain
    Upon her hand.

25   Rest, rest, for evermore
Upon a mossy shore;
Rest, rest at the heart's core
    Till time shall cease:
Sleep that no pain shall wake;
30   Night that no morn shall break,
Till joy shall overtake
    Her perfect peace.

AT HOME.

When I was dead, my spirit turned
    To seek the much frequented house:
I passed the door, and saw my friends
    Feasting beneath green orange boughs;
5   From hand to hand they pushed the wine,
    They sucked the pulp of plum and peach;
They sang, they jested, and they laughed,
    For each was loved of each.

I listened to their honest chat:
10   Said one: "Tomorrow we shall be
Plod plod along the featureless sands
    And coasting miles and miles of sea."
Said one: "Before the turn of tide
    We will achieve the eyrie-seat."
15 Said one: "Tomorrow shall be like
    Today, but much more sweet."

"Tomorrow," said they, strong with hope,
    And dwelt upon the pleasant way:
"Tomorrow," cried they one and all,
20   While no one spoke of yesterday.
Their life stood full at blessed noon;
    I, only I, had passed away:
"Tomorrow and today," they cried;
    I was of yesterday.

25 I shivered comfortless, but cast
    No chill across the tablecloth;
I all-forgotten shivered, sad
    To stay and yet to part how loth:
I passed from the familiar room,
30   I who from love had passed away,
Like the remembrance of a guest
    That tarrieth but a day.

A TRIAD.

Three sang of love together: one with lips
    Crimson, with cheeks and bosom in a glow,
Flushed to the yellow hair and finger tips;
    And one there sang who soft and smooth as snow
5   Bloomed like a tinted hyacinth at a show;
And one was blue with famine after love,
    Who like a harpstring snapped rang harsh and low
The burden of what those were singing of.
One shamed herself in love; one temperately
10   Grew gross in soulless love, a sluggish wife;
One famished died for love. Thus two of three
    Took death for love and won him after strife;
One droned in sweetness like a fattened bee:
    All on the threshold, yet all short of life.

LOVE FROM THE NORTH.

I had a love in soft south land,
    Beloved thro' April far in May;
He waited on my lightest breath,
    And never dared to say me nay.

5   He saddened if my cheer was sad,
    But gay he grew if I was gay;
We never differed on a hair,
    My yes his yes, my nay his nay.

The wedding hour was come, the aisles
10   Were flushed with sun and flowers that day;
I pacing balanced in my thoughts:
    "It's quite too late to think of nay."—

My bridegroom answered in his turn,
    Myself had almost answered "yea:"

15   When thro' the flashing nave I heard
        A struggle and resounding "nay".

     Bridemaids and bridegroom shrank in fear,
        But I stood high who stood at bay:
     "And if I answer yea, fair Sir,
20   What man art thou to bar with nay?"

     He was a strong man from the north,
        Light-locked, with eyes of dangerous grey:
     "Put yea by for another time
        In which I will not say thee nay."

25   He took me in his strong white arms,
        He bore me on his horse away
     O'er crag, morass, and hairbreadth pass,
        But never asked me yea or nay.

     He made me fast with book and bell,
30   With links of love he makes me stay;
     Till now I've neither heart nor power
        Nor will nor wish to say him nay.

WINTER RAIN.

     Every valley drinks,
        Every dell and hollow:
     Where the kind rain sinks and sinks,
        Green of Spring will follow.

5   Yet a lapse of weeks
        Buds will burst their edges,
     Strip their wool-coats, glue-coats, streaks,
        In the woods and hedges;

     Weave a bower of love
10   For birds to meet each other,
     Weave a canopy above
        Nest and egg and mother.

But for fattening rain
  We should have no flowers,
15 Never a bud or leaf again
  But for soaking showers;

Never a mated bird
  In the rocking tree-tops,
Never indeed a flock or herd
20   To graze upon the lea-crops.

Lambs so woolly white,
  Sheep the sun-bright leas on,
They could have no grass to bite
  But for rain in season.

25 We should find no moss
  In the shadiest places,
Find no waving meadow grass
  Pied with broad-eyed daisies:

But miles of barren sand,
30   With never a son or daughter,
Not a lily on the land,
  Or lily on the water.

COUSIN KATE.

I was a cottage maiden
  Hardened by sun and air,
Contented with my cottage mates,
  Not mindful I was fair.
5 Why did a great lord find me out,
  And praise my flaxen hair?
Why did a great lord find me out
  To fill my heart with care?

He lured me to his palace home—
10   Woe's me for joy thereof—

To lead a shameless shameful life,
  His plaything and his love.
He wore me like a silken knot,
  He changed me like a glove;
15 So now I moan, an unclean thing,
  Who might have been a dove.

O Lady Kate, my cousin Kate,
  You grew more fair than I:
He saw you at your father's gate,
20   Chose you, and cast me by.
He watched your steps along the lane,
  Your work among the rye;
He lifted you from mean estate
  To sit with him on high.

25 Because you were so good and pure
  He bound you with his ring:
The neighbours call you good and pure,
  Call me an outcast thing.
Even so I sit and howl in dust,
30   You sit in gold and sing:
Now which of us has tenderer heart?
  You had the stronger wing.

O cousin Kate, my love was true,
  Your love was writ in sand:
35 If he had fooled not me but you,
  If you stood where I stand,
He'd not have won me with his love
  Nor bought me with his land;
I would have spit into his face
40   And not have taken his hand.

Yet I've a gift you have not got,
  And seem not like to get:
For all your clothes and wedding-ring
  I've little doubt you fret.
45 My fair-haired son, my shame, my pride,
  Cling closer, closer yet:
Your father would give lands for one
  To wear his coronet.

NOBLE SISTERS.

"Now did you mark a falcon,
  Sister dear, sister dear,
Flying toward my window
  In the morning cool and clear?
5 With jingling bells about her neck,
  But what beneath her wing?
It may have been a ribbon,
  Or it may have been a ring."—
    "I marked a falcon swooping
10   At the break of day:
    And for your love, my sister dove,
    I 'frayed the thief away."—

"Or did you spy a ruddy hound,
  Sister fair and tall,
15 Went snuffing round my garden bound,
  Or crouched by my bower wall?
With a silken leash about his neck;
  But in his mouth may be
A chain of gold and silver links,
20 Or a letter writ to me."—
    "I heard a hound, highborn sister,
    Stood baying at the moon:
    I rose and drove him from your wall
    Lest you should wake too soon."—

25 "Or did you meet a pretty page
  Sat swinging on the gate;
Sat whistling whistling like a bird,
  Or may be slept too late:
With eaglets broidered on his cap,
30 And eaglets on his glove?
If you had turned his pockets out,
  You had found some pledge of love."—
    "I met him at this daybreak,
    Scarce the east was red:
35   Lest the creaking gate should anger you,
    I packed him home to bed."—

"Oh patience, sister. Did you see
  A young man tall and strong,
Swift-footed to uphold the right
40   And to uproot the wrong,
Come home across the desolate sea
  To woo me for his wife?
And in his heart my heart is locked,
  And in his life my life."—
45   "I met a nameless man, sister,
        Who loitered round our door:
        I said: Her husband loves her much,
        And yet she loves him more."—

"Fie, sister, fie, a wicked lie,
50   A lie, a wicked lie,
I have none other love but him,
  Nor will have till I die.
And you have turned him from our door,
  And stabbed him with a lie:
55 I will go seek him thro' the world
  In sorrow till I die."—
        "Go seek in sorrow, sister,
        And find in sorrow too:
        If thus you shame our father's name
60   My curse go forth with you."

SPRING.

Frost-locked all the winter,
Seeds, and roots, and stones of fruits,
What shall make their sap ascend
That they may put forth shoots?
5 Tips of tender green,
Leaf, or blade, or sheath;
Telling of the hidden life
That breaks forth underneath,
Life nursed in its grave by Death.

10　Blows the thaw-wind pleasantly,
　　Drips the soaking rain,
　　By fits looks down the waking sun:
　　Young grass springs on the plain;
　　Young leaves clothe early hedgerow trees;
15　Seeds, and roots, and stones of fruits,
　　Swollen with sap put forth their shoots;
　　Curled-headed ferns sprout in the lane;
　　Birds sing and pair again.

　　There is no time like Spring,
20　When life's alive in everything,
　　Before new nestlings sing,
　　Before cleft swallows speed their journey back
　　Along the trackless track—
　　God guides their wing,
25　He spreads their table that they nothing lack,—
　　Before the daisy grows a common flower,
　　Before the sun has power
　　To scorch the world up in his noontide hour.

　　There is no time like Spring,
30　Like Spring that passes by;
　　There is no life like Spring-life born to die,—
　　Piercing the sod,
　　Clothing the uncouth clod,
　　Hatched in the nest,
35　Fledged on the windy bough,
　　Strong on the wing:
　　There is no time like Spring that passes by,
　　Now newly born, and now
　　Hastening to die.

THE LAMBS OF GRASMERE, 1860.

The upland flocks grew starved and thinned:
　　Their shepherds scarce could feed the lambs

Whose milkless mothers butted them,
    Or who were orphaned of their dams.
5 The lambs athirst for mother's milk
    Filled all the place with piteous sounds:
Their mothers' bones made white for miles
    The pastureless wet pasture grounds.

Day after day, night after night,
10   From lamb to lamb the shepherds went,
With teapots for the bleating mouths
    Instead of nature's nourishment.
The little shivering gaping things
    Soon knew the step that brought them aid,
15 And fondled the protecting hand,
    And rubbed it with a woolly head.

Then, as the days waxed on to weeks,
    It was a pretty sight to see
These lambs with frisky heads and tails
20   Skipping and leaping on the lea,
Bleating in tender, trustful tones,
    Resting on rocky crag or mound,
And following the beloved feet
    That once had sought for them and found.

25 These very shepherds of their flocks,
    These loving lambs so meek to please,
Are worthy of recording words
    And honour in their due degrees:
So I might live a hundred years,
30   And roam from strand to foreign strand,
Yet not forget this flooded spring
    And scarce-saved lambs of Westmoreland.

A BIRTHDAY.

My heart is like a singing bird
    Whose nest is in a watered shoot;

My heart is like an apple tree
　　Whose boughs are bent with thickset fruit;
My heart is like a rainbow shell
　　That paddles in a halcyon sea;
My heart is gladder than all these
　　Because my love is come to me.

Raise me a dais of silk and down;
　　Hang it with vair and purple dyes;
Carve it in doves and pomegranates,
　　And peacocks with a hundred eyes;
Work it in gold and silver grapes,
　　In leaves and silver fleurs-de-lys;
Because the birthday of my life
　　Is come, my love is come to me.

REMEMBER.

Remember me when I am gone away,
　　Gone far away into the silent land;
　　When you can no more hold me by the hand,
Nor I half turn to go yet turning stay.
Remember me when no more day by day
　　You tell me of our future that you planned:
　　Only remember me; you understand
It will be late to counsel then or pray.
Yet if you should forget me for a while
　　And afterwards remember, do not grieve:
　　For if the darkness and corruption leave
A vestige of the thoughts that once I had,
Better by far you should forget and smile
　　Than that you should remember and be sad.

AFTER DEATH.

The curtains were half drawn, the floor was swept
　　And strewn with rushes, rosemary and may

Lay thick upon the bed on which I lay,
Where thro' the lattice ivy-shadows crept.
5   He leaned above me, thinking that I slept
       And could not hear him; but I heard him say:
       "Poor child, poor child:" and as he turned away
Came a deep silence, and I knew he wept.
He did not touch the shroud, or raise the fold
10   That hid my face, or take my hand in his,
          Or ruffle the smooth pillows for my head:
          He did not love me living; but once dead
       He pitied me; and very sweet it is
To know he still is warm tho' I am cold.

AN END.

Love, strong as Death, is dead.
Come, let us make his bed
Among the dying flowers:
A green turf at his head;
5   And a stone at his feet,
Whereon we may sit
In the quiet evening hours.

He was born in the Spring,
And died before the harvesting:
10   On the last warm Summer day
He left us; he would not stay
For Autumn twilight cold and gray.
Sit we by his grave, and sing
He is gone away.

15   To few chords and sad and low
Sing we so:
Be our eyes fixed on the grass
Shadow-veiled as the years pass,
While we think of all that was
20   In the long ago.

MY DREAM.

Hear now a curious dream I dreamed last night,
Each word whereof is weighed and sifted truth.

I stood beside Euphrates while it swelled
Like overflowing Jordan in its youth:
5   It waxed and coloured sensibly to sight,
Till out of myriad pregnant waves there welled
Young crocodiles, a gaunt blunt-featured crew,
Fresh-hatched perhaps and daubed with birthday dew.
The rest if I should tell, I fear my friend,
10   My closest friend would deem the facts untrue;
And therefore it were wisely left untold;
Yet if you will, why, hear it to the end.

Each crocodile was girt with massive gold
And polished stones that with their wearers grew:
15   But one there was who waxed beyond the rest,
Wore kinglier girdle and a kingly crown,
Whilst crowns and orbs and sceptres starred his breast.
All gleamed compact and green with scale on scale,
But special burnishment adorned his mail
20   And special terror weighed upon his frown;
His punier brethren quaked before his tail,
Broad as a rafter, potent as a flail.
So he grew lord and master of his kin:
But who shall tell the tale of all their woes?
25   An execrable appetite arose,
He battened on them, crunched, and sucked them in.
He knew no law, he feared no binding law,
But ground them with inexorable jaw:
The luscious fat distilled upon his chin,
30   Exuded from his nostrils and his eyes,
While still like hungry death he fed his maw;
Till every minor crocodile being dead
And buried too, himself gorged to the full,
He slept with breath oppressed and unstrung claw.
35   Oh marvel passing strange which next I saw:
In sleep he dwindled to the common size,

And all the empire faded from his coat.
Then from far off a wingèd vessel came,
Swift as a swallow, subtle as a flame:
40   I know not what it bore of freight or host,
But white it was as an avenging ghost.
It levelled strong Euphrates in its course;
Supreme yet weightless as an idle mote
It seemed to tame the waters without force
45   Till not a murmur swelled or billow beat:
Lo, as the purple shadow swept the sands,
The prudent crocodile rose on his feet
And shed appropriate tears and wrung his hands.

What can it mean? you ask. I answer not
50   For meaning, but myself must echo, What?
And tell it as I saw it on the spot.

SONG.

Oh roses for the flush of youth,
   And laurel for the perfect prime;
But pluck an ivy branch for me
   Grown old before my time.

5   Oh violets for the grave of youth,
   And bay for those dead in their prime;
Give me the withered leaves I chose
   Before in the old time.

THE HOUR AND THE GHOST.

BRIDE.
O love, love, hold me fast,
He draws me away from thee;
I cannot stem the blast,
Nor the cold strong sea:
5   Far away a light shines
Beyond the hills and pines;
It is lit for me.

BRIDEGROOM.

I have thee close, my dear,
No terror can come near;
10   Only far off the northern light shines clear.

GHOST.

Come with me, fair and false,
To our home, come home.
It is my voice that calls:
Once thou wast not afraid
15   When I woo'd, and said,
"Come, our nest is newly made"—
Now cross the tossing foam.

BRIDE.

Hold me one moment longer,
He taunts me with the past,
20   His clutch is waxing stronger,
Hold me fast, hold me fast.
He draws me from thy heart,
And I cannot withhold:
He bids my spirit depart
25   With him into the cold:—
Oh bitter vows of old!

BRIDEGROOM.

Lean on me, hide thine eyes:
Only ourselves, earth and skies,
Are present here: be wise.

GHOST.

30   Lean on me, come away,
I will guide and steady:
Come, for I will not stay:
Come, for house and bed are ready.
Ah, sure bed and house,
35   For better and worse, for life and death:
Goal won with shortened breath:
Come, crown our vows.

BRIDE.

One moment, one more word,
While my heart beats still,
40 While my breath is stirred
By my fainting will.
O friend forsake me not,
Forget not as I forgot:
But keep thy heart for me,
45 Keep thy faith true and bright;
Thro' the lone cold winter night
Perhaps I may come to thee.

BRIDEGROOM.

Nay peace, my darling, peace:
Let these dreams and terrors cease:
50 Who spoke of death or change or aught but ease?

GHOST.

O fair frail sin,
O poor harvest gathered in!
Thou shalt visit him again
To watch his heart grow cold;
55 To know the gnawing pain
I knew of old;
To see one much more fair
Fill up the vacant chair,
Fill his heart, his children bear:—
60 While thou and I together
In the outcast weather
Toss and howl and spin.

A SUMMER WISH.

Live all thy sweet life thro',
    Sweet Rose, dew-sprent,
Drop down thine evening dew
To gather it anew
5 When day is bright:

I fancy thou wast meant
Chiefly to give delight.

Sing in the silent sky,
    Glad soaring bird;
10 Sing out thy notes on high
To sunbeam straying by
Or passing cloud;
    Heedless if thou art heard
Sing thy full song aloud.

15 Oh that it were with me
    As with the flower;
Blooming on its own tree
For butterfly and bee
Its summer morns:
20   That I might bloom mine hour
A rose in spite of thorns.

Oh that my work were done
    As birds' that soar
Rejoicing in the sun:
25 That when my time is run
And daylight too,
    I so might rest once more
Cool with refreshing dew.

AN APPLE-GATHERING.

I plucked pink blossoms from mine apple tree
    And wore them all that evening in my hair:
Then in due season when I went to see
    I found no apples there.

5 With dangling basket all along the grass
    As I had come I went the selfsame track:
My neighbours mocked me while they saw me pass
    So empty-handed back.

Lilian and Lilias smiled in trudging by,
10   Their heaped-up basket teazed me like a jeer;

Sweet-voiced they sang beneath the sunset sky,
  Their mother's home was near.

Plump Gertrude passed me with her basket full,
  A stronger hand than hers helped it along;
15 A voice talked with her thro' the shadows cool
  More sweet to me than song.

Ah Willie, Willie, was my love less worth
  Than apples with their green leaves piled above?
I counted rosiest apples on the earth
20   Of far less worth than love.

So once it was with me you stooped to talk
  Laughing and listening in this very lane:
To think that by this way we used to walk
  We shall not walk again!

25 I let my neighbours pass me, ones and twos
  And groups; the latest said the night grew chill,
And hastened: but I loitered, while the dews
  Fell fast I loitered still.

SONG.

Two doves upon the selfsame branch,
  Two lilies on a single stem,
Two butterflies upon one flower:—
  Oh happy they who look on them.

5 Who look upon them hand in hand
  Flushed in the rosy summer light;
Who look upon them hand in hand
  And never give a thought to night.

MAUDE CLARE.

Out of the church she followed them
  With a lofty step and mien:

His bride was like a village maid,
    Maude Clare was like a queen.

5   "Son Thomas," his lady mother said,
    With smiles, almost with tears:
  "May Nell and you but live as true
    As we have done for years;

  "Your father thirty years ago
10   Had just your tale to tell;
  But he was not so pale as you,
    Nor I so pale as Nell."

My lord was pale with inward strife,
    And Nell was pale with pride;
15 My lord gazed long on pale Maude Clare
    Or ever he kissed the bride.

"Lo, I have brought my gift, my lord,
    Have brought my gift," she said:
"To bless the hearth, to bless the board,
20   To bless the marriage-bed.

"Here's my half of the golden chain
    You wore about your neck,
That day we waded ankle-deep
    For lilies in the beck:

25 "Here's my half of the faded leaves
    We plucked from budding bough,
With feet amongst the lily leaves,—
    The lilies are budding now."

He strove to match her scorn with scorn,
30   He faltered in his place:
"Lady," he said,—"Maude Clare," he said,—
    "Maude Clare:"—and hid his face.

She turn'd to Nell: "My Lady Nell,
    I have a gift for you;
35 Tho', were it fruit, the bloom were gone,
    Or, were it flowers, the dew.

"Take my share of a fickle heart,
    Mine of a paltry love:
Take it or leave it as you will,
40   I wash my hands thereof."

"And what you leave," said Nell, "I'll take,
    And what you spurn, I'll wear;
For he's my lord for better and worse,
    And him I love, Maude Clare.

45 "Yea, tho' you're taller by the head,
    More wise, and much more fair;
I'll love him till he loves me best,
    Me best of all, Maude Clare."

ECHO.

Come to me in the silence of the night;
    Come in the speaking silence of a dream;
Come with soft rounded cheeks and eyes as bright
    As sunlight on a stream;
5   Come back in tears,
O memory, hope, love of finished years.

Oh dream how sweet, too sweet, too bitter sweet,
    Whose wakening should have been in Paradise,
Where souls brimfull of love abide and meet;
10   Where thirsting longing eyes
        Watch the slow door
That opening, letting in, lets out no more.

Yet come to me in dreams, that I may live
    My very life again tho' cold in death:
15 Come back to me in dreams, that I may give
        Pulse for pulse, breath for breath:
        Speak low, lean low,
As long ago, my love, how long ago.

WINTER: MY SECRET.

I tell my secret? No indeed, not I:
Perhaps some day, who knows?
But not today; it froze, and blows, and snows,
And you're too curious: fie!
5   You want to hear it? well:
Only, my secret's mine, and I won't tell.

Or, after all, perhaps there's none:
Suppose there is no secret after all,
But only just my fun.
10   Today's a nipping day, a biting day;
In which one wants a shawl,
A veil, a cloak, and other wraps:
I cannot ope to every one who taps,
And let the draughts come whistling thro' my hall;
15   Come bounding and surrounding me,
Come buffeting, astounding me,
Nipping and clipping thro' my wraps and all.
I wear my mask for warmth: who ever shows
His nose to Russian snows
20   To be pecked at by every wind that blows?
You would not peck? I thank you for good will,
Believe, but leave that truth untested still.

Spring's an expansive time: yet I don't trust
March with its peck of dust,
25   Nor April with its rainbow-crowned brief showers,
Nor even May, whose flowers
One frost may wither thro' the sunless hours.

Perhaps some languid summer day,
When drowsy birds sing less and less,
30   And golden fruit is ripening to excess,
If there's not too much sun nor too much cloud,
And the warm wind is neither still nor loud,
Perhaps my secret I may say,
Or you may guess.

ANOTHER SPRING.

If I might see another Spring
   I'd not plant summer flowers and wait:
I'd have my crocuses at once,
My leafless pink mezereons,
5   My chill-veined snowdrops, choicer yet
   My white or azure violet,
Leaf-nested primrose; anything
    To blow at once, not late.

If I might see another Spring
10   I'd listen to the daylight birds
That build their nests and pair and sing,
Nor wait for mateless nightingale;
   I'd listen to the lusty herds,
   The ewes with lambs as white as snow,
15 I'd find out music in the hail
    And all the winds that blow.

If I might see another Spring—
   Oh stinging comment on my past
That all my past results in "if"—
20   If I might see another Spring
I'd laugh today, today is brief;
I would not wait for anything:
   I'd use today that cannot last,
    Be glad today and sing.

A PEAL OF BELLS.

Strike the bells wantonly,
   Tinkle tinkle well;
Bring me wine, bring me flowers,
   Ring the silver bell.
5 All my lamps burn scented oil,
   Hung on laden orange trees,

Whose shadowed foliage is the foil
   To golden lamps and oranges.
Heap my golden plates with fruit,
10   Golden fruit, fresh-plucked and ripe;
   Strike the bells and breathe the pipe;
Shut out showers from summer hours—
Silence that complaining lute—
   Shut out thinking, shut out pain,
15   From hours that cannot come again.

Strike the bells solemnly,
   Ding dong deep:
My friend is passing to his bed,
   Fast asleep;
20   There's plaited linen round his head,
   While foremost go his feet—
His feet that cannot carry him.
My feast's a show, my lights are dim;
   Be still, your music is not sweet,—
25   There is no music more for him:
   His lights are out, his feast is done;
His bowl that sparkled to the brim
Is drained, is broken, cannot hold;
My blood is chill, his blood is cold;
30   His death is full, and mine begun.

FATA MORGANA.

A blue-eyed phantom far before
   Is laughing, leaping toward the sun:
Like lead I chase it evermore,
   I pant and run.

5   It breaks the sunlight bound on bound:
   Goes singing as it leaps along
To sheep-bells with a dreamy sound
   A dreamy song.

I laugh, it is so brisk and gay;
10   It is so far before, I weep:
I hope I shall lie down some day,
    Lie down and sleep.

"NO, THANK YOU, JOHN."

I never said I loved you, John:
    Why will you teaze me day by day,
And wax a weariness to think upon
    With always "do" and "pray"?

5   You know I never loved you, John;
    No fault of mine made me your toast:
Why will you haunt me with a face as wan
    As shows an hour-old ghost?

I dare say Meg or Moll would take
10   Pity upon you, if you'd ask:
And pray don't remain single for my sake
    Who can't perform that task.

I have no heart?—Perhaps I have not;
    But then you're mad to take offence
15 That I don't give you what I have not got:
    Use your own common sense.

Let bygones be bygones:
    Don't call me false, who owed not to be true:
I'd rather answer "No" to fifty Johns
20   Than answer "Yes" to you.

Let's mar our pleasant days no more,
    Song-birds of passage, days of youth:
Catch at today, forget the days before:
    I'll wink at your untruth.

25 Let us strike hands as hearty friends;
    No more, no less; and friendship's good:

Only don't keep in view ulterior ends,
  And points not understood

In open treaty. Rise above
30   Quibbles and shuffling off and on:
Here's friendship for you if you like; but love,—
  No, thank you, John.

MAY.

I cannot tell you how it was;
But this I know: it came to pass
Upon a bright and breezy day
When May was young; ah pleasant May!
5   As yet the poppies were not born
Between the blades of tender corn;
The last eggs had not hatched as yet,
Nor any bird foregone its mate.

I cannot tell you what it was;
10   But this I know: it did but pass.
It passed away with sunny May,
With all sweet things it passed away,
And left me old, and cold, and grey.

A PAUSE OF THOUGHT.

I looked for that which is not, nor can be,
  And hope deferred made my heart sick in truth:
  But years must pass before a hope of youth
    Is resigned utterly.

5   I watched and waited with a steadfast will:
  And though the object seemed to flee away

That I so longed for, ever day by day
I watched and waited still.

Sometimes I said: This thing shall be no more;
10   My expectation wearies and shall cease;
I will resign it now and be at peace:
Yet never gave it o'er.

Sometimes I said: It is an empty name
I long for; to a name why should I give
15   The peace of all the days I have to live?—
Yet gave it all the same.

Alas, thou foolish one! alike unfit
For healthy joy and salutary pain:
Thou knowest the chase useless, and again
20   Turnest to follow it.

TWILIGHT CALM.

Oh pleasant eventide!
Clouds on the western side
Grow grey and greyer hiding the warm sun:
The bees and birds, their happy labours done,
5   Seek their close nests and bide.

Screened in the leafy wood
The stock-doves sit and brood:
The very squirrel leaps from bough to bough
But lazily; pauses; and settles now
10   Where once he stored his food.

One by one the flowers close,
Lily and dewy rose
Shutting their tender petals from the moon:
The grasshoppers are still; but not so soon
15   Are still the noisy crows.

The dormouse squats and eats
Choice little dainty bits
Beneath the spreading roots of a broad lime;
Nibbling his fill he stops from time to time
20   And listens where he sits.

From far the lowings come
Of cattle driven home:
From farther still the wind brings fitfully
The vast continual murmur of the sea,
25   Now loud, now almost dumb.

The gnats whirl in the air,
The evening gnats; and there
The owl opes broad his eyes and wings to sail
For prey; the bat wakes; and the shell-less snail
30   Comes forth, clammy and bare.

Hark! that's the nightingale,
Telling the selfsame tale
Her song told when this ancient earth was young:
So echoes answered when her song was sung
35   In the first wooded vale.

We call it love and pain
The passion of her strain;
And yet we little understand or know:
Why should it not be rather joy that so
40   Throbs in each throbbing vein?

In separate herds the deer
Lie; here the bucks, and here
The does, and by its mother sleeps the fawn:
Through all the hours of night until the dawn
45   They sleep, forgetting fear.

The hare sleeps where it lies,
With wary half-closed eyes;
The cock has ceased to crow, the hen to cluck:
Only the fox is out, some heedless duck
50   Or chicken to surprise.

Remote, each single star
Comes out, till there they are
All shining brightly: how the dews fall damp!
While close at hand the glow-worm lights her lamp
55   Or twinkles from afar.

But evening now is done
As much as if the sun
Day-giving had arisen in the East:
For night has come; and the great calm has ceased,
60   The quiet sands have run.

WIFE TO HUSBAND.

Pardon the faults in me,
     For the love of years ago:
          Good bye.
I must drift across the sea,
5   I must sink into the snow,
          I must die.

You can bask in this sun,
     You can drink wine, and eat:
          Good bye.
10   I must gird myself and run,
     Tho' with unready feet:
          I must die.

Blank sea to sail upon,
     Cold bed to sleep in:
15   Good bye.
While you clasp, I must be gone
     For all your weeping:
          I must die.

A kiss for one friend,
20   And a word for two,—
          Good bye:—

A lock that you must send,
 A kindness you must do:
  I must die.

25 Not a word for you,
 Not a lock or kiss,
  Good bye.
We, one, must part in two;
 Verily death is this:
30   I must die.

THREE SEASONS.

 "A cup for hope!" she said,
In springtime ere the bloom was old:
The crimson wine was poor and cold
 By her mouth's richer red.

5 "A cup for love!" how low,
How soft the words; and all the while
Her blush was rippling with a smile
 Like summer after snow.

 "A cup for memory!"
10 Cold cup that one must drain alone:
While autumn winds are up and moan
 Across the barren sea.

 Hope, memory, love:
Hope for fair morn, and love for day,
15 And memory for the evening grey
 And solitary dove.

MIRAGE.

The hope I dreamed of was a dream,
 Was but a dream; and now I wake

Exceeding comfortless, and worn, and old,
    For a dream's sake.

5   I hang my harp upon a tree,
      A weeping willow in a lake;
    I hang my silenced harp there, wrung and snapt
      For a dream's sake.

Lie still, lie still, my breaking heart;
10   My silent heart, lie still and break:
Life, and the world, and mine own self, are changed
    For a dream's sake.

SHUT OUT.

The door was shut. I looked between
    Its iron bars; and saw it lie,
    My garden, mine, beneath the sky,
Pied with all flowers bedewed and green:

5   From bough to bough the song-birds crossed,
      From flower to flower the moths and bees;
      With all its nests and stately trees
It had been mine, and it was lost.

A shadowless spirit kept the gate,
10   Blank and unchanging like the grave.
      I peering thro' said: "Let me have
Some buds to cheer my outcast state."

He answered not. "Or give me, then,
    But one small twig from shrub or tree;
15   And bid my home remember me
Until I come to it again."

The spirit was silent; but he took
    Mortar and stone to build a wall;
    He left no loophole great or small
20   Thro' which my straining eyes might look:

So now I sit here quite alone
    Blinded with tears; nor grieve for that,
    For nought is left worth looking at
Since my delightful land is gone.

25   A violet bed is budding near,
    Wherein a lark has made her nest:
    And good they are, but not the best;
And dear they are, but not so dear.

SOUND SLEEP.

Some are laughing, some are weeping;
She is sleeping, only sleeping.
Round her rest wild flowers are creeping;
There the wind is heaping, heaping
5   Sweetest sweets of Summer's keeping,
By the corn fields ripe for reaping.

There are lilies, and there blushes
The deep rose, and there the thrushes
Sing till latest sunlight flushes
10   In the west; a fresh wind brushes
Thro' the leaves while evening hushes.

There by day the lark is singing
And the grass and weeds are springing;
There by night the bat is winging;
15   There for ever winds are bringing
Far-off chimes of church-bells ringing.

Night and morning, noon and even,
Their sound fills her dreams with Heaven:
The long strife at length is striven:
20   Till her grave-bands shall be riven,
Such is the good portion given
To her soul at rest and shriven.

SONG.

She sat and sang alway
  By the green margin of a stream,
Watching the fishes leap and play
  Beneath the glad sunbeam.

5   I sat and wept alway
  Beneath the moon's most shadowy beam,
Watching the blossoms of the May
  Weep leaves into the stream.

I wept for memory;
10 She sang for hope that is so fair:
My tears were swallowed by the sea;
  Her songs died on the air.

SONG.

When I am dead, my dearest,
  Sing no sad songs for me;
Plant thou no roses at my head,
  Nor shady cypress tree:
5 Be the green grass above me
  With showers and dewdrops wet;
And if thou wilt, remember,
  And if thou wilt, forget.

I shall not see the shadows,
10 I shall not feel the rain;
I shall not hear the nightingale
  Sing on, as if in pain:
And dreaming through the twilight
  That doth not rise nor set,
15 Haply I may remember,
  And haply may forget.

DEAD BEFORE DEATH.

Ah! changed and cold, how changed and very cold!
  With stiffened smiling lips and cold calm eyes:
  Changed, yet the same; much knowing, little wise;
This was the promise of the days of old!
5 Grown hard and stubborn in the ancient mould,
  Grown rigid in the sham of lifelong lies:
  We hoped for better things as years would rise,
But it is over as a tale once told.
All fallen the blossom that no fruitage bore,
10 All lost the present and the future time,
All lost, all lost, the lapse that went before:
So lost till death shut-to the opened door,
  So lost from chime to everlasting chime,
So cold and lost for ever evermore.

BITTER FOR SWEET.

Summer is gone with all its roses,
  Its sun and perfumes and sweet flowers,
  Its warm air and refreshing showers:
  And even Autumn closes.

5 Yea, Autumn's chilly self is going,
  And Winter comes which is yet colder;
  Each day the hoar-frost waxes bolder,
  And the last buds cease blowing.

SISTER MAUDE.

Who told my mother of my shame,
  Who told my father of my dear?

Oh who but Maude, my sister Maude,
  Who lurked to spy and peer.

5 Cold he lies, as cold as stone,
  With his clotted curls about his face:
The comeliest corpse in all the world
  And worthy of a queen's embrace.

You might have spared his soul, sister,
10   Have spared my soul, your own soul too:
Though I had not been born at all,
  He'd never have looked at you.

My father may sleep in Paradise,
  My mother at Heaven-gate:
15 But sister Maude shall get no sleep
  Either early or late.

My father may wear a golden gown,
  My mother a crown may win;
If my dear and I knocked at Heaven-gate
20   Perhaps they'd let us in:
But sister Maude, oh sister Maude,
  Bide *you* with death and sin.

REST.

O Earth, lie heavily upon her eyes;
  Seal her sweet eyes weary of watching, Earth;
  Lie close around her; leave no room for mirth
With its harsh laughter, nor for sound of sighs.
5 She hath no questions, she hath no replies,
  Hushed in and curtained with a blessèd dearth
  Of all that irked her from the hour of birth;
With stillness that is almost Paradise.
Darkness more clear than noon-day holdeth her,
10   Silence more musical than any song;
Even her very heart has ceased to stir:

Until the morning of Eternity
Her rest shall not begin nor end, but be;
　And when she wakes she will not think it long.

THE FIRST SPRING DAY.

I wonder if the sap is stirring yet,
If wintry birds are dreaming of a mate,
If frozen snowdrops feel as yet the sun
And crocus fires are kindling one by one:
5　　　Sing, robin, sing;
I still am sore in doubt concerning Spring.

I wonder if the springtide of this year
Will bring another Spring both lost and dear;
If heart and spirit will find out their Spring,
10　Or if the world alone will bud and sing:
　　　Sing, hope, to me;
Sweet notes, my hope, soft notes for memory.

The sap will surely quicken soon or late,
The tardiest bird will twitter to a mate;
15　So Spring must dawn again with warmth and bloom,
Or in this world, or in the world to come:
　　　Sing, voice of Spring,
Till I too blossom and rejoice and sing.

THE CONVENT THRESHOLD.

There's blood between us, love, my love,
There's father's blood, there's brother's blood;
And blood's a bar I cannot pass:
I choose the stairs that mount above,
5　Stair after golden skyward stair,

To city and to sea of glass.
My lily feet are soiled with mud,
With scarlet mud which tells a tale
Of hope that was, of guilt that was,
10   Of love that shall not yet avail;
Alas, my heart, if I could bare
My heart, this selfsame stain is there:
I seek the sea of glass and fire
To wash the spot, to burn the snare;
15   Lo, stairs are meant to lift us higher:
Mount with me, mount the kindled stair.

Your eyes look earthward, mine look up.
I see the far-off city grand,
Beyond the hills a watered land,
20   Beyond the gulf a gleaming strand
Of mansions where the righteous sup;
Who sleep at ease among their trees,
Or wake to sing a cadenced hymn
With Cherubim and Seraphim;
25   They bore the Cross, they drained the cup,
Racked, roasted, crushed, wrenched limb from limb,
They the offscouring of the world:
The heaven of starry heavens unfurled,
The sun before their face is dim.

30   You looking earthward, what see you?
Milk-white, wine-flushed among the vines,
Up and down leaping, to and fro,
Most glad, most full, made strong with wines,
Blooming as peaches pearled with dew,
35   Their golden windy hair afloat,
Love-music warbling in their throat,
Young men and women come and go.

You linger, yet the time is short:
Flee for your life, gird up your strength
40   To flee; the shadows stretched at length
Show that day wanes, that night draws nigh;
Flee to the mountain, tarry not.

Is this a time for smile and sigh,
For songs among the secret trees
45   Where sudden blue birds nest and sport?
The time is short and yet you stay:
Today while it is called today
Kneel, wrestle, knock, do violence, pray;
Today is short, tomorrow nigh:
50   Why will you die? why will you die?

You sinned with me a pleasant sin:
Repent with me, for I repent.
Woe's me the lore I must unlearn!
Woe's me that easy way we went,
55   So rugged when I would return!
How long until my sleep begin,
How long shall stretch these nights and days?
Surely, clean Angels cry, she prays;
She laves her soul with tedious tears:
60   How long must stretch these years and years?

I turn from you my cheeks and eyes,
My hair which you shall see no more—
Alas for joy that went before,
For joy that dies, for love that dies.
65   Only my lips still turn to you,
My livid lips that cry, Repent.
Oh weary life, Oh weary Lent,
Oh weary time whose stars are few.

How should I rest in Paradise,
70   Or sit on steps of heaven alone?
If Saints and Angels spoke of love
Should I not answer from my throne:
Have pity upon me, ye my friends,
For I have heard the sound thereof:
75   Should I not turn with yearning eyes,
Turn earthwards with a pitiful pang?
Oh save me from a pang in heaven.
By all the gifts we took and gave,
Repent, repent, and be forgiven:

80   This life is long, but yet it ends;
      Repent and purge your soul and save:
      No gladder song the morning stars
      Upon their birthday morning sang
      Than Angels sing when one repents.

85   I tell you what I dreamed last night:
      A spirit with transfigured face
      Fire-footed clomb an infinite space.
      I heard his hundred pinions clang,
      Heaven-bells rejoicing rang and rang,
90   Heaven-air was thrilled with subtle scents,
      Worlds spun upon their rushing cars:
      He mounted shrieking: "Give me light."
      Still light was poured on him, more light;
      Angels, Archangels he outstripped
95   Exultant in exceeding might,
      And trod the skirts of Cherubim.
      Still "Give me light," he shrieked; and dipped
      His thirsty face, and drank a sea,
      Athirst with thirst it could not slake.
100   I saw him, drunk with knowledge, take
      From aching brows the aureole crown—
      His locks writhed like a cloven snake—
      He left his throne to grovel down
      And lick the dust of Seraphs' feet:
105   For what is knowledge duly weighed?
      Knowledge is strong, but love is sweet;
      Yea all the progress he had made
      Was but to learn that all is small
      Save love, for love is all in all.

110   I tell you what I dreamed last night:
      It was not dark, it was not light,
      Cold dews had drenched my plenteous hair
      Thro' clay; you came to seek me there.
      And "Do you dream of me?" you said.
115   My heart was dust that used to leap
      To you; I answered half asleep:
      "My pillow is damp, my sheets are red,

There's a leaden tester to my bed:
Find you a warmer playfellow,
120 A warmer pillow for your head,
A kinder love to love than mine."
You wrung your hands; while I like lead
Crushed downwards thro' the sodden earth:
You smote your hands but not in mirth,
125 And reeled but were not drunk with wine.

For all night long I dreamed of you:
I woke and prayed against my will,
Then slept to dream of you again.
At length I rose and knelt and prayed:
130 I cannot write the words I said,
My words were slow, my tears were few;
But thro' the dark my silence spoke
Like thunder. When this morning broke,
My face was pinched, my hair was grey,
135 And frozen blood was on the sill
Where stifling in my struggle I lay.

If now you saw me you would say:
Where is the face I used to love?
And I would answer: Gone before;
140 It tarries veiled in paradise.
When once the morning star shall rise,
When earth with shadow flees away
And we stand safe within the door,
Then you shall lift the veil thereof.
145 Look up, rise up: for far above
Our palms are grown, our place is set;
There we shall meet as once we met
And love with old familiar love.

UP-HILL.

Does the road wind up-hill all the way?
    Yes, to the very end.

Will the day's journey take the whole long day?
  From morn to night, my friend.

5 But is there for the night a resting-place?
  A roof for when the slow dark hours begin.
May not the darkness hide it from my face?
  You cannot miss that inn.

Shall I meet other wayfarers at night?
10   Those who have gone before.
Then must I knock, or call when just in sight?
  They will not keep you standing at that door.

Shall I find comfort, travel-sore and weak?
  Of labour you shall find the sum.
15 Will there be beds for me and all who seek?
  Yea, beds for all who come.

"THE LOVE OF CHRIST WHICH PASSETH KNOWLEDGE."

I bore with thee long weary days and nights,
  Through many pangs of heart, through many tears;
I bore with thee, thy hardness, coldness, slights,
  For three and thirty years.

5 Who else had dared for thee what I have dared?
  I plunged the depth most deep from bliss above;
I not My flesh, I not My spirit spared:
  Give thou Me love for love.

For thee I thirsted in the daily drouth,
10   For thee I trembled in the nightly frost:
Much sweeter thou than honey to My mouth:
  Why wilt thou still be lost?

I bore thee on My shoulders and rejoiced:
  Men only marked upon My shoulders borne
15 The branding cross; and shouted hungry-voiced,
  Or wagged their heads in scorn.

Thee did nails grave upon My hands, thy name
   Did thorns for frontlets stamp between Mine eyes:
I, Holy One, put on thy guilt and shame;
20   I, God, Priest, Sacrifice.

A thief upon My right hand and My left;
   Six hours alone, athirst, in misery:
At length in death one smote My heart and cleft
   A hiding-place for thee.

25 Nailed to the racking cross, than bed of down
   More dear, whereon to stretch Myself and sleep:
So did I win a kingdom,—share My crown;
   A harvest,—come and reap.

"A BRUISED REED SHALL HE NOT BREAK."

I will accept thy will to do and be,
   Thy hatred and intolerance of sin,
   Thy will at least to love, that burns within
   And thirsteth after Me:
5 So will I render fruitful, blessing still
   The germs and small beginnings in thy heart,
   Because thy will cleaves to the better part.—
   Alas, I cannot will.

Dost not thou will, poor soul? Yet I receive
10   The inner unseen longings of the soul,
   I guide them turning towards Me; I control
   And charm hearts till they grieve:
If thou desire, it yet shall come to pass,
   Tho' thou but wish indeed to choose My love;
15   For I have power in earth and heaven above.—
   I cannot wish, alas!

What, neither choose nor wish to choose? and yet
   I still must strive to win thee and constrain:
   For thee I hung upon the cross in pain,
20   How then can I forget?

If thou as yet dost neither love, nor hate,
   Nor choose, nor wish,—resign thyself, be still
   Till I infuse love, hatred, longing, will.—
     I do not deprecate.

A BETTER RESURRECTION.

I have no wit, no words, no tears;
   My heart within me like a stone
Is numbed too much for hopes or fears;
   Look right, look left, I dwell alone;
5   I lift mine eyes, but dimmed with grief
     No everlasting hills I see;
My life is in the falling leaf:
     O Jesus, quicken me.

My life is like a faded leaf,
10   My harvest dwindled to a husk;
Truly my life is void and brief
   And tedious in the barren dusk;
My life is like a frozen thing,
   No bud nor greenness can I see:
15   Yet rise it shall—the sap of Spring;
     O Jesus, rise in me.

My life is like a broken bowl,
   A broken bowl that cannot hold
One drop of water for my soul
20   Or cordial in the searching cold;
Cast in the fire the perished thing,
   Melt and remould it, till it be
A royal cup for Him my King:
     O Jesus, drink of me.

ADVENT.

This Advent moon shines cold and clear,
   These Advent nights are long;

Our lamps have burned year after year
    And still their flame is strong.
5 "Watchman, what of the night?" we cry
    Heart-sick with hope deferred:
"No speaking signs are in the sky,"
    Is still the watchman's word.

The Porter watches at the gate,
10   The servants watch within;
The watch is long betimes and late,
    The prize is slow to win.
"Watchman, what of the night?" but still
    His answer sounds the same:
15 "No daybreak tops the utmost hill,
    Nor pale our lamps of flame."

One to another hear them speak
    The patient virgins wise:
"Surely He is not far to seek"—
20   "All night we watch and rise."
"The days are evil looking back,
    The coming days are dim;
Yet count we not His promise slack,
    But watch and wait for Him."

25 One with another, soul with soul,
    They kindle fire from fire:
"Friends watch us who have touched the goal."
    "They urge us, come up higher."
"With them shall rest our waysore feet,
30   With them is built our home,
With Christ."—"They sweet, but He most sweet,
    Sweeter than honeycomb."

There no more parting, no more pain,
    The distant ones brought near,
35 The lost so long are found again,
    Long lost but longer dear:
Eye hath not seen, ear hath not heard,
    Nor heart conceived that rest,
With them our good things long deferred,
40   With Jesus Christ our Best.

We weep because the night is long,
  We laugh for day shall rise,
We sing a slow contented song
  And knock at Paradise.
45 Weeping we hold Him fast, Who wept
  For us, we hold Him fast;
And will not let Him go except
  He bless us first or last.

Weeping we hold Him fast tonight;
50 We will not let Him go
Till daybreak smite our wearied sight
  And summer smite the snow:
Then figs shall bud, and dove with dove
  Shall coo the livelong day;
55 Then He shall say, "Arise, My love,
  My fair one, come away."

THE THREE ENEMIES.

THE FLESH.
"Sweet, thou art pale."
   "More pale to see,
Christ hung upon the cruel tree
And bore His Father's wrath for me."

5 "Sweet, thou art sad."
   "Beneath a rod
More heavy, Christ for my sake trod
The winepress of the wrath of God."

"Sweet, thou art weary."
10   "Not so Christ:
Whose mighty love of me sufficed
For Strength, Salvation, Eucharist."

"Sweet, thou art footsore."
   "If I bleed,

15 His feet have bled: yea, in my need
    His Heart once bled for mine indeed."

            THE WORLD.
    "Sweet, thou art young."
        "So He was young
    Who for my sake in silence hung
20 Upon the Cross with Passion wrung."

    "Look, thou art fair."
        "He was more fair
    Than men, Who deigned for me to wear
    A visage marred beyond compare."

25 "And thou hast riches."
        "Daily bread:
    All else is His; Who living, dead,
    For me lacked where to lay His Head."

    "And life is sweet."
30   "It was not so
    To Him, Whose Cup did overflow
    With mine unutterable woe."

            THE DEVIL.
    "Thou drinkest deep."
        "When Christ would sup
35 He drained the dregs from out my cup:
    So how should I be lifted up?"

    "Thou shalt win Glory."
        "In the skies,
    Lord Jesus, cover up mine eyes
40 Lest they should look on vanities."

    "Thou shalt have Knowledge."
        "Helpless dust,
    In Thee, O Lord, I put my trust:
    Answer Thou for me, Wise and Just."

45 "And Might."—
        "Get thee behind me. Lord,

Who hast redeemed and not abhorred
My soul, oh keep it by Thy Word."

ONE CERTAINTY.

Vanity of vanities, the Preacher saith,
  All things are vanity. The eye and ear
  Cannot be filled with what they see and hear.
Like early dew, or like the sudden breath
5 Of wind, or like the grass that withereth,
    Is man, tossed to and fro by hope and fear:
    So little joy hath he, so little cheer,
Till all things end in the long dust of death.
Today is still the same as yesterday,
10   Tomorrow also even as one of them;
And there is nothing new under the sun:
Until the ancient race of Time be run,
    The old thorns shall grow out of the old stem,
And morning shall be cold and twilight grey.

CHRISTIAN AND JEW.
A DIALOGUE.

"Oh happy happy land!
Angels like rushes stand
  About the wells of light."—
  "Alas, I have not eyes for this fair sight:
5 Hold fast my hand."—

"As in a soft wind, they
Bend all one blessed way,
  Each bowed in his own glory, star with star."—
  "I cannot see so far,
10 Here shadows are."—

"White-winged the cherubim,
Yet whiter seraphim,
   Glow white with intense fire of love."—
"Mine eyes are dim:
15   I look in vain above,
And miss their hymn."—

"Angels, Archangels cry
One to other ceaselessly
   (I hear them sing)
20   One 'Holy, Holy, Holy' to their King."—
"I do not hear them, I."—

"Joy to thee, Paradise,—
   Garden and goal and nest!
Made green for wearied eyes;
25   Much softer than the breast
Of mother-dove clad in a rainbow's dyes.

"All precious souls are there
   Most safe, elect by grace,
All tears are wiped for ever from their face:
30 Untired in prayer
   They wait and praise
Hidden for a little space.

"Boughs of the Living Vine
They spread in summer shine
35   Green leaf with leaf:
Sap of the Royal Vine it stirs like wine
   In all both less and chief.

"Sing to the Lord,
   All spirits of all flesh, sing;
40 For He hath not abhorred
Our low estate nor scorn'd our offering:
Shout to our King."—

"But Zion said:
   My Lord forgetteth me.
45 Lo, she hath made her bed
   In dust; forsaken weepeth she
Where alien rivers swell the sea.

"She laid her body as the ground,
    Her tender body as the ground to those
50 Who passed; her harpstrings cannot sound
In a strange land; discrowned
    She sits, and drunk with woes."—

"O drunken not with wine,
    Whose sins and sorrows have fulfilled the sum,—
55 Be not afraid, arise, be no more dumb;
Arise, shine,
    For thy light is come."—

"Can these bones live?"—
              "God knows:
60 The prophet saw such clothed with flesh and skin,
A wind blew on them and life entered in,
    They shook and rose.
    Hasten the time, O Lord, blot out their sin,
    Let life begin."

SWEET DEATH.

The sweetest blossoms die.
    And so it was that, going day by day
    Unto the Church to praise and pray,
And crossing the green churchyard thoughtfully,
5   I saw how on the graves the flowers
    Shed their fresh leaves in showers,
And how their perfume rose up to the sky
    Before it passed away.

The youngest blossoms die.
10   They die and fall and nourish the rich earth
    From which they lately had their birth;
Sweet life, but sweeter death that passeth by
    And is as though it had not been:—
    All colours turn to green;

15   The bright hues vanish and the odours fly,
       The grass hath lasting worth.

    And youth and beauty die.
       So be it, O my God, Thou God of truth:
       Better than beauty and than youth
20   Are Saints and Angels, a glad company;
       And Thou, O Lord, our Rest and Ease,
       Art better far than these.
    Why should we shrink from our full harvest? why
       Prefer to glean with Ruth?

SYMBOLS.

    I watched a rosebud very long
       Brought on by dew and sun and shower,
       Waiting to see the perfect flower:
    Then, when I thought it should be strong,
5   It opened at the matin hour
         And fell at evensong.

    I watched a nest from day to day,
       A green nest full of pleasant shade,
       Wherein three speckled eggs were laid:
10   But when they should have hatched in May,
       The two old birds had grown afraid
         Or tired, and flew away.

    Then in my wrath I broke the bough
       That I had tended so with care,
15   Hoping its scent should fill the air;
    I crushed the eggs, not heeding how
       Their ancient promise had been fair:
         I would have vengeance now.

    But the dead branch spoke from the sod,
20   And the eggs answered me again:
       Because we failed dost thou complain?

Is thy wrath just? And what if God,
  Who waiteth for thy fruits in vain,
  Should also take the rod?

"CONSIDER THE LILIES OF THE FIELD."

Flowers preach to us if we will hear:—
The rose saith in the dewy morn:
I am most fair;
Yet all my loveliness is born
5 Upon a thorn.
The poppy saith amid the corn:
Let but my scarlet head appear
And I am held in scorn;
Yet juice of subtle virtue lies
10 Within my cup of curious dyes.
The lilies say: Behold how we
Preach without words of purity.
The violets whisper from the shade
Which their own leaves have made:
15 Men scent our fragrance on the air,
Yet take no heed
Of humble lessons we would read.

But not alone the fairest flowers:
The merest grass
20 Along the roadside where we pass,
Lichen and moss and sturdy weed,
Tell of His love who sends the dew,
The rain and sunshine too,
To nourish one small seed.

THE WORLD.

By day she wooes me, soft, exceeding fair:
  But all night as the moon so changeth she;
  Loathsome and foul with hideous leprosy

And subtle serpents gliding in her hair.
5 By day she wooes me to the outer air,
    Ripe fruits, sweet flowers, and full satiety:
    But thro' the night, a beast she grins at me,
A very monster void of love and prayer.
By day she stands a lie: by night she stands
10   In all the naked horror of the truth
With pushing horns and clawed and clutching hands.
Is this a friend indeed; that I should sell
    My soul to her, give her my life and youth,
Till my feet, cloven too, take hold on hell?

A TESTIMONY.

I said of laughter: it is vain.
    Of mirth I said: what profits it?
    Therefore I found a book, and writ
Therein how ease and also pain,
5 How health and sickness, every one
Is vanity beneath the sun

Man walks in a vain shadow; he
    Disquieteth himself in vain.
    The things that were shall be again:
10 The rivers do not fill the sea,
But turn back to their secret source;
The winds too turn upon their course.

Our treasures moth and rust corrupt,
    Or thieves break thro' and steal, or they
15   Make themselves wings and fly away.
One man made merry as he supped,
Nor guessed how when that night grew dim
His soul would be required of him.

We build our houses on the sand
20   Comely withoutside and within;
    But when the winds and rains begin

To beat on them, they cannot stand:
They perish, quickly overthrown,
Loose from the very basement stone.

25   All things are vanity, I said:
     Yea vanity of vanities.
      The rich man dies; and the poor dies:
The worm feeds sweetly on the dead.
Whate'er thou lackest, keep this trust:
30   All in the end shall have but dust:

The one inheritance, which best
     And worst alike shall find and share:
      The wicked cease from troubling there,
And there the weary be at rest;
35   There all the wisdom of the wise
Is vanity of vanities.

Man flourishes as a green leaf,
     And as a leaf doth pass away;
      Or as a shade that cannot stay
40   And leaves no track, his course is brief:
Yet man doth hope and fear and plan
Till he is dead:—oh foolish man!

Our eyes cannot be satisfied
     With seeing, nor our ears be filled
45   With hearing: yet we plant and build
And buy and make our borders wide;
We gather wealth, we gather care,
But know not who shall be our heir.

Why should we hasten to arise
50   So early, and so late take rest?
      Our labour is not good; our best
Hopes fade; our heart is stayed on lies:
Verily, we sow wind; and we
Shall reap the whirlwind, verily.

55   He who hath little shall not lack;
     He who hath plenty shall decay:
      Our fathers went; we pass away;

Our children follow on our track:
So generations fail, and so
60   They are renewed and come and go.

The earth is fattened with our dead;
  She swallows more and doth not cease:
  Therefore her wine and oil increase
And her sheaves are not numberèd;
65 Therefore her plants are green, and all
Her pleasant trees lusty and tall.

Therefore the maidens cease to sing,
  And the young men are very sad;
  Therefore the sowing is not glad,
70 And mournful is the harvesting.
Of high and low, of great and small,
Vanity is the lot of all.

A King dwelt in Jerusalem;
  He was the wisest man on earth;
75   He had all riches from his birth,
And pleasures till he tired of them;
Then, having tested all things, he
Witnessed that all are vanity.

SLEEP AT SEA.

Sound the deep waters:—
  Who shall sound that deep?—
Too short the plummet
  And the watchmen sleep.
5 Some dream of effort
  Up a toilsome steep;
Some dream of pasture grounds
  For harmless sheep.

White shapes flit to and fro
10   From mast to mast;

They feel the distant tempest
    That nears them fast:
Great rocks are straight ahead,
    Great shoals not past;
15 They shout to one another
    Upon the blast.

Oh soft the streams drop music
    Between the hills,
And musical the birds' nests
20   Beside those rills:
The nests are types of home
    Love-hidden from ills,
The nests are types of spirits
    Love-music fills.

25 So dream the sleepers,
    Each man in his place;
The lightning shows the smile
    Upon each face:
The ship is driving, driving,
30   It drives apace:
And sleepers smile, and spirits
    Bewail their case.

The lightning glares and reddens
    Across the skies;
35 It seems but sunset
    To those sleeping eyes.
When did the sun go down
    On such a wise?
From such a sunset
40   When shall day arise?

"Wake," call the spirits:
    But to heedless ears;
They have forgotten sorrows
    And hopes and fears;
45 They have forgotten perils
    And smiles and tears;

Their dream has held them long,
  Long years and years.

"Wake," call the spirits again:
50   But it would take
A louder summons
  To bid them awake.
Some dream of pleasure
  For another's sake;
55 Some dream, forgetful
  Of a lifelong ache.

One by one slowly,
  Ah how sad and slow—
Wailing and praying
60   The spirits rise and go:
Clear stainless spirits
  White as white as snow;
Pale spirits, wailing
  For an overthrow.

65 One by one flitting,
  Like a mournful bird
Whose song is tired at last
  For no mate heard.
The loving voice is silent,
70   The useless word;
One by one flitting
  Sick with hope deferred.

Driving and driving,
  The ship drives amain:
75 While swift from mast to mast
  Shapes flit again,
Flit silent as the silence
  Where men lie slain;
Their shadow cast upon the sails
80   Is like a stain.

No voice to call the sleepers,
  No hand to raise:

They sleep to death in dreaming
    Of length of days.
85 Vanity of vanities,
    The Preacher says:
Vanity is the end
    Of all their ways.

FROM HOUSE TO HOME.

The first was like a dream thro' summer heat,
    The second like a tedious numbing swoon,
While the half-frozen pulses lagged to beat
    Beneath a winter moon.

5   "But," says my friend, "what was this thing and where?"
    It was a pleasure-place within my soul;
An earthly paradise supremely fair
    That lured me from the goal.

The first part was a tissue of hugged lies;
10   The second was its ruin fraught with pain:
Why raise the fair delusion to the skies
    But to be dashed again?

My castle stood of white transparent glass
    Glittering and frail with many a fretted spire,
15 But when the summer sunset came to pass
    It kindled into fire.

My pleasaunce was an undulating green,
    Stately with trees whose shadows slept below,
With glimpses of smooth garden-beds between
20   Like flame or sky or snow.

Swift squirrels on the pastures took their ease,
    With leaping lambs safe from the unfeared knife;
All singing-birds rejoicing in those trees
    Fulfilled their careless life.

25 Wood-pigeons cooed there, stockdoves nestled there,

My trees were full of songs and flowers and fruit,
Their branches spread a city to the air
    And mice lodged in their root.

My heath lay farther off, where lizards lived
30   In strange metallic mail, just spied and gone;
Like darted lightnings here and there perceived
    But no where dwelt upon.

Frogs and fat toads were there to hop or plod
    And propagate in peace, an uncouth crew,
35 Where velvet-headed rushes rustling nod
    And spill the morning dew.

All caterpillars throve beneath my rule,
    With snails and slugs in corners out of sight;
I never marred the curious sudden stool
40   That perfects in a night.

Safe in his excavated gallery
    The burrowing mole groped on from year to year;
No harmless hedgehog curled because of me
    His prickly back for fear.

45 Ofttimes one like an angel walked with me,
    With spirit-discerning eyes like flames of fire,
But deep as the unfathomed endless sea
    Fulfilling my desire:

And sometimes like a snowdrift he was fair,
50   And sometimes like a sunset glorious red,
And sometimes he had wings to scale the air
    With aureole round his head.

We sang our songs together by the way,
    Calls and recalls and echoes of delight;
55 So communed we together all the day,
    And so in dreams by night.

I have no words to tell what way we walked,
    What unforgotten path now closed and sealed;
I have no words to tell all things we talked,
60   All things that he revealed:

This only can I tell: that hour by hour
 I waxed more feastful, lifted up and glad;
I felt no thorn-prick when I plucked a flower,
 Felt not my friend was sad.

65 "Tomorrow," once I said to him with smiles:
 "Tonight," he answered gravely and was dumb,
But pointed out the stones that numbered miles
 And miles and miles to come.

"Not so," I said: "tomorrow shall be sweet;
70 Tonight is not so sweet as coming days."
Then first I saw that he had turned his feet,
 Had turned from me his face:

Running and flying miles and miles he went,
 But once looked back to beckon with his hand
75 And cry: "Come home, O love, from banishment:
 Come to the distant land."—

That night destroyed me like an avalanche;
 One night turned all my summer back to snow:
Next morning not a bird upon my branch,
80 Not a lamb woke below;

No bird, no lamb, no living breathing thing;
 No squirrel scampered on my breezy lawn,
No mouse lodged by his hoard: all joys took wing
 And fled before that dawn.

85 Azure and sun were starved from heaven above,
 No dew had fallen but biting frost lay hoar:
O love, I knew that I should meet my love,
 Should find my love no more.

"My love no more," I muttered, stunned with pain:
90 I shed no tear, I wrung no passionate hand,
Till something whispered: "You shall meet again,
 Meet in a distant land."

Then with a cry like famine I arose,
 I lit my candle, searched from room to room,
95 Searched up and down; a war of winds that froze
 Swept thro' the blank of gloom.

I searched day after day, night after night;
　　Scant change there came to me of night or day:
"No more," I wailed, "no more:" and trimmed my light,
100　　　And gnashed but did not pray,

Until my heart broke and my spirit broke:
　　Upon the frost-bound floor I stumbled, fell,
And moaned: "It is enough: withhold the stroke.
　　Farewell, O love, farewell."

105　Then life swooned from me. And I heard the song
　　Of spheres and spirits rejoicing over me:
One cried: "Our sister, she hath suffered long "—
　　One answered: "Make her see "—

One cried: "Oh blessed she who no more pain,
110　　Who no more disappointment shall receive "—
One answered: "Not so: she must live again;
　　Strengthen thou her to live."

So while I lay entranced a curtain seemed
　　To shrivel with crackling from before my face;
115　Across mine eyes a waxing radiance beamed
　　And showed a certain place.

I saw a vision of a woman, where
　　Night and new morning strive for domination;
Incomparably pale, and almost fair,
120　　And sad beyond expression.

Her eyes were like some fire-enshrining gem,
　　Were stately like the stars, and yet were tender;
Her figure charmed me like a windy stem
　　Quivering and drooped and slender.

125　I stood upon the outer barren ground,
　　She stood on inner ground that budded flowers;
While circling in their never-slackening round
　　Danced by the mystic hours.

But every flower was lifted on a thorn,
130　　And every thorn shot upright from its sands
To gall her feet; hoarse laughter pealed in scorn
　　With cruel clapping hands.

She bled and wept, yet did not shrink; her strength
Was strung up until daybreak of delight:
135   She measured measureless sorrow toward its length,
And breadth, and depth, and height.

Then marked I how a chain sustained her form,
A chain of living links not made nor riven:
It stretched sheer up thro' lightning, wind, and storm,
140   And anchored fast in heaven.

One cried: "How long? yet founded on the Rock
She shall do battle, suffer, and attain "—
One answered: "Faith quakes in the tempest shock:
Strengthen her soul again."

145   I saw a cup sent down and come to her
Brim full of loathing and of bitterness:
She drank with livid lips that seemed to stir
The depth, not make it less.

But as she drank I spied a hand distil
150   New wine and virgin honey; making it
First bitter-sweet, then sweet indeed, until
She tasted only sweet.

Her lips and cheeks waxed rosy-fresh and young;
Drinking she sang: "My soul shall nothing want;"
155   And drank anew: while soft a song was sung,
A mystical slow chant.

One cried: "The wounds are faithful of a friend:
The wilderness shall blossom as a rose "—
One answered: "Rend the veil, declare the end,
160   Strengthen her ere she goes."

Then earth and heaven were rolled up like a scroll;
Time and space, change and death, had passed away;
Weight, number, measure, each had reached its whole;
The day had come, that day.

165   Multitudes—multitudes—stood up in bliss,
Made equal to the angels, glorious, fair;
With harps, palms, wedding-garments, kiss of peace,
And crowned and haloed hair.

They sang a song, a new song in the height,
170   Harping with harps to Him Who is Strong and True:
They drank new wine, their eyes saw with new light,
    Lo, all things were made new.

Tier beyond tier they rose and rose and rose
    So high that it was dreadful, flames with flames:
175 No man could number them, no tongue disclose
    Their secret sacred names.

As tho' one pulse stirred all, one rush of blood
    Fed all, one breath swept thro' them myriad-voiced,
They struck their harps, cast down their crowns, they stood
180   And worshipped and rejoiced.

Each face looked one way like a moon new-lit,
    Each face looked one way towards its Sun of Love;
Drank love and bathed in love and mirrored it
    And knew no end thereof.

185 Glory touched glory on each blessed head,
    Hands locked dear hands never to sunder more:
These were the new-begotten from the dead
    Whom the great birthday bore.

Heart answered heart, soul answered soul at rest,
190   Double against each other, filled, sufficed:
All loving, loved of all; but loving best
    And best beloved of Christ.

I saw that one who lost her love in pain,
    Who trod on thorns, who drank the loathsome cup;
195 The lost in night, in day was found again;
    The fallen was lifted up.

They stood together in the blessed noon,
    They sang together thro' the length of days;
Each loving face bent Sunwards like a moon
200   New-lit with love and praise.

Therefore, O friend, I would not if I might
    Rebuild my house of lies, wherein I joyed
One time to dwell: my soul shall walk in white,
    Cast down but not destroyed.

205   Therefore in patience I possess my soul;
      Yea, therefore as a flint I set my face,
    To pluck down, to build up again the whole—
      But in a distant place.

    These thorns are sharp, yet I can tread on them;
210   This cup is loathsome, yet He makes it sweet:
    My face is steadfast toward Jerusalem,
      My heart remembers it.

    I lift the hanging hands, the feeble knees—
      I, precious more than seven times molten gold—
215   Until the day when from His storehouses
      God shall bring new and old;

    Beauty for ashes, oil of joy for grief,
      Garment of praise for spirit of heaviness:
    Altho' today I fade as doth a leaf,
220   I languish and grow less.

    Altho' today He prunes my twigs with pain,
      Yet doth His blood nourish and warm my root:
    Tomorrow I shall put forth buds again
      And clothe myself with fruit.

225   Altho' today I walk in tedious ways,
      Today His staff is turned into a rod,
    Yet will I wait for Him the appointed days
      And stay upon my God.

OLD AND NEW YEAR DITTIES.

1.

New Year met me somewhat sad:
    Old Year leaves me tired,
Stripped of favourite things I had,
    Baulked of much desired:
5   Yet farther on my road today
God willing, farther on my way.

New Year coming on apace
  What have you to give me?
Bring you scathe, or bring you grace,
10 Face me with an honest face;
  You shall not deceive me:
Be it good or ill, be it what you will,
It needs shall help me on my road,
My rugged way to heaven, please God.

2.

Watch with me, men, women, and children dear,
You whom I love, for whom I hope and fear,
Watch with me this last vigil of the year.
Some hug their business, some their pleasure scheme;
5 Some seize the vacant hour to sleep or dream;
Heart locked in heart some kneel and watch apart.

Watch with me, blessed spirits, who delight
All thro' the holy night to walk in white,
Or take your ease after the long-drawn fight.
10 I know not if they watch with me: I know
They count this eve of resurrection slow,
And cry, "How long?" with urgent utterance strong.

Watch with me, Jesus, in my loneliness:
Tho' others say me nay, yet say Thou yes;
15 Tho' others pass me by, stop Thou to bless.
Yea, Thou dost stop with me this vigil night;
Tonight of pain, tomorrow of delight:
I, Love, am Thine; Thou, Lord my God, art mine.

3.

Passing away, saith the World, passing away:
Chances, beauty and youth sapped day by day:
Thy life never continueth in one stay.
Is the eye waxen dim, is the dark hair changing to grey
5 That hath won neither laurel nor bay?
I shall clothe myself in Spring and bud in May:
Thou, root-stricken, shalt not rebuild thy decay
On my bosom for aye.
Then I answered: Yea.

10 Passing away, saith my Soul, passing away:
    With its burden of fear and hope, of labour and play;
    Hearken what the past doth witness and say:
    Rust in thy gold, a moth is in thine array,
    A canker is in thy bud, thy leaf must decay.
15 At midnight, at cockcrow, at morning, one certain day
    Lo the bridegroom shall come and shall not delay:
    Watch thou and pray.
    Then I answered: Yea.

    Passing away, saith my God, passing away:
20 Winter passeth after the long delay:
    New grapes on the vine, new figs on the tender spray,
    Turtle calleth turtle in Heaven's May.
    Tho' I tarry, wait for Me, trust Me, watch and pray.
    Arise, come away, night is past and lo it is day,
25 My love, My sister, My spouse, thou shalt hear Me say.
    Then I answered: Yea.

AMEN.

    It is over. What is over?
      Nay, how much is over truly:
    Harvest days we toiled to sow for;
      Now the sheaves are gathered newly,
5   Now the wheat is garnered duly.

    It is finished. What is finished?
      Much is finished known or unknown:
    Lives are finished; time diminished;
      Was the fallow field left unsown?
10   Will these buds be always unblown?

    It suffices. What suffices?
      All suffices reckoned rightly:

Spring shall bloom where now the ice is,
  Roses make the bramble sightly,
15   And the quickening sun shine brightly,
  And the latter wind blow lightly,
And my garden teem with spices.

II The Prince's Progress and Other Poems

(1866)

THE PRINCE'S PROGRESS.

Till all sweet gums and juices flow,
Till the blossom of blossoms blow,
The long hours go and come and go,
   The bride she sleepeth, waketh, sleepeth,
5 Waiting for one whose coming is slow:—
     Hark! the bride weepeth.

"How long shall I wait, come heat come rime?"—
"Till the strong Prince comes, who must come in time"
(Her women say), "there's a mountain to climb,
10   A river to ford. Sleep, dream and sleep:
Sleep" (they say): "we've muffled the chime,
     Better dream than weep."

In his world-end palace the strong Prince sat,
Taking his ease on cushion and mat,
15 Close at hand lay his staff and his hat.
   "When wilt thou start? the bride waits, O youth."—
"Now the moon's at full; I tarried for that,
     Now I start in truth.

"But tell me first, true voice of my doom,
20 Of my veiled bride in her maiden bloom;
Keeps she watch thro' glare and thro' gloom,
   Watch for me asleep and awake?"—
"Spell-bound she watches in one white room,
     And is patient for thy sake.

25 "By her head lilies and rosebuds grow;
The lilies droop, will the rosebuds blow?

The silver slim lilies hang the head low;
 Their stream is scanty, their sunshine rare;
Let the sun blaze out, and let the stream flow,
30 They will blossom and wax fair.

"Red and white poppies grow at her feet,
The blood-red wait for sweet summer heat,
Wrapped in bud-coats hairy and neat;
 But the white buds swell, one day they will burst,
35 Will open their death-cups drowsy and sweet—
  Which will open the first?"

Then a hundred sad voices lifted a wail,
And a hundred glad voices piped on the gale:
"Time is short, life is short," they took up the tale:
40 "Life is sweet, love is sweet, use today while you may;
Love is sweet, and tomorrow may fail;
  Love is sweet, use today."

While the song swept by, beseeching and meek,
Up rose the Prince with a flush on his cheek,
45 Up he rose to stir and to seek,
 Going forth in the joy of his strength;
Strong of limb if of purpose weak,
  Starting at length.

Forth he set in the breezy morn,
50 Across green fields of nodding corn,
As goodly a Prince as ever was born,
 Carolling with the carolling lark;—
Sure his bride will be won and worn,
  Ere fall of the dark.

55 So light his step, so merry his smile,
A milkmaid loitered beside a stile,
Set down her pail and rested awhile,
 A wave-haired milkmaid, rosy and white;
The Prince, who had journeyed at least a mile,
60 Grew athirst at the sight.

"Will you give me a morning draught?"—
"You're kindly welcome," she said, and laughed.

He lifted the pail, new milk he quaffed;
   Then wiping his curly black beard like silk:
65 "Whitest cow that ever was calved
     Surely gave you this milk."

Was it milk now, or was it cream?
Was she a maid, or an evil dream?
Her eyes began to glitter and gleam;
70   He would have gone, but he stayed instead;
Green they gleamed as he looked in them:
     "Give me my fee," she said.—

"I will give you a jewel of gold."—
"Not so; gold is heavy and cold."—
75 "I will give you a velvet fold
     Of foreign work your beauty to deck."—
"Better I like my kerchief rolled
     Light and white round my neck."—

"Nay," cried he, "but fix your own fee."—
80 She laughed, "You may give the full moon to me;
Or else sit under this apple-tree
     Here for one idle day by my side;
After that I'll let you go free,
     And the world is wide."

85 Loth to stay, yet to leave her slack,
He half turned away, then he quite turned back:
For courtesy's sake he could not lack
     To redeem his own royal pledge;
Ahead too the windy heaven lowered black
90   With a fire-cloven edge.

So he stretched his length in the apple-tree shade,
Lay and laughed and talked to the maid,
Who twisted her hair in a cunning braid
     And writhed it in shining serpent-coils,
95 And held him a day and night fast laid
     In her subtle toils.

At the death of night and the birth of day,
When the owl left off his sober play,

And the bat hung himself out of the way,
100   Woke the song of mavis and merle,
And heaven put off its hodden grey
        For mother-o'-pearl.

Peeped up daisies here and there,
Here, there, and everywhere;
105   Rose a hopeful lark in the air,
        Spreading out towards the sun his breast;
While the moon set solemn and fair
        Away in the West.

"Up, up, up," called the watchman lark,
110   In his clear réveillée: "Hearken, oh hark!
Press to the high goal, fly to the mark.
        Up, O sluggard, new morn is born;
If still asleep when the night falls dark,
        Thou must wait a second morn."

115   "Up, up, up," sad glad voices swelled:
"So the tree falls and lies as it's felled.
Be thy bands loosed, O sleeper, long held
        In sweet sleep whose end is not sweet.
Be the slackness girt and the softness quelled
120   And the slowness fleet."

Off he set. The grass grew rare,
A blight lurked in the darkening air,
The very moss grew hueless and spare,
        The last daisy stood all astunt;
125   Behind his back the soil lay bare,
        But barer in front.

A land of chasm and rent, a land
Of rugged blackness on either hand:
If water trickled its track was tanned
130   With an edge of rust to the chink;
If one stamped on stone or on sand
        It returned a clink.

A lifeless land, a loveless land,
Without lair or nest on either hand:

135　Only scorpions jerked in the sand,
　　　　Black as black iron, or dusty pale;
　　　From point to point sheer rock was manned
　　　　By scorpions in mail.

　　　A land of neither life nor death,
140　Where no man buildeth or fashioneth,
　　　Where none draws living or dying breath;
　　　　No man cometh or goeth there,
　　　No man doeth, seeketh, saith,
　　　　In the stagnant air.

145　Some old volcanic upset must
　　　Have rent the crust and blackened the crust;
　　　Wrenched and ribbed it beneath its dust
　　　　Above earth's molten centre at seethe,
　　　Heaved and heaped it by huge upthrust
150　　Of fire beneath.

　　　Untrodden before, untrodden since:
　　　Tedious land for a social Prince;
　　　Halting, he scanned the outs and ins,
　　　　Endless, labyrinthine, grim,
155　Of the solitude that made him wince,
　　　　Laying wait for him.

　　　By bulging rock and gaping cleft,
　　　Even of half mere daylight reft,
　　　Rueful he peered to right and left,
160　　Muttering in his altered mood:
　　　"The fate is hard that weaves my weft,
　　　　Tho' my lot be good."

　　　Dim the changes of day to night,
　　　Of night scarce dark to day not bright.
165　Still his road wound towards the right,
　　　　Still he went, and still he went,
　　　Till one night he spied a light,
　　　　In his discontent.

　　　Out it flashed from a yawn-mouthed cave,
170　Like a red-hot eye from a grave.

No man stood there of whom to crave
    Rest for wayfarer plodding by:
Tho' the tenant were churl or knave
    The Prince might try.

175 In he passed and tarried not,
Groping his way from spot to spot,
Towards where the cavern flare glowed hot:—
    An old, old mortal, cramped and double,
Was peering into a seething-pot,
180   In a world of trouble.

The veriest atomy he looked,
With grimy fingers clutching and crooked,
Tight skin, a nose all bony and hooked,
    And a shaking, sharp, suspicious way;
185 Blinking, his eyes had scarcely brooked
      The light of day.

Stared the Prince, for the sight was new;
Stared, but asked without more ado:
"May a weary traveller lodge with you,
190   Old father, here in your lair?
In your country the inns seem few,
    And scanty the fare."

The head turned not to hear him speak;
The old voice whistled as thro' a leak
195 (Out it came in a quavering squeak):
    "Work for wage is a bargain fit:
If there's aught of mine that you seek
      You must work for it.

"Buried alive from light and air
200 This year is the hundredth year,
I feed my fire with a sleepless care,
    Watching my potion wane or wax:
Elixir of Life is simmering there,
      And but one thing lacks.

205 "If you're fain to lodge here with me,
Take that pair of bellows you see—

Too heavy for my old hands they be—
    Take the bellows and puff and puff:
When the steam curls rosy and free
₂₁₀   The broth's boiled enough.

"Then take your choice of all I have;
I will give you life if you crave.
Already I'm mildewed for the grave,
    So first myself I must drink my fill:
₂₁₅ But all the rest may be yours, to save
    Whomever you will."

"Done," quoth the Prince, and the bargain stood.
First he piled on resinous wood,
Next plied the bellows in hopeful mood;
₂₂₀   Thinking, "My love and I will live.
If I tarry, why life is good,
    And she may forgive."

The pot began to bubble and boil;
The old man cast in essence and oil,
₂₂₅ He stirred all up with a triple coil
    Of gold and silver and iron wire,
Dredged in a pinch of virgin soil,
    And fed the fire.

But still the steam curled watery white;
₂₃₀ Night turned to day and day to night;
One thing lacked, by his feeble sight
    Unseen, unguessed by his feeble mind:
Life might miss him, but Death the blight
    Was sure to find.

₂₃₅ So when the hundredth year was full
The thread was cut and finished the school.
Death snapped the old worn-out tool,
    Snapped him short while he stood and stirred
(Tho' stiff he stood as a stiff-necked mule)
₂₄₀   With never a word.

Thus at length the old crab was nipped.
The dead hand slipped, the dead finger dipped

In the broth as the dead man slipped,—
   That same instant, a rosy red
245 Flushed the steam, and quivered and clipped
   Round the dead old head.

The last ingredient was supplied
(Unless the dead man mistook or lied).
Up started the Prince, he cast aside
250   The bellows plied thro' the tedious trial,
Made sure that his host had died,
   And filled a phial.

"One night's rest," thought the Prince: "This done,
Forth I speed with the rising sun:
255 With the morrow I rise and run,
   Come what will of wind or of weather.
This draught of Life when my Bride is won
   We'll drink together."

Thus the dead man stayed in his grave,
260 Self-chosen, the dead man in his cave;
There he stayed, were he fool or knave,
   Or honest seeker who had not found:
While the Prince outside was prompt to crave
   Sleep on the ground.

265 "If she watches, go bid her sleep;
Bid her sleep, for the road is steep:
He can sleep who holdeth her cheap,
   Sleep and wake and sleep again.
Let him sow, one day he shall reap,
270   Let him sow the grain.

"When there blows a sweet garden rose,
Let it bloom and wither if no man knows:
But if one knows when the sweet thing blows,
   Knows, and lets it open and drop,
275 If but a nettle his garden grows
   He hath earned the crop."

Thro' his sleep the summons rang,
Into his ears it sobbed and it sang.

Slow he woke with a drowsy pang,
280   Shook himself without much debate,
Turned where he saw green branches hang,
        Started tho' late.

For the black land was travelled o'er,
He should see the grim land no more.
285   A flowering country stretched before
        His face when the lovely day came back:
He hugged the phial of Life he bore,
        And resumed his track.

By willow courses he took his path,
290   Spied what a nest the kingfisher hath,
Marked the fields green to aftermath,
        Marked where the red-brown field-mouse ran,
Loitered awhile for a deep-stream bath,
        Yawned for a fellow-man.

295   Up on the hills not a soul in view,
In the vale not many nor few;
Leaves, still leaves, and nothing new.
        It's oh for a second maiden, at least,
To bear the flagon, and taste it too,
300   And flavour the feast.

Lagging he moved, and apt to swerve;
Lazy of limb, but quick of nerve.
At length the water-bed took a curve,
        The deep river swept its bankside bare;
305   Waters streamed from the hill-reserve—
        Waters here, waters there.

High above, and deep below,
Bursting, bubbling, swelling the flow,
Like hill-torrents after the snow,—
310   Bubbling, gurgling, in whirling strife,
Swaying, sweeping, to and fro,—
        He must swim for his life.

Which way?—which way?—his eyes grew dim
With the dizzying whirl—which way to swim?

315   The thunderous downshoot deafened him;
         Half he choked in the lashing spray:
      Life is sweet, and the grave is grim—
         Which way?—which way?

      A flash of light, a shout from the strand:
320   "This way—this way; here lies the land!"
      His phial clutched in one drowning hand;
         He catches—misses—catches a rope;
      His feet slip on the slipping sand:
         Is there life?—is there hope?

325   Just saved, without pulse or breath,—
      Scarcely saved from the gulp of death;
      Laid where a willow shadoweth—
         Laid where a swelling turf is smooth.
      (O Bride! but the Bridegroom lingereth
330   For all thy sweet youth.)

      Kind hands do and undo,
      Kind voices whisper and coo:
      "I will chafe his hands"—"And I"—"And you
         Raise his head, put his hair aside."
335   (If many laugh, one well may rue:
         Sleep on, thou Bride.)

      So the Prince was tended with care:
      One wrung foul ooze from his clustered hair;
      Two chafed his hands, and did not spare;
340   But one propped his head that drooped awry:
      Till his eyes oped, and at unaware
         They met eye to eye.

      Oh a moon face in a shadowy place,
      And a light touch and a winsome grace,
345   And a thrilling tender voice which says:
         "Safe from waters that seek the sea—
      Cold waters by rugged ways—
         Safe with me."

      While overhead bird whistles to bird,
350   And round about plays a gamesome herd:

"Safe with us"—some take up the word—
"Safe with us, dear lord and friend:
All the sweeter if long deferred
        Is rest in the end."

355 Had he stayed to weigh and to scan,
He had been more or less than a man:
He did what a young man can,
        Spoke of toil and an arduous way—
Toil tomorrow, while golden ran
360   The sands of today.

Slip past, slip fast,
Uncounted hours from first to last,
Many hours till the last is past,
        Many hours dwindling to one—
365 One hour whose die is cast,
        One last hour gone.

Come, gone—gone for ever—
Gone as an unreturning river—
Gone as to death the merriest liver—
370   Gone as the year at the dying fall—
Tomorrow, today, yesterday, never—
        Gone once for all.

Came at length the starting-day,
With last words, and last, last words to say,
375 With bodiless cries from far away—
        Chiding wailing voices that rang
Like a trumpet-call to the tug and fray;
        And thus they sang:

"Is there life?—the lamp burns low;
380 Is there hope?—the coming is slow:
The promise promised so long ago,
        The long promise, has not been kept.
Does she live?—does she die?—she slumbers so
        Who so oft has wept.

385 "Does she live?—does she die?—she languisheth
As a lily drooping to death,

As a drought-worn bird with failing breath,
 As a lovely vine without a stay,
As a tree whereof the owner saith,
390 'Hew it down today.'"

Stung by that word the Prince was fain
To start on his tedious road again.
He crossed the stream where a ford was plain,
 He clomb the opposite bank tho' steep,
395 And swore to himself to strain and attain
  Ere he tasted sleep.

Huge before him a mountain frowned
With foot of rock on the valley ground,
And head with snows incessant crowned,
400 And a cloud mantle about its strength,
And a path which the wild goat hath not found
  In its breadth and length.

But he was strong to do and dare:
If a host had withstood him there,
405 He had braved a host with little care
  In his lusty youth and his pride,
Tough to grapple tho' weak to snare.
  He comes, O Bride.

Up he went where the goat scarce clings,
410 Up where the eagle folds her wings,
Past the green line of living things,
  Where the sun cannot warm the cold,—
Up he went as a flame enrings
  Where there seems no hold.

415 Up a fissure barren and black,
Till the eagles tired upon his track,
And the clouds were left behind his back,
  Up till the utmost peak was past.
Then he gasped for breath and his strength fell slack;
420 He paused at last.

Before his face a valley spread
Where fatness laughed, wine, oil, and bread,

Where all fruit-trees their sweetness shed,
   Where all birds made love to their kind,
425 Where jewels twinkled, and gold lay red
     And not hard to find.

Midway down the mountain side
(On its green slope the path was wide)
Stood a house for a royal bride,
430   Built all of changing opal stone,
The royal palace, till now descried
     In his dreams alone.

Less bold than in days of yore,
Doubting now tho' never before,
435 Doubting he goes and lags the more:
   Is the time late? does the day grow dim?
Rose, will she open the crimson core
     Of her heart to him?

Above his head a tangle glows
440 Of wine-red roses, blushes, snows,
Closed buds and buds that unclose,
   Leaves, and moss, and prickles too;
His hand shook as he plucked a rose,
     And the rose dropped dew.

445 Take heart of grace! the potion of Life
May go far to woo him a wife:
If she frown, yet a lover's strife
   Lightly raised can be laid again:
A hasty word is never the knife
450   To cut love in twain.

Far away stretched the royal land,
Fed by dew, by a spice-wind fanned:
Light labour more, and his foot would stand
   On the threshold, all labour done;
455 Easy pleasure laid at his hand,
     And the dear Bride won.

His slackening steps pause at the gate—
Does she wake or sleep?—the time is late—

Does she sleep now, or watch and wait?
460   She has watched, she has waited long,
Watching athwart the golden grate
        With a patient song.

Fling the golden portals wide,
The Bridegroom comes to his promised Bride;
465   Draw the gold-stiff curtains aside,
        Let them look on each other's face,
She in her meekness, he in his pride—
        Day wears apace.

Day is over, the day that wore.
470   What is this that comes thro' the door,
The face covered, the feet before?
        This that coming takes his breath;
This Bride not seen, to be seen no more
        Save of Bridegroom Death?

475   Veiled figures carrying her
Sweep by yet make no stir;
There is a smell of spice and myrrh,
        A bride-chant burdened with one name;
The bride-song rises steadier
480   Than the torches' flame:

"Too late for love, too late for joy,
        Too late, too late!
You loitered on the road too long,
        You trifled at the gate:
485   The enchanted dove upon her branch
        Died without a mate;
The enchanted princess in her tower
        Slept, died, behind the grate;
Her heart was starving all this while
490   You made it wait.

"Ten years ago, five years ago,
        One year ago,
Even then you had arrived in time,
        Tho' somewhat slow;

495 Then you had known her living face
        Which now you cannot know:
     The frozen fountain would have leaped,
        The buds gone on to blow,
     The warm south wind would have awaked
500   To melt the snow.

     "Is she fair now as she lies?
        Once she was fair;
     Meet queen for any kingly king,
        With gold-dust on her hair.
505 Now these are poppies in her locks,
        White poppies she must wear;
     Must wear a veil to shroud her face
        And the want graven there:
     Or is the hunger fed at length,
510   Cast off the care?

     "We never saw her with a smile
        Or with a frown;
     Her bed seemed never soft to her,
        Tho' tossed of down;
515 She little heeded what she wore,
        Kirtle, or wreath, or gown;
     We think her white brows often ached
        Beneath her crown,
     Till silvery hairs showed in her locks
520   That used to be so brown.

     "We never heard her speak in haste:
        Her tones were sweet,
     And modulated just so much
        As it was meet:
525 Her heart sat silent thro' the noise
        And concourse of the street.
     There was no hurry in her hands,
        No hurry in her feet;
     There was no bliss drew nigh to her,
530   That she might run to greet.

"You should have wept her yesterday,
     Wasting upon her bed:
But wherefore should you weep today
     That she is dead?
535   Lo, we who love weep not today,
     But crown her royal head.
Let be these poppies that we strew,
     Your roses are too red:
Let be these poppies, not for you
540   Cut down and spread."

MAIDEN-SONG.

Long ago and long ago,
     And long ago still,
There dwelt three merry maidens
     Upon a distant hill.
5   One was tall Meggan,
     And one was dainty May,
But one was fair Margaret,
     More fair than I can say,
Long ago and long ago.

10   When Meggan plucked the thorny rose,
     And when May pulled the brier,
Half the birds would swoop to see,
     Half the beasts draw nigher;
Half the fishes of the streams
15   Would dart up to admire:
But when Margaret plucked a flag-flower,
     Or poppy hot aflame,
All the beasts and all the birds
     And all the fishes came
20   To her hand more soft than snow.

Strawberry leaves and May-dew
     In brisk morning air,

Strawberry leaves and May-dew
   Make maidens fair.
25 "I go for strawberry leaves,"
   Meggan said one day:
"Fair Margaret can bide at home,
   But you come with me, May;
Up the hill and down the hill,
30   Along the winding way
You and I are used to go."

So these two fair sisters
   Went with innocent will
Up the hill and down again,
35   And round the homestead hill:
While the fairest sat at home,
   Margaret like a queen,
Like a blush-rose, like the moon
   In her heavenly sheen,
40 Fragrant-breathed as milky cow
   Or field of blossoming bean,
Graceful as an ivy bough
   Born to cling and lean;
Thus she sat to sing and sew.

45 When she raised her lustrous eyes
   A beast peeped at the door;
When she downward cast her eyes
   A fish gasped on the floor;
When she turned away her eyes
50   A bird perched on the sill,
Warbling out its heart of love,
   Warbling warbling still,
With pathetic pleadings low.

Light-foot May with Meggan
55   Sought the choicest spot,
Clothed with thyme-alternate grass:
   Then, while day waxed hot,
Sat at ease to play and rest,
   A gracious rest and play;

60   The loveliest maidens near or far,
       When Margaret was away,
     Who sat at home to sing and sew.

     Sun-glow flushed their comely cheeks,
       Wind-play tossed their hair,
65   Creeping things among the grass
       Stroked them here and there;
     Meggan piped a merry note,
       A fitful wayward lay,
     While shrill as bird on topmost twig
70   Piped merry May;
     Honey-smooth the double flow.

     Sped a herdsman from the vale,
       Mounting like a flame,
     All on fire to hear and see,
75   With floating locks he came.
     Looked neither north nor south,
       Neither east nor west,
     But sat him down at Meggan's feet
       As love-bird on his nest,
80   And wooed her with a silent awe,
       With trouble not expressed;
     She sang the tears into his eyes,
       The heart out of his breast:
     So he loved her, listening so.

85   She sang the heart out of his breast,
       The words out of his tongue;
     Hand and foot and pulse he paused
       Till her song was sung.
     Then he spoke up from his place
90   Simple words and true:
     "Scanty goods have I to give,
       Scanty skill to woo;
     But I have a will to work,
       And a heart for you:
95   Bid me stay or bid me go."

Then Meggan mused within herself:
  "Better be first with him,
Than dwell where fairer Margaret sits,
  Who shines my brightness dim,
100 For ever second where she sits,
  However fair I be:
I will be lady of his love,
  And he shall worship me;
I will be lady of his herds
105   And stoop to his degree,
At home where kids and fatlings grow."

Sped a shepherd from the height
  Headlong down to look,
(White lambs followed, lured by love
110   Of their shepherd's crook):
He turned neither east nor west,
  Neither north nor south,
But knelt right down to May, for love
  Of her sweet-singing mouth;
115 Forgot his flocks, his panting flocks
  In parching hill-side drouth;
Forgot himself for weal or woe.

Trilled her song and swelled her song
  With maiden coy caprice
120 In a labyrinth of throbs,
  Pauses, cadences;
Clear-noted as a dropping brook,
  Soft-noted like the bees,
Wild-noted as the shivering wind
125   Forlorn thro' forest trees:
Love-noted like the wood-pigeon
  Who hides herself for love,
Yet cannot keep her secret safe,
  But cooes and cooes thereof:
130 Thus the notes rang loud or low.

He hung breathless on her breath;
  Speechless, who listened well;

Could not speak or think or wish
   Till silence broke the spell.
135 Then he spoke, and spread his hands,
   Pointing here and there:
"See my sheep and see the lambs,
   Twin lambs which they bare.
All myself I offer you,
140   All my flocks and care,
Your sweet song hath moved me so."

In her fluttered heart young May
   Mused a dubious while:
"If he loves me as he says"—
145   Her lips curved with a smile:
"Where Margaret shines like the sun
   I shine but like a moon;
If sister Meggan makes her choice
   I can make mine as soon;
150 At cockcrow we were sister-maids,
   We may be brides at noon."
Said Meggan, "Yes;" May said not "No."

Fair Margaret stayed alone at home,
   Awhile she sang her song,
155 Awhile sat silent, then she thought:
   "My sisters loiter long."
That sultry noon had waned away,
   Shadows had waxen great:
"Surely," she thought within herself,
160   "My sisters loiter late."
She rose, and peered out at the door,
   With patient heart to wait,
And heard a distant nightingale
   Complaining of its mate;
165 Then down the garden slope she walked,
   Down to the garden gate,
Leaned on the rail and waited so.

The slope was lightened by her eyes
   Like summer lightning fair,

170   Like rising of the haloed moon
      Lightened her glimmering hair,
   While her face lightened like the sun
      Whose dawn is rosy white.
   Thus crowned with maiden majesty
175   She peered into the night,
   Looked up the hill and down the hill,
      To left hand and to right,
   Flashing like fire-flies to and fro.

   Waiting thus in weariness
180   She marked the nightingale
   Telling, if any one would heed,
      Its old complaining tale.
   Then lifted she her voice and sang,
      Answering the bird:
185   Then lifted she her voice and sang,
      Such notes were never heard
   From any bird where Spring's in blow.

   The king of all that country
      Coursing far, coursing near,
190   Curbed his amber-bitted steed,
      Coursed amain to hear;
   All his princes in his train,
      Squire, and knight, and peer,
   With his crown upon his head,
195   His sceptre in his hand,
   Down he fell at Margaret's knees
      Lord king of all that land,
   To her highness bending low.

   Every beast and bird and fish
200   Came mustering to the sound,
   Every man and every maid
      From miles of country round:
   Meggan on her herdsman's arm,
      With her shepherd May,
205   Flocks and herds trooped at their heels
      Along the hill-side way;

No foot too feeble for the ascent,
　　Not any head too grey;
Some were swift and none were slow.

210　So Margaret sang her sisters home
　　In their marriage mirth;
Sang free birds out of the sky,
　　Beasts along the earth,
Sang up fishes of the deep—
215　　All breathing things that move
Sang from far and sang from near
　　To her lovely love;
Sang together friend and foe;

Sang a golden-bearded king
220　　Straightway to her feet,
Sang him silent where he knelt
　　In eager anguish sweet.
But when the clear voice died away,
　　When longest echoes died,
225　He stood up like a royal man
　　And claimed her for his bride.
So three maids were wooed and won
　　In a brief May-tide,
Long ago and long ago.

JESSIE CAMERON.

"Jessie, Jessie Cameron,
　　Hear me but this once," quoth he.
"Good luck go with you, neighbour's son,
　　But I'm no mate for you," quoth she.
5　Day was verging toward the night
　　There beside the moaning sea,
Dimness overtook the light
　　There where the breakers be.

"O Jessie, Jessie Cameron,
10   I have loved you long and true."—
"Good luck go with you, neighbour's son,
    But I'm no mate for you."

She was a careless, fearless girl,
    And made her answer plain,
15   Outspoken she to earl or churl,
    Kindhearted in the main,
But somewhat heedless with her tongue
    And apt at causing pain;
A mirthful maiden she and young,
20   Most fair for bliss or bane.
"Oh long ago I told you so,
    I tell you so today:
Go you your way, and let me go
    Just my own free way."

25   The sea swept in with moan and foam
    Quickening the stretch of sand;
They stood almost in sight of home;
    He strove to take her hand.
"Oh can't you take your answer then,
30   And won't you understand?
For me you're not the man of men,
    I've other plans are planned.
You're good for Madge, or good for Cis,
    Or good for Kate, may be:
35   But what's to me the good of this
    While you're not good for me?"

They stood together on the beach,
    They two alone,
And louder waxed his urgent speech,
40   His patience almost gone:
"Oh say but one kind word to me,
    Jessie, Jessie Cameron."—
"I'd be too proud to beg," quoth she,
    And pride was in her tone.

45   And pride was in her lifted head,
     And in her angry eye,
   And in her foot, which might have fled,
     But would not fly.

   Some say that he had gipsy blood,
50   That in his heart was guile:
   Yet he had gone thro' fire and flood
     Only to win her smile.
   Some say his grandam was a witch,
     A black witch from beyond the Nile,
55   Who kept an image in a niche
     And talked with it the while.
   And by her hut far down the lane
     Some say they would not pass at night,
   Lest they should hear an unked strain
60   Or see an unked sight.

   Alas for Jessie Cameron!—
     The sea crept moaning, moaning nigher:
   She should have hastened to begone,—
     The sea swept higher, breaking by her:
65   She should have hastened to her home
     While yet the west was flushed with fire,
   But now her feet are in the foam,
     The sea-foam sweeping higher.
   O mother, linger at your door,
70   And light your lamp to make it plain;
   But Jessie she comes home no more,
     No more again.

   They stood together on the strand,
     They only each by each;
75   Home, her home, was close at hand,
     Utterly out of reach.
   Her mother in the chimney nook
     Heard a startled sea-gull screech,
   But never turned her head to look
80   Towards the darkening beach:
   Neighbours here and neighbours there
     Heard one scream, as if a bird

Shrilly screaming cleft the air:—
That was all they heard.

85 Jessie she comes home no more,
Comes home never;
Her lover's step sounds at his door
No more for ever.
And boats may search upon the sea
90 And search along the river,
But none know where the bodies be:
Sea-winds that shiver,
Sea-birds that breast the blast,
Sea-waves swelling,
95 Keep the secret first and last
Of their dwelling.

Whether the tide so hemmed them round
With its pitiless flow,
That when they would have gone they found
100 No way to go;
Whether she scorned him to the last
With words flung to and fro,
Or clung to him when hope was past,
None will ever know:
105 Whether he helped or hindered her,
Threw up his life or lost it well,
The troubled sea for all its stir
Finds no voice to tell.

Only watchers by the dying
110 Have thought they heard one pray
Wordless, urgent; and replying
One seem to say him nay:
And watchers by the dead have heard
A windy swell from miles away,
115 With sobs and screams, but not a word
Distinct for them to say:
And watchers out at sea have caught
Glimpse of a pale gleam here or there,
Come and gone as quick as thought,
120 Which might be hand or hair.

SPRING QUIET.

Gone were but the Winter,
   Come were but the Spring,
I would go to a covert
   Where the birds sing;

5 Where in the whitethorn
   Singeth a thrush,
And a robin sings
   In the holly-bush.

Full of fresh scents
10 Are the budding boughs
Arching high over
   A cool green house:

Full of sweet scents,
   And whispering air
15 Which sayeth softly:
   "We spread no snare;

"Here dwell in safety,
   Here dwell alone,
With a clear stream
20 And a mossy stone.

"Here the sun shineth
   Most shadily;
Here is heard an echo
   Of the far sea,
25 Tho' far off it be."

THE POOR GHOST.

"Oh whence do you come, my dear friend, to me,
With your golden hair all fallen below your knee,
And your face as white as snowdrops on the lea,
And your voice as hollow as the hollow sea?"

5   "From the other world I come back to you,
    My locks are uncurled with dripping drenching dew.
    You know the old, whilst I know the new:
    But tomorrow you shall know this too."

    "Oh not tomorrow into the dark, I pray;
10   Oh not tomorrow, too soon to go away:
    Here I feel warm and well-content and gay:
    Give me another year, another day."

    "Am I so changed in a day and a night
    That mine own only love shrinks from me with fright,
15   Is fain to turn away to left or right
    And cover up his eyes from the sight?"

    "Indeed I loved you, my chosen friend,
    I loved you for life, but life has an end;
    Thro' sickness I was ready to tend:
20   But death mars all, which we cannot mend.

    "Indeed I loved you; I love you yet
    If you will stay where your bed is set,
    Where I have planted a violet
    Which the wind waves, which the dew makes wet."

25   "Life is gone, then love too is gone,
    It was a reed that I leant upon:
    Never doubt I will leave you alone
    And not wake you rattling bone with bone.

    "I go home alone to my bed,
30   Dug deep at the foot and deep at the head,
    Roofed in with a load of lead,
    Warm enough for the forgotten dead.

    "But why did your tears soak thro' the clay,
    And why did your sobs wake me where I lay?
35   I was away, far enough away:
    Let me sleep now till the Judgment Day."

A PORTRAIT.

I.

She gave up beauty in her tender youth,
  Gave all her hope and joy and pleasant ways;
  She covered up her eyes lest they should gaze
On vanity, and chose the bitter truth.
5 Harsh towards herself, towards others full of ruth,
  Servant of servants, little known to praise,
  Long prayers and fasts trenched on her nights and days:
She schooled herself to sights and sounds uncouth
That with the poor and stricken she might make
10 A home, until the least of all sufficed
Her wants; her own self learned she to forsake,
Counting all earthly gain but hurt and loss.
So with calm will she chose and bore the cross
  And hated all for love of Jesus Christ.

II.

15 They knelt in silent anguish by her bed,
  And could not weep; but calmly there she lay;
  All pain had left her; and the sun's last ray
Shone through upon her, warming into red
The shady curtains. In her heart she said:
20 "Heaven opens; I leave these and go away;
  The Bridegroom calls,—shall the Bride seek to stay?"
Then low upon her breast she bowed her head.
O lily flower, O gem of priceless worth,
  O dove with patient voice and patient eyes,
25 O fruitful vine amid a land of dearth,
  O maid replete with loving purities,
Thou bowedst down thy head with friends on earth
  To raise it with the saints in Paradise.

DREAM-LOVE.

Young Love lies sleeping
   In May-time of the year,
Among the lilies,
   Lapped in the tender light:
5 White lambs come grazing,
   White doves come building there;
And round about him
   The May-bushes are white.

Soft moss the pillow
10   For oh, a softer cheek;
Broad leaves cast shadow
   Upon the heavy eyes:
There winds and waters
   Grow lulled and scarcely speak;
15 There twilight lingers
   The longest in the skies.

Young Love lies dreaming;
   But who shall tell the dream?
A perfect sunlight
20   On rustling forest tips;
Or perfect moonlight
   Upon a rippling stream;
Or perfect silence,
   Or song of cherished lips.

25 Burn odours round him
   To fill the drowsy air;
Weave silent dances
   Around him to and fro;
For oh, in waking
30   The sights are not so fair,
And song and silence
   Are not like these below.

Young Love lies dreaming
   Till summer days are gone,—

35 Dreaming and drowsing
    Away to perfect sleep:
He sees the beauty
    Sun hath not looked upon,
And tastes the fountain
40 Unutterably deep.

Him perfect music
    Doth hush unto his rest,
And thro' the pauses
    The perfect silence calms:
45 Oh poor the voices
    Of earth from east to west,
And poor earth's stillness
    Between her stately palms.

Young Love lies drowsing
50 Away to poppied death;
Cool shadows deepen
    Across the sleeping face:
So fails the summer
    With warm, delicious breath;
55 And what hath autumn
    To give us in its place?

Draw close the curtains
    Of branched evergreen;
Change cannot touch them
60 With fading fingers sere:
Here the first violets
    Perhaps will bud unseen,
And a dove, may be,
    Return to nestle here.

TWICE.

I took my heart in my hand
    (O my love, O my love),

I said: Let me fall or stand,
　　Let me live or die,
5 But this once hear me speak—
　　(O my love, O my love)—
Yet a woman's words are weak;
　　You should speak, not I.

You took my heart in your hand
10 　　With a friendly smile,
With a critical eye you scanned,
　　Then set it down,
And said: It is still unripe,
　　Better wait awhile;
15 Wait while the skylarks pipe,
　　Till the corn grows brown.

As you set it down it broke—
　　Broke, but I did not wince;
I smiled at the speech you spoke,
20 　　At your judgment that I heard:
But I have not often smiled
　　Since then, nor questioned since,
Nor cared for corn-flowers wild,
　　Nor sung with the singing bird.

25 I take my heart in my hand,
　　O my God, O my God,
My broken heart in my hand:
　　Thou hast seen, judge Thou.
My hope was written on sand,
30 　　O my God, O my God;
Now let Thy judgment stand—
　　Yea, judge me now.

This contemned of a man,
　　This marred one heedless day,
35 This heart take Thou to scan
　　Both within and without:
Refine with fire its gold,
　　Purge Thou its dross away—
Yea hold it in Thy hold,
40 　　Whence none can pluck it out.

I take my heart in my hand—
  I shall not die, but live—
Before Thy face I stand;
  I, for Thou callest such:
45 All that I have I bring,
  All that I am I give,
Smile Thou and I shall sing,
  But shall not question much.

SONGS IN A CORNFIELD.

A song in a cornfield
  Where corn begins to fall,
Where reapers are reaping,
  Reaping one, reaping all.
5 Sing pretty Lettice,
  Sing Rachel, sing May;
Only Marian cannot sing
  While her sweetheart's away.

Where is he gone to
10 And why does he stay?
He came across the green sea
  But for a day,
Across the deep green sea
  To help with the hay.
15 His hair was curly yellow
  And his eyes were grey,
He laughed a merry laugh
  And said a sweet say.
Where is he gone to
20 That he comes not home?
Today or tomorrow
  He surely will come.
Let him haste to joy
  Lest he lag for sorrow,

25   For one weeps today
            Who'll not weep tomorrow:
        Today she must weep
            For gnawing sorrow,
        Tonight she may sleep
30   And not wake tomorrow.

        May sang with Rachel
            In the waxing warm weather,
        Lettice sang with them,
            They sang all together:—

35   "Take the wheat in your arm
            Whilst day is broad above,
        Take the wheat to your bosom,
            But not a false false love.
        Out in the fields
40   Summer heat gloweth,
        Out in the fields
            Summer wind bloweth,
        Out in the fields
            Summer friend showeth,
45   Out in the fields
            Summer wheat groweth:
        But in the winter
            When summer heat is dead
        And summer wind has veered
50   And summer friend has fled,
        Only summer wheat remaineth,
            White cakes and bread.
        Take the wheat, clasp the wheat
            That's food for maid and dove;
55   Take the wheat to your bosom,
            But not a false false love."

    A silence of full noontide heat
        Grew on them at their toil:
    The farmer's dog woke up from sleep,
60   The green snake hid her coil
    Where grass stood thickest: bird and beast
        Sought shadows as they could,

The reaping men and women paused
  And sat down where they stood;
65 They ate and drank and were refreshed,
  For rest from toil is good.

While the reapers took their ease,
  Their sickles lying by,
Rachel sang a second strain,
70   And singing seemed to sigh:—

    "There goes the swallow—
    Could we but follow!
    Hasty swallow stay,
    Point us out the way;
75 Look back swallow, turn back swallow, stop swallow.

    "There went the swallow—
    Too late to follow:
    Lost our note of way,
    Lost our chance today;
80 Good bye swallow, sunny swallow, wise swallow.

    "After the swallow
    All sweet things follow:
    All things go their way,
    Only we must stay,
85 Must not follow; good bye swallow, good swallow."

Then listless Marian raised her head
  Among the nodding sheaves;
Her voice was sweeter than that voice;
  She sang like one who grieves:
90 Her voice was sweeter than its wont
  Among the nodding sheaves;
All wondered while they heard her sing
  Like one who hopes and grieves:—

    "Deeper than the hail can smite,
95   Deeper than the frost can bite,
    Deep asleep thro' day and night,
      Our delight.

"Now thy sleep no pang can break,
No tomorrow bid thee wake,
100   Not our sobs who sit and ache
      For thy sake.

"Is it dark or light below?
Oh but is it cold like snow?
Dost thou feel the green things grow
105   Fast or slow?

"Is it warm or cold beneath,
Oh but is it cold like death?
Cold like death, without a breath,
      Cold like death?"

110   If he comes today
      He will find her weeping;
If he comes tomorrow
      He will find her sleeping;
If he comes the next day
115   He'll not find her at all,
He may tear his curling hair,
      Beat his breast and call.

A YEAR'S WINDFALLS.

On the wind of January
    Down flits the snow,
Travelling from the frozen North
    As cold as it can blow.
5   Poor robin redbreast,
    Look where he comes;
Let him in to feel your fire,
    And toss him of your crumbs.

On the wind in February
10 Snowflakes float still,
Half inclined to turn to rain,
    Nipping, dripping, chill.
Then the thaws swell the streams,
    And swollen rivers swell the sea:—
15 If the winter ever ends
    How pleasant it will be.

In the wind of windy March
    The catkins drop down,
Curly, caterpillar-like,
20 Curious green and brown.
With concourse of nest-building birds
    And leaf-buds by the way,
We begin to think of flowers
    And life and nuts some day.

25 With the gusts of April
    Rich fruit-tree blossoms fall,
On the hedged-in orchard-green,
    From the southern wall.
Apple trees and pear trees
30 Shed petals white or pink,
Plum trees and peach trees;
    While sharp showers sink and sink.

Little brings the May breeze
    Beside pure scent of flowers,
35 While all things wax and nothing wanes
    In lengthening daylight hours.
Across the hyacinth beds
    The wind lags warm and sweet,
Across the hawthorn tops,
40 Across the blades of wheat.

In the wind of sunny June
    Thrives the red-rose crop,
Every day fresh blossoms blow
    While the first leaves drop;

45 White rose and yellow rose
    And moss rose choice to find,
And the cottage cabbage rose
    Not one whit behind.

On the blast of scorched July
50   Drives the pelting hail,
From thunderous lightning-clouds, that blot
    Blue heaven grown lurid-pale.
Weedy waves are tossed ashore,
    Sea-things strange to sight
55 Gasp upon the barren shore
    And fade away in light.

In the parching August wind
    Cornfields bow the head,
Sheltered in round valley depths,
60   On low hills outspread.
Early leaves drop loitering down
    Weightless on the breeze,
Firstfruits of the year's decay
    From the withering trees.

65 In brisk wind of September
    The heavy-headed fruits
Shake upon their bending boughs
    And drop from the shoots;
Some glow golden in the sun,
70   Some show green and streaked,
Some set forth a purple bloom,
    Some blush rosy-cheeked.

In strong blast of October
    At the equinox,
75 Stirred up in his hollow bed
    Broad ocean rocks;
Plunge the ships on his bosom,
    Leaps and plunges the foam,—
It's oh! for mothers' sons at sea,
80   That they were safe at home.

In slack wind of November
  The fog forms and shifts;
All the world comes out again
  When the fog lifts.
85 Loosened from their sapless twigs
  Leaves drop with every gust;
Drifting, rustling, out of sight
  In the damp or dust.

Last of all, December,
90   The year's sands nearly run,
Speeds on the shortest day,
  Curtails the sun;
With its bleak raw wind
  Lays the last leaves low,
95 Brings back the nightly frosts,
  Brings back the snow.

THE QUEEN OF HEARTS.

How comes it, Flora, that, whenever we
Play cards together, you invariably,
  However the pack parts,
  Still hold the Queen of Hearts?

5 I've scanned you with a scrutinizing gaze,
Resolved to fathom these your secret ways:
  But, sift them as I will,
  Your ways are secret still.

I cut and shuffle; shuffle, cut, again;
10 But all my cutting, shuffling, proves in vain:
  Vain hope, vain forethought too;
  That Queen still falls to you.

I dropped her once, prepense; but, ere the deal
Was dealt, your instinct seemed her loss to feel:
15   "There should be one card more,"
  You said, and searched the floor.

I cheated once; I made a private notch
In Heart-Queen's back, and kept a lynx-eyed watch;
    Yet such another back
20   Deceived me in the pack:

The Queen of Clubs assumed by arts unknown
An imitative dint that seemed my own;
    This notch, not of my doing,
       Misled me to my ruin.

25 It baffles me to puzzle out the clue,
Which must be skill, or craft, or luck in you:
    Unless, indeed, it be
       Natural affinity.

ONE DAY.

I will tell you when they met:
In the limpid days of Spring;
Elder boughs were budding yet,
Oaken boughs looked wintry still,
5 But primrose and veined violet
In the mossful turf were set,
While meeting birds made haste to sing
And build with right good will.

I will tell you when they parted:
10 When plenteous Autumn sheaves were brown,
Then they parted heavy-hearted;
The full rejoicing sun looked down
As grand as in the days before;
Only they had lost a crown;
15 Only to them those days of yore
Could come back nevermore.

When shall they meet? I cannot tell,
Indeed, when they shall meet again,
Except some day in Paradise:
20 For this they wait, one waits in pain.

Beyond the sea of death love lies
For ever, yesterday, today;
Angels shall ask them, "Is it well?"
And they shall answer, "Yea."

A BIRD'S-EYE VIEW.

"Croak, croak, croak,"
Thus the Raven spoke,
Perched on his crooked tree
As hoarse as hoarse could be.
5   Shun him and fear him,
Lest the Bridegroom hear him;
Scout him and rout him
With his ominous eye about him.

Yet, "Croak, croak, croak,"
10   Still tolled from the oak;
From that fatal black bird,
Whether heard or unheard:
"O ship upon the high seas,
Freighted with lives and spices,
15   Sink, O ship," croaked the Raven:
"Let the Bride mount to heaven."

In a far foreign land
Upon the wave-edged sand,
Some friends gaze wistfully
20   Across the glittering sea.
"If we could clasp our sister,"
Three say, "now we have missed her!"
"If we could kiss our daughter!"
Two sigh across the water.

25   Oh the ship sails fast
With silken flags at the mast,
And the home-wind blows soft;

But a Raven sits aloft,
Chuckling and choking,
30 Croaking, croaking, croaking:—
Let the beacon-fire blaze higher;
Bridegroom, watch; the Bride draws nigher.

On a sloped sandy beach,
Which the spring-tide billows reach,
35 Stand a watchful throng
Who have hoped and waited long:
"Fie on this ship, that tarries
With the priceless freight it carries.
The time seems long and longer:
40 O languid wind, wax stronger;"—

Whilst the Raven perched at east
Still croaks and does not cease,
One monotonous note
Tolled from his iron throat:
45 "No father, no mother,
But I have a sable brother:
He sees where ocean flows to,
And he knows what he knows too."

A day and a night
50 They kept watch worn and white;
A night and a day
For the swift ship on its way:
For the Bride and her maidens
—Clear chimes the bridal cadence—
55 For the tall ship that never
Hove in sight for ever.

On either shore, some
Stand in grief loud or dumb
As the dreadful dread
60 Grows certain tho' unsaid.
For laughter there is weeping,
And waking instead of sleeping,
And a desperate sorrow
Morrow after morrow.

65   Oh who knows the truth,
How she perished in her youth,
And like a queen went down
Pale in her royal crown:
How she went up to glory
70   From the sea-foam chill and hoary,
From the sea-depth black and riven
To the calm that is in Heaven?

They went down, all the crew,
The silks and spices too,
75   The great ones and the small,
One and all, one and all.
Was it thro' stress of weather,
Quicksands, rocks, or all together?
Only the Raven knows this,
80   And he will not disclose this.—

After a day and a year
The bridal bells chime clear;
After a year and a day
The Bridegroom is brave and gay:
85   Love is sound, faith is rotten;
The old Bride is forgotten:—
Two ominous Ravens only
Remember, black and lonely.

LIGHT LOVE.

"Oh sad thy lot before I came,
    But sadder when I go;
My presence but a flash of flame,
    A transitory glow
5   Between two barren wastes like snow.
What wilt thou do when I am gone,
    Where wilt thou rest, my dear?

For cold thy bed to rest upon,
   And cold the falling year
10   Whose withered leaves are lost and sere."

She hushed the baby at her breast,
   She rocked it on her knee:
"And I will rest my lonely rest,
   Warmed with the thought of thee,
15   Rest lulled to rest by memory."
She hushed the baby with her kiss,
   She hushed it with her breast:
"Is death so sadder much than this—
   Sure death that builds a nest
20   For those who elsewhere cannot rest?"

"Oh sad thy note, my mateless dove,
   With tender nestling cold;
But hast thou ne'er another love
   Left from the days of old,
25   To build thy nest of silk and gold,
To warm thy paleness to a blush
   When I am far away—
To warm thy coldness to a flush,
   And turn thee back to May,
30   And turn thy twilight back to day?"

She did not answer him again,
   But leaned her face aside,
Wrung with the pang of shame and pain,
   And sore with wounded pride:
35   He knew his very soul had lied.
She strained his baby in her arms,
   His baby to her heart:
"Even let it go, the love that harms:
   We twain will never part;
40   Mine own, his own, how dear thou art."

"Now never teaze me, tender-eyed,
   Sigh-voiced," he said in scorn:
"For nigh at hand there blooms a bride,
   My bride before the morn;
45   Ripe-blooming she, as thou forlorn.

Ripe-blooming she, my rose, my peach;
   She wooes me day and night:
I watch her tremble in my reach;
   She reddens, my delight;
50   She ripens, reddens in my sight."

"And is she like a sunlit rose?
   Am I like withered leaves?
Haste where thy spicèd garden blows:
   But in bare Autumn eves
55   Wilt thou have store of harvest sheaves?
Thou leavest love, true love behind,
   To seek a love as true;
Go, seek in haste: but wilt thou find?
   Change new again for new;
60   Pluck up, enjoy—yea, trample too.

"Alas for her, poor faded rose,
   Alas for her, like me,
Cast down and trampled in the snows."
   "Like thee? nay, not like thee:
65   She leans, but from a guarded tree.
Farewell, and dream as long ago,
   Before we ever met:
Farewell; my swift-paced horse seems slow."
   She raised her eyes, not wet
70   But hard, to Heaven: "Does God forget?"

ON THE WING.

Once in a dream (for once I dreamed of you)
   We stood together in an open field;
   Above our heads two swift-winged pigeons wheeled,
Sporting at ease and courting full in view.
5   When loftier still a broadening darkness flew,
   Down-swooping, and a ravenous hawk revealed;
   Too weak to fight, to fond to fly, they yield;
So farewell life and love and pleasures new.

Then as their plumes fell fluttering to the ground,
10   Their snow-white plumage flecked with crimson drops,
           I wept, and thought I turned towards you to weep:
           But you were gone; while rustling hedgerow tops
Bent in a wind which bore to me a sound
           Of far-off piteous bleat of lambs and sheep.

A RING POSY.

Jess and Jill are pretty girls,
     Plump and well to do,
In a cloud of windy curls:
     Yet I know who
5   Loves me more than curls or pearls.

I'm not pretty, not a bit;
     Thin and sallow-pale;
When I trudge along the street
     I don't need a veil:
10 Yet I have one fancy hit.

Jess and Jill can trill and sing
     With a flute-like voice,
Dance as light as bird on wing,
     Laugh for careless joys:
15 Yet it's I who wear the ring.

Jess and Jill will mate some day,
     Surely, surely;
Ripen on to June thro' May,
While the sun shines make their hay,
20   Slacken steps demurely:
Yet even there I lead the way.

BEAUTY IS VAIN.

While roses are so red,
     While lilies are so white,

Shall a woman exalt her face
Because it gives delight?
5 She's not so sweet as a rose,
A lily's straighter than she,
And if she were as red or white
She'd be but one of three.

Whether she flush in love's summer
10 Or in its winter grow pale,
Whether she flaunt her beauty
Or hide it away in a veil,
Be she red or white,
And stand she erect or bowed,
15 Time will win the race he runs with her
And hide her away in a shroud.

MAGGIE A LADY.

You must not call me Maggie, you must not call me Dear,
For I'm Lady of the Manor now stately to see;
And if there comes a babe, as there may some happy year,
'Twill be little lord or lady at my knee.

5 Oh but what ails you, my sailor cousin Phil,
That you shake and turn white like a cockcrow ghost?
You're as white as I turned once down by the mill,
When one told me you and ship and crew were lost:

Philip my playfellow, when we were boy and girl
10 (It was the Miller's Nancy told it to me),
Philip with the merry life in lip and curl,
Philip my playfellow drowned in the sea!

I thought I should have fainted, but I did not faint;
I stood stunned at the moment, scarcely sad,
15 Till I raised my wail of desolate complaint
For you, my cousin, brother, all I had.

They said I looked so pale—some say so fair—
    My lord stopped in passing to soothe me back to life:
I know I missed a ringlet from my hair
20   Next morning; and now I am his wife.

Look at my gown, Philip, and look at my ring,
    I'm all crimson and gold from top to toe:
All day long I sit in the sun and sing,
    Where in the sun red roses blush and blow.

25 And I'm the rose of roses, says my lord;
    And to him I'm more than the sun in the sky,
While I hold him fast with the golden cord
    Of a curl, with the eyelash of an eye.

His mother said "fie," and his sisters cried "shame,"
30   His highborn ladies cried "shame" from their place:
They said "fie" when they only heard my name,
    But fell silent when they saw my face.

Am I so fair, Philip? Philip, did you think
    I was so fair when we played boy and girl,
35 Where blue forget-me-nots bloomed on the brink
    Of our stream which the mill-wheel sent awhirl?

If I was fair then sure I'm fairer now,
    Sitting where a score of servants stand,
With a coronet on high days for my brow
40   And almost a sceptre for my hand.

You're but a sailor, Philip, weatherbeaten brown,
    A stranger on land and at home on the sea,
Coasting as best you may from town to town:
    Coasting along do you often think of me?

45 I'm a great lady in a sheltered bower,
    With hands grown white thro' having nought to do:
Yet sometimes I think of you hour after hour
    Till I nigh wish myself a child with you.

WHAT WOULD I GIVE?

What would I give for a heart of flesh to warm me thro',
Instead of this heart of stone ice-cold whatever I do;
Hard and cold and small, of all hearts the worst of all.

What would I give for words, if only words would come;
5   But now in its misery my spirit has fallen dumb:
O merry friends, go your way, I have never a word to say.

What would I give for tears, not smiles but scalding tears,
To wash the black mark clean, and to thaw the frost of years,
To wash the stain ingrain and to make me clean again.

THE BOURNE.

Underneath the growing grass,
    Underneath the living flowers,
    Deeper than the sound of showers:
    There we shall not count the hours
5   By the shadows as they pass.

Youth and health will be but vain,
    Beauty reckoned of no worth:
    There a very little girth
    Can hold round what once the earth
10   Seemed too narrow to contain.

SUMMER.

Winter is cold-hearted,
    Spring is yea and nay,
Autumn is a weathercock
    Blown every way:
5   Summer days for me
When every leaf is on its tree;

When Robin's not a beggar,
   And Jenny Wren's a bride,
And larks hang singing, singing, singing,
10   Over the wheat-fields wide,
   And anchored lilies ride,
And the pendulum spider
   Swings from side to side,

And blue-black beetles transact business,
15   And gnats fly in a host,
And furry caterpillars hasten
   That no time be lost,
And moths grow fat and thrive,
   And ladybirds arrive.

20 Before green apples blush,
   Before green nuts embrown,
Why, one day in the country
   Is worth a month in town;
   Is worth a day and a year
25 Of the dusty, musty, lag-last fashion
   That days drone elsewhere.

AUTUMN.

I dwell alone—I dwell alone, alone,
   Whilst full my river flows down to the sea,
     Gilded with flashing boats
     That bring no friend to me:
5 O love-songs, gurgling from a hundred throats,
     O love-pangs, let me be.

Fair fall the freighted boats which gold and stone
     And spices bear to sea:
Slim, gleaming maidens swell their mellow notes,
10   Love-promising, entreating—
     Ah! sweet, but fleeting—
Beneath the shivering, snow-white sails.
   Hush! the wind flags and fails—

Hush! they will lie becalmed in sight of strand—
15   Sight of my strand, where I do dwell alone;
Their songs wake singing echoes in my land—
    They cannot hear me moan.

One latest, solitary swallow flies
    Across the sea, rough autumn-tempest tost,
20   Poor bird, shall it be lost?
Dropped down into this uncongenial sea,
        With no kind eyes
        To watch it while it dies,
    Unguessed, uncared for, free:
25   Set free at last,
        The short pang past,
In sleep, in death, in dreamless sleep locked fast.

Mine avenue is all a growth of oaks,
    Some rent by thunder strokes,
30 Some rustling leaves and acorns in the breeze;
    Fair fall my fertile trees,
That rear their goodly heads, and live at ease.

A spider's web blocks all mine avenue;
    He catches down and foolish painted flies,
35   That spider wary and wise.
Each morn it hangs a rainbow strung with dew
    Betwixt boughs green with sap,
    So fair, few creatures guess it is a trap:
        I will not mar the web,
40 Tho' sad I am to see the small lives ebb.

It shakes—my trees shake—for a wind is roused
        In cavern where it housed:
    Each white and quivering sail,
    Of boats among the water leaves
45 Hollows and strains in the full-throated gale:
        Each maiden sings again—
Each languid maiden, whom the calm
Had lulled to sleep with rest and spice and balm.
        Miles down my river to the sea
50   They float and wane,
    Long miles away from me.

Perhaps they say: "She grieves,
  Uplifted, like a beacon, on her tower."
Perhaps they say: "One hour
55 More, and we dance among the golden sheaves."
Perhaps they say: "One hour
  More, and we stand,
  Face to face, hand in hand;
Make haste, O slack gale, to the looked-for land!"

60   My trees are not in flower,
    I have no bower,
    And gusty creaks my tower,
And lonesome, very lonesome, is my strand.

THE GHOST'S PETITION.

"There's a footstep coming; look out and see."—
  "The leaves are falling, the wind is calling;
No one cometh across the lea."—

"There's a footstep coming; O sister, look."—
5   "The ripple flashes, the white foam dashes;
No one cometh across the brook."—

"But he promised that he would come:
  Tonight, tomorrow, in joy or sorrow,
He must keep his word, and must come home.

10 "For he promised that he would come:
  His word was given; from earth or heaven,
He must keep his word, and must come home.

"Go to sleep, my sweet sister Jane;
  You can slumber, who need not number
15 Hour after hour, in doubt and pain.

"I shall sit here awhile, and watch;
  Listening, hoping, for one hand groping
In deep shadow to find the latch."

After the dark, and before the light,
20   One lay sleeping; and one sat weeping,
Who had watched and wept the weary night.

After the night, and before the day,
    One lay sleeping; and one sat weeping—
Watching, weeping for one away.

25 There came a footstep climbing the stair;
    Some one standing out on the landing
Shook the door like a puff of air—

Shook the door and in he passed.
    Did he enter? In the room centre
30 Stood her husband: the door shut fast.

"O Robin, but you are cold—
    Chilled with the night-dew: so lily-white you
Look like a stray lamb from our fold.

"O Robin, but you are late:
35   Come and sit near me—sit here and cheer me."—
(Blue the flame burnt in the grate.)

"Lay not down your head on my breast:
    I cannot hold you, kind wife, nor fold you
In the shelter that you love best.

40 "Feel not after my clasping hand:
    I am but a shadow, come from the meadow
Where many lie, but no tree can stand.

"We are trees which have shed their leaves:
    Our heads lie low there, but no tears flow there;
45 Only I grieve for my wife who grieves.

"I could rest if you would not moan
    Hour after hour; I have no power
To shut my ears where I lie alone.

"I could rest if you would not cry;
50   But there's no sleeping while you sit weeping—
Watching, weeping so bitterly."—

"Woe's me! woe's me! for this I have heard.
    Oh night of sorrow!—oh black tomorrow!
Is it thus that you keep your word?

55 "O you who used so to shelter me
    Warm from the least wind—why, now the east wind
Is warmer than you, whom I quake to see.

"O my husband of flesh and blood,
    For whom my mother I left, and brother,
60 And all I had, accounting it good,

"What do you do there, underground,
    In the dark hollow? I'm fain to follow.
What do you do there?—what have you found?"—

"What I do there I must not tell:
65 But I have plenty: kind wife, content ye:
It is well with us—it is well.

"Tender hand hath made our nest;
    Our fear is ended, our hope is blended
With present pleasure, and we have rest."—

70 "Oh but Robin, I'm fain to come,
    If your present days are so pleasant;
For my days are so wearisome.

"Yet I'll dry my tears for your sake:
    Why should I tease you, who cannot please you
75 Any more with the pains I take?"

MEMORY.

I

I nursed it in my bosom while it lived,
    I hid it in my heart when it was dead;
In joy I sat alone, even so I grieved
    Alone and nothing said.

5   I shut the door to face the naked truth,
       I stood alone—I faced the truth alone,
     Stripped bare of self-regard or forms or ruth
         Till first and last were shown.

     I took the perfect balances and weighed;
10   No shaking of my hand disturbed the poise;
     Weighed, found it wanting: not a word I said,
         But silent made my choice.

     None know the choice I made; I make it still.
       None know the choice I made and broke my heart,
15   Breaking mine idol: I have braced my will
         Once, chosen for once my part.

     I broke it at a blow, I laid it cold,
       Crushed in my deep heart where it used to live.
     My heart dies inch by inch; the time grows old,
20   Grows old in which I grieve.

                         II

     I have a room whereinto no one enters
         Save I myself alone:
       There sits a blessed memory on a throne,
     There my life centres;

25   While winter comes and goes—oh tedious comer!—
         And while its nip-wind blows;
       While bloom the bloodless lily and warm rose
     Of lavish summer.

     If any should force entrance he might see there
30   One buried yet not dead,
       Before whose face I no more bow my head
     Or bend my knee there;

     But often in my worn life's autumn weather
         I watch there with clear eyes,
35   And think how it will be in Paradise
     When we're together.

A ROYAL PRINCESS.

I, a princess, king-descended, decked with jewels, gilded,
    drest,
Would rather be a peasant with her baby at her breast,
For all I shine so like the sun, and am purple like the west.

Two and two my guards behind, two and two before,
5   Two and two on either hand, they guard me evermore;
Me, poor dove that must not coo—eagle that must not soar.

All my fountains cast up perfumes, all my gardens grow
Scented woods and foreign spices, with all flowers in blow
That are costly, out of season as the seasons go.

10   All my walls are lost in mirrors, whereupon I trace
Self to right hand, self to left hand, self in every place,
Self-same solitary figure, self-same seeking face.

Then I have an ivory chair high to sit upon,
Almost like my father's chair, which is an ivory throne;
15   There I sit uplift and upright, there I sit alone.

Alone by day, alone by night, alone days without end;
My father and my mother give me treasures, search and
    spend—
O my father! O my mother! have you ne'er a friend?

As I am a lofty princess, so my father is
20   A lofty king, accomplished in all kingly subtilties,
Holding in his strong right hand world-kingdoms' balances.

He has quarrelled with his neighbours, he has scourged his
    foes;
Vassal counts and princes follow where his pennon goes,
Long-descended valiant lords whom the vulture knows,

25   On whose track the vulture swoops, when they ride in state
To break the strength of armies and topple down the great:
Each of these my courteous servant, none of these my mate.

My father counting up his strength sets down with equal pen
So many head of cattle, head of horses, head of men;
30   These for slaughter, these for labour, with the how and when.

Some to work on roads, canals; some to man his ships;
Some to smart in mines beneath sharp overseers' whips;
Some to trap fur-beasts in lands where utmost winter nips.

Once it came into my heart and whelmed me like a flood,
35   That these too are men and women, human flesh and blood;
Men with hearts and men with souls, tho' trodden down like
        mud.

Our feasting was not glad that night, our music was not gay;
On my mother's graceful head I marked a thread of grey,
My father frowning at the fare seemed every dish to weigh.

40   I sat beside them sole princess in my exalted place,
My ladies and my gentlemen stood by me on the dais:
A mirror showed me I look old and haggard in the face;

It showed me that my ladies all are fair to gaze upon,
Plump, plenteous-haired, to every one love's secret lore is
        known,
45   They laugh by day, they sleep by night; ah, me, what is a
        throne?

The singing men and women sang that night as usual,
The dancers danced in pairs and sets, but music had a fall,
A melancholy windy fall as at a funeral.

Amid the toss of torches to my chamber back we swept;
50   My ladies loosed my golden chain; meantime I could have
        wept
To think of some in galling chains whether they waked or
        slept.

I took my bath of scented milk, delicately waited on,
They burned sweet things for my delight, cedar and
        cinnamon,
They lit my shaded silver lamp, and left me there alone.

55 A day went by, a week went by. One day I heard it said:
"Men are clamouring, women, children, clamouring to be
        fed;
Men like famished dogs are howling in the streets for bread."

So two whispered by my door, not thinking I could hear,
Vulgar naked truth, ungarnished for a royal ear;
60 Fit for cooping in the background, not to stalk so near.

But I strained my utmost sense to catch this truth, and mark:
"There are families out grazing like cattle in the park."
"A pair of peasants must be saved, even if we build an ark."

A merry jest, a merry laugh, each strolled upon his way;
65 One was my page, a lad I reared and bore with day by day;
One was my youngest maid, as sweet and white as cream in
        May.

Other footsteps followed softly with a weightier tramp;
Voices said: "Picked soldiers have been summoned from the
        camp,
To quell these base-born ruffians who make free to howl and
        stamp."

70 "Howl and stamp?" one answered: "They made free to hurl a
        stone
At the minister's state coach, well aimed and stoutly thrown."
"There's work then for the soldiers, for this rank crop must
        be mown."

"One I saw, a poor old fool with ashes on his head,
Whimpering because a girl had snatched his crust of bread:
75 Then he dropped; when some one raised him, it turned out
        he was dead."

"After us the deluge," was retorted with a laugh:
"If bread's the staff of life, they must walk without a staff."
"While I've a loaf they're welcome to my blessing and the
        chaff."

These passed. "The king:" stand up. Said my father with a
        smile:

80 "Daughter mine, your mother comes to sit with you awhile,
She's sad today, and who but you her sadness can beguile?"

He too left me. Shall I touch my harp now while I wait,—
(I hear them doubling guard below before our palace gate)—
Or shall I work the last gold stitch into my veil of state;

85 Or shall my woman stand and read some unimpassioned
         scene,
There's music of a lulling sort in words that pause between;
Or shall she merely fan me while I wait here for the queen?

Again I caught my father's voice in sharp word of command:
"Charge!" a clash of steel: "Charge again, the rebels stand.
90 Smite and spare not, hand to hand; smite and spare not, hand
         to hand."

There swelled a tumult at the gate, high voices waxing higher;
A flash of red reflected light lit the cathedral spire;
I heard a cry for faggots, then I heard a yell for fire.

"Sit and roast there with your meat, sit and bake there with
         your bread,
95 You who sat to see us starve," one shrieking woman said:
"Sit on your throne and roast with your crown upon your
         head."

Nay, this thing will I do, while my mother tarrieth,
I will take my fine spun gold, but not to sew therewith,
I will take my gold and gems, and rainbow fan and wreath;

100 With a ransom in my lap, a king's ransom in my hand,
I will go down to this people, will stand face to face, will stand
Where they curse king, queen, and princess of this cursed
         land.

They shall take all to buy them bread, take all I have to give;
I, if I perish, perish; they today shall eat and live;
105 I, if I perish, perish; that's the goal I half conceive:

Once to speak before the world, rend bare my heart and show
The lesson I have learned, which is death, is life, to know.
I, if I perish, perish; in the name of God I go.

SHALL I FORGET?

Shall I forget on this side of the grave?
I promise nothing: you must wait and see
    Patient and brave.
(O my soul, watch with him and he with me.)

5   Shall I forget in peace of Paradise?
I promise nothing: follow, friend, and see
    Faithful and wise.
(O my soul, lead the way he walks with me.)

VANITY OF VANITIES.

Ah woe is me for pleasure that is vain,
    Ah woe is me for glory that is past:
    Pleasure that bringeth sorrow at the last,
Glory that at the last bringeth no gain!
5   So saith the sinking heart; and so again
    It shall say till the mighty angel-blast
    Is blown, making the sun and moon aghast,
And showering down the stars like sudden rain.
And evermore men shall go fearfully
10   Bending beneath their weight of heaviness;
And ancient men shall lie down wearily,
    And strong men shall rise up in weariness;
Yea, even the young shall answer sighingly,
    Saying one to another: How vain it is!

L. E. L.
"Whose heart was breaking for a little love."

Downstairs I laugh, I sport and jest with all:
    But in my solitary room above

I turn my face in silence to the wall;
   My heart is breaking for a little love.
5   Tho' winter frosts are done,
      And birds pair every one,
And leaves peep out, for springtide is begun.

I feel no spring, while spring is wellnigh blown,
   I find no nest, while nests are in the grove:
10 Woe's me for mine own heart that dwells alone,
   My heart that breaketh for a little love.
      While golden in the sun
      Rivulets rise and run,
While lilies bud, for springtide is begun.

15 All love, are loved, save only I; their hearts
   Beat warm with love and joy, beat full thereof:
They cannot guess, who play the pleasant parts,
   My heart is breaking for a little love.
      While beehives wake and whirr,
20   And rabbit thins his fur,
In living spring that sets the world astir.

I deck myself with silks and jewelry,
   I plume myself like any mated dove:
They praise my rustling show, and never see
25 My heart is breaking for a little love.
      While sprouts green lavender
      With rosemary and myrrh,
For in quick spring the sap is all astir.

Perhaps some saints in glory guess the truth,
30   Perhaps some angels read it as they move,
And cry one to another full of ruth,
   "Her heart is breaking for a little love."
      Tho' other things have birth,
      And leap and sing for mirth,
35 When springtime wakes and clothes and feeds the earth.

Yet saith a saint: "Take patience for thy scathe;"
   Yet saith an angel: "Wait, for thou shalt prove
True best is last, true life is born of death,
   O thou, heart-broken for a little love.

40   Then love shall fill thy girth,
        And love make fat thy dearth,
When new spring builds new heaven and clean new earth."

LIFE AND DEATH.

Life is not sweet. One day it will be sweet
      To shut our eyes and die:
Nor feel the wild flowers blow, nor birds dart by
      With flitting butterfly,
5 Nor grass grow long above our heads and feet,
Nor hear the happy lark that soars sky high,
Nor sigh that spring is fleet and summer fleet,
      Nor mark the waxing wheat,
Nor know who sits in our accustomed seat.

10 Life is not good. One day it will be good
      To die, then live again;
To sleep meanwhile: so not to feel the wane
Of shrunk leaves dropping in the wood,
Nor hear the foamy lashing of the main,
15 Nor mark the blackened bean-fields, nor where stood
      Rich ranks of golden grain
Only dead refuse stubble clothe the plain:
Asleep from risk, asleep from pain.

BIRD OR BEAST?

Did any bird come flying
   After Adam and Eve,
When the door was shut against them
   And they sat down to grieve?

5   I think not Eve's peacock
        Splendid to see,
    And I think not Adam's eagle;
        But a dove may be.

    Did any beast come pushing
10   Thro' the thorny hedge
    Into the thorny thistly world
        Out from Eden's edge?

    I think not a lion
        Tho' his strength is such;
15 But an innocent loving lamb
        May have done as much.

    If the dove preached from her bough
        And the lamb from his sod,
    The lamb and the dove
20   Were preachers sent from God.

EVE.

    "While I sit at the door
    Sick to gaze within
    Mine eye weepeth sore
    For sorrow and sin:
5   As a tree my sin stands
    To darken all lands;
    Death is the fruit it bore.

    "How have Eden bowers grown
    Without Adam to bend them!
10 How have Eden flowers blown
    Squandering their sweet breath
    Without me to tend them!
    The Tree of Life was ours,
    Tree twelvefold-fruited,

15 Most lofty tree that flowers,
    Most deeply rooted:
    I chose the tree of death.

    "Hadst thou but said me nay,
    Adam, my brother,
20 I might have pined away;
    I, but none other:
    God might have let thee stay
    Safe in our garden,
    By putting me away
25 Beyond all pardon.

    "I, Eve, sad mother
    Of all who must live,
    I, not another,
    Plucked bitterest fruit to give
30 My friend, husband, lover;—
    O wanton eyes, run over;
    Who but I should grieve?—
    Cain hath slain his brother:
    Of all who must die mother,
35 Miserable Eve!"

    Thus she sat weeping,
    Thus Eve our mother,
    Where one lay sleeping
    Slain by his brother.
40 Greatest and least
    Each piteous beast
    To hear her voice
    Forgot his joys
    And set aside his feast.

45 The mouse paused in his walk
    And dropped his wheaten stalk;
    Grave cattle wagged their heads
    In rumination;
    The eagle gave a cry
50 From his cloud station;

Larks on thyme beds
Forbore to mount or sing;
Bees drooped upon the wing;
The raven perched on high
55   Forgot his ration;
The conies in their rock,
A feeble nation,
Quaked sympathetical;
The mocking-bird left off to mock;
60   Huge camels knelt as if
In deprecation;
The kind hart's tears were falling;
Chattered the wistful stork;
Dove-voices with a dying fall
65   Cooed desolation
Answering grief by grief.

Only the serpent in the dust
Wriggling and crawling,
Grinned an evil grin and thrust
70   His tongue out with its fork.

GROWN AND FLOWN.

I loved my love from green of Spring
    Until sere Autumn's fall;
But now that leaves are withering
    How should one love at all?
5   One heart's too small
For hunger, cold, love, everything.

I loved my love on sunny days
    Until late Summer's wane;
But now that frost begins to glaze
10   How should one love again?
        Nay, love and pain
Walk wide apart in diverse ways.

I loved my love—alas to see
   That this should be, alas!
15 I thought that this could scarcely be,
   Yet has it come to pass:
   Sweet sweet love was,
Now bitter bitter grown to me.

A FARM WALK.

The year stood at its equinox
   And bluff the North was blowing,
A bleat of lambs came from the flocks,
   Green hardy things were growing;
5 I met a maid with shining locks
   Where milky kine were lowing.

She wore a kerchief on her neck,
   Her bare arm showed its dimple,
Her apron spread without a speck,
10 Her air was frank and simple.

She milked into a wooden pail
   And sang a country ditty,
An innocent fond lovers' tale,
   That was not wise nor witty,
15 Pathetically rustical,
   Too pointless for the city.

She kept in time without a beat
   As true as church-bell ringers,
Unless she tapped time with her feet,
20 Or squeezed it with her fingers;
Her clear unstudied notes were sweet
   As many a practised singer's.

I stood a minute out of sight,
   Stood silent for a minute
25 To eye the pail, and creamy white
   The frothing milk within it;

To eye the comely milking maid
  Herself so fresh and creamy:
"Good day to you," at last I said;
30   She turned her head to see me:
"Good day," she said with lifted head;
  Her eyes looked soft and dreamy,

And all the while she milked and milked
  The grave cow heavy-laden:
35 I've seen grand ladies plumed and silked,
  But not a sweeter maiden;

But not a sweeter fresher maid
  Than this in homely cotton
Whose pleasant face and silky braid
40   I have not yet forgotten.

Seven springs have passed since then, as I
  Count with a sober sorrow;
Seven springs have come and passed me by,
  And spring sets in tomorrow.

45 I've half a mind to shake myself
  Free just for once from London,
To set my work upon the shelf
  And leave it done or undone;

To run down by the early train,
50   Whirl down with shriek and whistle,
And feel the bluff North blow again,
  And mark the sprouting thistle
Set up on waste patch of the lane
  Its green and tender bristle,

55 And spy the scarce-blown violet banks,
  Crisp primrose leaves and others,
And watch the lambs leap at their pranks
  And butt their patient mothers.

Alas, one point in all my plan
60   My serious thoughts demur to:
Seven years have passed for maid and man,
  Seven years have passed for her too;

Perhaps my rose is overblown,
 Not rosy or too rosy;
65 Perhaps in farmhouse of her own
 Some husband keeps her cosy,
Where I should show a face unknown.
 Good bye, my wayside posy.

SOMEWHERE OR OTHER.

Somewhere or other there must surely be
 The face not seen, the voice not heard,
The heart that not yet—never yet—ah me!
 Made answer to my word.

5 Somewhere or other, may be near or far;
 Past land and sea, clean out of sight;
Beyond the wandering moon, beyond the star
 That tracks her night by night.

Somewhere or other, may be far or near;
10 With just a wall, a hedge, between;
With just the last leaves of the dying year
 Fallen on a turf grown green.

A CHILL.

 What can lambkins do
 All the keen night thro'?
Nestle by their woolly mother
 The careful ewe.

5 What can nestlings do
 In the nightly dew?
Sleep beneath their mother's wing
 Till day breaks anew.

If in field or tree
10   There might only be
Such a warm soft sleeping-place
Found for me!

CHILD'S TALK IN APRIL.

I wish you were a pleasant wren,
    And I your small accepted mate;
How we'd look down on toilsome men!
    We'd rise and go to bed at eight
5   Or it may be not quite so late.

Then you should see the nest I'd build,
    The wondrous nest for you and me;
The outside rough perhaps, but filled
    With wool and down: ah, you should see
10   The cosy nest that it would be.

We'd have our change of hope and fear,
    Small quarrels, reconcilements sweet:
I'd perch by you to chirp and cheer,
    Or hop about on active feet
15   And fetch you dainty bits to eat.

We'd be so happy by the day,
    So safe and happy thro' the night,
We both should feel, and I should say,
    It's all one season of delight,
20   And we'll make merry whilst we may.

Perhaps some day there'd be an egg
    When spring had blossomed from the snow:
I'd stand triumphant on one leg;
    Like chanticleer I'd almost crow
25   To let our little neighbours know.

Next you should sit and I would sing
Thro' lengthening days of sunny spring;
   Till, if you wearied of the task,
I'd sit; and you should spread your wing
30   From bough to bough; I'd sit and bask.

Fancy the breaking of the shell,
   The chirp, the chickens wet and bare,
The untried proud paternal swell;
   And you with housewife-matron air
35   Enacting choicer bills of fare.

Fancy the embryo coats of down,
   The gradual feathers soft and sleek;
Till clothed and strong from tail to crown,
   With virgin warblings in their beak,
40   They too go forth to soar and seek.

So would it last an April thro'
And early summer fresh with dew:
   Then should we part and live as twain,
Love-time would bring me back to you
45   And build our happy nest again.

GONE FOR EVER.

O happy rose-bud blooming
   Upon thy parent tree,
Nay, thou art too presuming;
For soon the earth entombing
5   Thy faded charms shall be,
And the chill damp consuming.

O happy skylark springing
   Up to the broad blue sky,
Too fearless in thy winging,
10 Too gladsome in thy singing,
   Thou also soon shalt lie
Where no sweet notes are ringing.

And through life's shine and shower
  We shall have joy and pain;
15 But in the summer bower,
And at the morning hour,
  We still shall look in vain
For the same bird and flower.

"THE INIQUITY OF THE FATHERS
UPON THE CHILDREN"

Oh the rose of keenest thorn!
One hidden summer morn
Under the rose I was born.

I do not guess his name
5 Who wrought my Mother's shame,
And gave me life forlorn,
But my Mother, Mother, Mother,
I know her from all other.
My Mother pale and mild,
10 Fair as ever was seen,
She was but scarce sixteen,
Little more than a child,
When I was born
To work her scorn.
15 With secret bitter throes,
In a passion of secret woes,
She bore me under the rose.

One who my Mother nursed
Took me from the first:—
20 "O nurse, let me look upon
This babe that costs so dear;
Tomorrow she will be gone:
Other mothers may keep
Their babes awake and asleep,
25 But I must not keep her here."—
Whether I know or guess,
I know this not the less.

So I was sent away
That none might spy the truth:
30 And my childhood waxed to youth
And I left off childish play.
I never cared to play
With the village boys and girls;
And I think they thought me proud,
35 I found so little to say
And kept so from the crowd:
But I had the longest curls
And I had the largest eyes,
And my teeth were small like pearls;
40 The girls might flout and scout me,
But the boys would hang about me
In sheepish mooning wise.

Our one-street village stood
A long mile from the town,
45 A mile of windy down
And bleak one-sided wood,
With not a single house.
Our town itself was small,
With just the common shops,
50 And throve in its small way.
Our neighbouring gentry reared
The good old-fashioned crops,
And made old-fashioned boasts
Of what John Bull would do
55 If Frenchman Frog appeared,
And drank old-fashioned toasts,
And made old-fashioned bows
To my Lady at the Hall.

My Lady at the Hall
60 Is grander than they all:
Hers is the oldest name
In all the neighbourhood;
But the race must die with her
Tho' she's a lofty dame,
65 For she's unmarried still.

Poor people say she's good
And has an open hand
As any in the land,
And she's the comforter
70 Of many sick and sad;
My nurse once said to me
That everything she had
Came of my Lady's bounty:
"Tho' she's greatest in the county
75 She's humble to the poor,
No beggar seeks her door
But finds help presently.
I pray both night and day
For her, and you must pray:
80 But she'll never feel distress
If needy folk can bless."

I was a little maid
When here we came to live
From somewhere by the sea.
85 Men spoke a foreign tongue
There where we used to be
When I was merry and young,
Too young to feel afraid;
The fisher-folk would give
90 A kind strange word to me,
There by the foreign sea:
I don't know where it was,
But I remember still
Our cottage on a hill,
95 And fields of flowering grass
On that fair foreign shore.

I liked my old home best,
But this was pleasant too:
So here we made our nest
100 And here I grew.
And now and then my Lady
In riding past our door
Would nod to Nurse and speak,
Or stoop and pat my cheek;

105 And I was always ready
    To hold the field-gate wide
    For my Lady to go thro';
    My Lady in her veil
    So seldom put aside,
110 My Lady grave and pale.

    I often sat to wonder
    Who might my parents be,
    For I knew of something under
    My simple-seeming state.
115 Nurse never talked to me
    Of mother or of father,
    But watched me early and late
    With kind suspicious cares:
    Or not suspicious, rather
120 Anxious, as if she knew
    Some secret I might gather
    And smart for unawares.
    Thus I grew.

    But Nurse waxed old and grey,
125 Bent and weak with years.
    There came a certain day
    That she lay upon her bed
    Shaking her palsied head,
    With words she gasped to say
130 Which had to stay unsaid.
    Then with a jerking hand
    Held out so piteously
    She gave a ring to me
    Of gold wrought curiously,
135 A ring which she had worn
    Since the day that I was born,
    She once had said to me:
    I slipped it on my finger;
    Her eyes were keen to linger
140 On my hand that slipped it on;
    Then she sighed one rattling sigh
    And stared on with sightless eyes:—
    The one who loved me was gone.

How long I stayed alone
145 With the corpse, I never knew,
For I fainted dead as stone:
When I came to life once more
I was down upon the floor,
With neighbours making ado
150 To bring me back to life.
I heard the sexton's wife
Say: "Up, my lad, and run
To tell it at the Hall;
She was my Lady's nurse,
155 And done can't be undone.
I'll watch by this poor lamb.
I guess my Lady's purse
Is always open to such:
I'd run up on my crutch
160 A cripple as I am,"
(For cramps had vexed her much)
"Rather than this dear heart
Lack one to take her part."

For days day after day
165 On my weary bed I lay
Wishing the time would pass;
Oh, so wishing that I was
Likely to pass away:
For the one friend whom I knew
170 Was dead, I knew no other,
Neither father nor mother;
And I, what should I do?

One day the sexton's wife
Said: "Rouse yourself, my dear:
175 My Lady has driven down
From the Hall into the town,
And we think she's coming here.
Cheer up, for life is life."

But I would not look or speak,
180 Would not cheer up at all.

My tears were like to fall,
So I turned round to the wall
And hid my hollow cheek
Making as if I slept,
185   As silent as a stone,
And no one knew I wept.
What was my Lady to me,
The grand lady from the Hall?
She might come, or stay away,
190   I was sick at heart that day:
The whole world seemed to be
Nothing, just nothing to me,
For aught that I could see.

Yet I listened where I lay:
195   A bustle came below,
A clear voice said: "I know;
I will see her first alone,
It may be less of a shock
If she's so weak today:"—
200   A light hand turned the lock,
A light step crossed the floor,
One sat beside my bed:
But never a word she said.

For me, my shyness grew
205   Each moment more and more:
So I said never a word
And neither looked nor stirred;
I think she must have heard
My heart go pit-a-pat:
210   Thus I lay, my Lady sat,
More than a mortal hour—
(I counted one and two
By the house-clock while I lay):
I seemed to have no power
215   To think of a thing to say,
Or do what I ought to do,
Or rouse myself to a choice.

At last she said: "Margaret,
Won't you even look at me?"
220 A something in her voice
Forced my tears to fall at last,
Forced sobs from me thick and fast;
Something not of the past,
Yet stirring memory;
225 A something new, and yet
Not new, too sweet to last,
Which I never can forget.

I turned and stared at her:
Her cheek showed hollow-pale;
230 Her hair like mine was fair,
A wonderful fall of hair
That screened her like a veil;
But her height was statelier,
Her eyes had depth more deep;
235 I think they must have had
Always a something sad,
Unless they were asleep.

While I stared, my Lady took
My hand in her spare hand
240 Jewelled and soft and grand,
And looked with a long long look
Of hunger in my face;
As if she tried to trace
Features she ought to know,
245 And half hoped, half feared, to find.
Whatever was in her mind
She heaved a sigh at last,
And began to talk to me.

"Your nurse was my dear nurse,
250 And her nursling's dear," said she:
"No one told me a word
Of her getting worse and worse,
Till her poor life was past"
(Here my Lady's tears dropped fast):

255 "I might have been with her,
    I might have promised and heard,
    But she had no comforter.
    She might have told me much
    Which now I shall never know,
260 Never never shall know."
    She sat by me sobbing so,
    And seemed so woe-begone,
    That I laid one hand upon
    Hers with a timid touch,
265 Scarce thinking what I did,
    Not knowing what to say:
    That moment her face was hid
    In the pillow close by mine,
    Her arm was flung over me,
270 She hugged me, sobbing so
    As if her heart would break,
    And kissed me where I lay.

    After this she often came
    To bring me fruit or wine,
275 Or sometimes hothouse flowers.
    And at nights I lay awake
    Often and often thinking
    What to do for her sake.
    Wet or dry it was the same:
280 She would come in at all hours,
    Set me eating and drinking
    And say I must grow strong;
    At last the day seemed long
    And home seemed scarcely home
285 If she did not come.

    Well, I grew strong again:
    In time of primroses,
    I went to pluck them in the lane;
    In time of nestling birds,
290 I heard them chirping round the house;
    And all the herds
    Were out at grass when I grew strong,

And days were waxen long,
And there was work for bees
295   Among the May-bush boughs,
And I had shot up tall,
And life felt after all
Pleasant, and not so long
When I grew strong.

300   I was going to the Hall
To be my Lady's maid:
"Her little friend," she said to me,
"Almost her child,"
She said and smiled
305   Sighing painfully;
Blushing, with a second flush
As if she blushed to blush.

Friend, servant, child: just this
My standing at the Hall;
310   The other servants call me "Miss,"
My Lady calls me "Margaret,"
With her clear voice musical.
She never chides when I forget
This or that; she never chides.
315   Except when people come to stay,
(And that's not often) at the Hall,
I sit with her all day
And ride out when she rides.
She sings to me and makes me sing;
320   Sometimes I read to her,
Sometimes we merely sit and talk.
She noticed once my ring
And made me tell its history:
That evening in our garden walk
325   She said she should infer
The ring had been my father's first,
Then my mother's, given for me
To the nurse who nursed
My mother in her misery,

330 That so quite certainly
     Some one might know me, who . . .
     Then she was silent, and I too.

     I hate when people come:
     The women speak and stare
335 And mean to be so civil.
     This one will stroke my hair,
     That one will pat my cheek
     And praise my Lady's kindness,
     Expecting me to speak;
340 I like the proud ones best
     Who sit as struck with blindness,
     As if I wasn't there.
     But if any gentleman
     Is staying at the Hall
345 (Tho' few come prying here),
     My Lady seems to fear
     Some downright dreadful evil,
     And makes me keep my room
     As closely as she can:
350 So I hate when people come,
     It is so troublesome.
     In spite of all her care,
     Sometimes to keep alive
     I sometimes do contrive
355 To get out in the grounds
     For a whiff of wholesome air,
     Under the rose you know:
     It's charming to break bounds,
     Stolen waters are sweet,
360 And what's the good of feet
     If for days they mustn't go?
     Give me a longer tether,
     Or I may break from it.

     Now I have eyes and ears
365 And just some little wit:
     "Almost my Lady's child;"

I recollect she smiled,
Sighed and blushed together;
Then her story of the ring
370 Sounds not improbable,
She told it me so well
It seemed the actual thing:—
Oh, keep your counsel close,
But I guess under the rose,
375 In long past summer weather
When the world was blossoming,
And the rose upon its thorn:
I guess not who he was
Flawed honour like a glass
380 And made my life forlorn,
But my Mother, Mother, Mother,
Oh, I know her from all other.

My Lady, you might trust
Your daughter with your fame.
385 Trust me, I would not shame
Our honourable name,
For I have noble blood
Tho' I was bred in dust
And brought up in the mud.
390 I will not press my claim,
Just leave me where you will:
But you might trust your daughter,
For blood is thicker than water
And you're my mother still.

395 So my Lady holds her own
With condescending grace,
And fills her lofty place
With an untroubled face
As a queen may fill a throne.
400 While I could hint a tale—
(But then I am her child)—
Would make her quail;
Would set her in the dust,
Lorn with no comforter,

405 Her glorious hair defiled
And ashes on her cheek:
The decent world would thrust
Its finger out at her,
Not much displeased I think
410 To make a nine days' stir;
The decent world would sink
Its voice to speak of her.

Now this is what I mean
To do, no more, no less:
415 Never to speak, or show
Bare sign of what I know.
Let the blot pass unseen;
Yea, let her never guess
I hold the tangled clue
420 She huddles out of view.
Friend, servant, almost child,
So be it and nothing more
On this side of the grave.
Mother, in Paradise,
425 You'll see with clearer eyes;
Perhaps in this world even
When you are like to die
And face to face with Heaven
You'll drop for once the lie:
430 But you must drop the mask, not I.

My Lady promises
Two hundred pounds with me
Whenever I may wed
A man she can approve:
435 And since besides her bounty
I'm fairest in the county
(For so I've heard it said,
Tho' I don't vouch for this),
Her promised pounds may move
440 Some honest man to see
My virtues and my beauties;
Perhaps the rising grazier,

Or temperance publican,
May claim my wifely duties.
445   Meanwhile I wait their leisure
And grace-bestowing pleasure,
I wait the happy man;
But if I hold my head
And pitch my expectations
450   Just higher than their level,
They must fall back on patience:
I may not mean to wed,
Yet I'll be civil.

Now sometimes in a dream
455   My heart goes out of me
To build and scheme,
Till I sob after things that seem
So pleasant in a dream:
A home such as I see
460   My blessed neighbours live in
With father and with mother,
All proud of one another,
Named by one common name
From baby in the bud
465   To full-blown workman father;
It's little short of Heaven.
I'd give my gentle blood
To wash my special shame
And drown my private grudge;
470   I'd toil and moil much rather
The dingiest cottage drudge
Whose mother need not blush,
Than live here like a lady
And see my Mother flush
475   And hear her voice unsteady
Sometimes, yet never dare
Ask to share her care.

Of course the servants sneer
Behind my back at me;
480   Of course the village girls,

Who envy me my curls
And gowns and idleness,
Take comfort in a jeer;
Of course the ladies guess
485 Just so much of my history
As points the emphatic stress
With which they laud my Lady;
The gentlemen who catch
A casual glimpse of me
490 And turn again to see,
Their valets on the watch
To speak a word with me,
All know and sting me wild;
Till I am almost ready
495 To wish that I were dead,
No faces more to see,
No more words to be said,
My Mother safe at last
Disburdened of her child,
500 And the past past.

"All equal before God"—
Our Rector has it so,
And sundry sleepers nod:
It may be so; I know
505 All are not equal here,
And when the sleepers wake
They make a difference.
"All equal in the grave"—
That shows an obvious sense:
510 Yet something which I crave
Not death itself brings near;
How should death half atone
For all my past; or make
The name I bear my own?

515 I love my dear old Nurse
Who loved me without gains;
I love my mistress even,
Friend, Mother, what you will:

But I could almost curse
520   My Father for his pains;
And sometimes at my prayer
Kneeling in sight of Heaven
I almost curse him still:
Why did he set his snare
525   To catch at unaware
My Mother's foolish youth;
Load me with shame that's hers,
And her with something worse,
A lifelong lie for truth?

530   I think my mind is fixed
On one point and made up:
To accept my lot unmixed;
Never to drug the cup
But drink it by myself.
535   I'll not be wooed for pelf;
I'll not blot out my shame
With any man's good name;
But nameless as I stand,
My hand is my own hand,
540   And nameless as I came
I go to the dark land.

"All equal in the grave"—
I bide my time till then:
"All equal before God"—
545   Today I feel His rod,
Tomorrow He may save:
                    Amen.

DESPISED AND REJECTED.

My sun has set, I dwell
In darkness as a dead man out of sight;
And none remains, not one, that I should tell
To him mine evil plight
5   This bitter night.

I will make fast my door
That hollow friends may trouble me no more.

"Friend, open to Me."—Who is this that calls?
Nay, I am deaf as are my walls:
10   Cease crying, for I will not hear
Thy cry of hope or fear.
Others were dear,
Others forsook me: what art thou indeed
That I should heed
15   Thy lamentable need?
Hungry should feed,
Or stranger lodge thee here?

"Friend, My Feet bleed.
Open thy door to Me and comfort Me."
20   I will not open, trouble me no more.
Go on thy way footsore,
I will not rise and open unto thee.

"Then is it nothing to thee? Open, see
Who stands to plead with thee.
25   Open, lest I should pass thee by, and thou
One day entreat My Face
And howl for grace,
And I be deaf as thou art now.
Open to Me."

30   Then I cried out upon him: Cease,
Leave me in peace:
Fear not that I should crave
Aught thou mayst have.
Leave me in peace, yea trouble me no more,
35   Lest I arise and chase thee from my door.
What, shall I not be let
Alone, that thou dost vex me yet?

But all night long that voice spake urgently:
"Open to Me."
40   Still harping in mine ears:
"Rise, let Me in."

Pleading with tears:
"Open to Me that I may come to thee."
While the dew dropped, while the dark hours were cold
45 "My Feet bleed, see My Face,
See My Hands bleed that bring thee grace,
My Heart doth bleed for thee,
Open to Me."

So till the break of day:
50 Then died away
That voice, in silence as of sorrow;
Then footsteps echoing like a sigh
Passed me by,
Lingering footsteps slow to pass.
55 On the morrow
I saw upon the grass
Each footprint marked in blood, and on my door
The mark of blood for evermore.

LONG BARREN.

Thou who didst hang upon a barren tree,
My God, for me;
  Tho' I till now be barren, now at length,
  Lord, give me strength
5   To bring forth fruit to Thee.

Thou who didst bear for me the crown of thorn,
Spitting and scorn;
  Tho' I till now have put forth thorns, yet now
  Strengthen me Thou
10 That better fruit be borne.

Thou Rose of Sharon, Cedar of broad roots,
Vine of sweet fruits,
  Thou Lily of the vale with fadeless leaf,
  Of thousands Chief,
15 Feed Thou my feeble shoots.

IF ONLY.

If I might only love my God and die!
  But now He bids me love Him and live on,
  Now when the bloom of all my life is gone,
The pleasant half of life has quite gone by.
5 My tree of hope is lopped that spread so high;
  And I forget how Summer glowed and shone,
  While Autumn grips me with its fingers wan,
And frets me with its fitful windy sigh.
When Autumn passes then must Winter numb,
10 And Winter may not pass a weary while,
    But when it passes Spring shall flower again:
And in that Spring who weepeth now shall smile,
  Yea, they shall wax who now are on the wane,
Yea, they shall sing for love when Christ shall come.

DOST THOU NOT CARE?

I love and love not: Lord, it breaks my heart
  To love and not to love.
Thou veiled within Thy glory, gone apart
  Into Thy shrine, which is above,
5 Dost Thou not love me, Lord, or care
  For this mine ill?—
I love thee here or there,
  I will accept they broken heart, lie still.

Lord, it was well with me in time gone by
10 That cometh not again,
When I was fresh and cheerful, who but I?
  I fresh, I cheerful: worn with pain
Now, out of sight and out of heart;
  O Lord, how long?—
15 *I watch thee as thou art,*
  I will accept thy fainting heart, be strong.

"Lie still," "be strong," today; but, Lord, tomorrow,
    What of tomorrow, Lord?
Shall there be rest from toil, be truce from sorrow,
20   Be living green upon the sward
Now but a barren grave to me,
    Be joy for sorrow?—
    Did I not die for thee?
    Do I not live for thee? leave Me tomorrow.

WEARY IN WELL-DOING.

I would have gone; God bade me stay:
    I would have worked; God bade me rest.
He broke my will from day to day,
    He read my yearnings unexpressed
5   And said them nay.

Now I would stay; God bids me go:
    Now I would rest; God bids me work.
He breaks my heart tossed to and fro,
    My soul is wrung with doubts that lurk
10   And vex it so.

I go, Lord, where Thou sendest me;
    Day after day I plod and moil:
But, Christ my God, when will it be
    That I may let alone my toil
15   And rest with Thee?

MARTYRS' SONG.

We meet in joy, tho' we part in sorrow;
We part tonight, but we meet tomorrow.

Be it flood or blood the path that's trod,
All the same it leads home to God:
5   Be it furnace-fire voluminous,
One like God's Son will walk with us.

What are these that glow from afar,
These that lean over the golden bar,
Strong as the lion, pure as the dove,
10 With open arms and hearts of love?
They the blessed ones gone before,
They the blessed for evermore.
Out of great tribulation they went
Home to their home of Heaven-content;
15 Thro' flood, or blood, or furnace-fire,
To the rest that fulfils desire.

What are these that fly as a cloud,
With flashing heads and faces bowed,
In their mouths a victorious psalm,
20 In their hands a robe and a palm?
Welcoming angels these that shine,
Your own angel, and yours, and mine;
Who have hedged us both day and night
On the left hand and on the right,
25 Who have watched us both night and day
Because the devil keeps watch to slay.

Light above light, and Bliss beyond bliss,
Whom words cannot utter, lo, Who is This?
As a King with many crowns He stands,
30 And our names are graven upon His hands;
As a Priest, with God-uplifted eyes,
He offers for us His Sacrifice;
As the Lamb of God for sinners slain,
That we too may live He lives again;
35 As our Champion behold Him stand,
Strong to save us, at God's Right Hand.

God the Father give us grace
To walk in the light of Jesus' Face.

God the Son give us a part
40 In the hiding-place of Jesus' Heart:
God the Spirit so hold us up
That we may drink of Jesus' cup.

Death is short and life is long;
Satan is strong, but Christ more strong.
45 At His Word, Who hath led us hither,
The Red Sea must part hither and thither.
At His Word, Who goes before us too,
Jordan must cleave to let us thro'.

Yet one pang searching and sore,
50 And then Heaven for evermore;
Yet one moment awful and dark,
Then safety within the Veil and the Ark;
Yet one effort by Christ His grace,
Then Christ for ever face to face.

55 God the Father we will adore,
In Jesus' Name, now and evermore:
God the Son we will love and thank
In this flood and on the farther bank:
God the Holy Ghost we will praise,
60 In Jesus' Name, thro' endless days:
God Almighty, God Three in One,
God Almighty, God alone.

AFTER THIS THE JUDGMENT.

As eager homebound traveller to the goal,
    Or steadfast seeker on an unsearched main,
Or martyr panting for an aureole,
    My fellow-pilgrims pass me, and attain
5   That hidden mansion of perpetual peace
    Where keen desire and hope dwell free from pain:

That gate stands open of perennial ease;
　　I view the glory till I partly long,
Yet lack the fire of love which quickens these.
10　　O passing Angel, speed me with a song,
A melody of heaven to reach my heart
　　And rouse me to the race and make me strong;
Till in such music I take up my part
　　Swelling those Hallelujahs full of rest,
15　One, tenfold, hundredfold, with heavenly art,
　　Fulfilling north and south and east and west,
Thousand, ten thousandfold, innumerable,
　　All blent in one yet each one manifest;
Each one distinguished and beloved as well
20　　As if no second voice in earth or heaven
Were lifted up the Love of God to tell.
　　Ah, Love of God, which Thine Own Self hast given
To me most poor, and made me rich in love,
　　Love that dost pass the tenfold seven times seven,
25　Draw Thou mine eyes, draw Thou my heart above,
　　My treasure and my heart store Thou in Thee,
Brood over me with yearnings of a dove;
　　Be Husband, Brother, closest Friend to me;
Love me as very mother loves her son,
30　　Her sucking firstborn fondled on her knee:
Yea, more than mother loves her little one;
　　For, earthly, even a mother may forget
And feel no pity for its piteous moan;
　　But Thou, O Love of God, remember yet,
35　Thro' the dry desert, thro' the waterflood
　　(Life, death), until the Great White Throne is set.
If now I am sick in chewing the bitter cud
　　Of sweet past sin, tho' solaced by Thy grace
And ofttimes strengthened by Thy Flesh and Blood,
40　　How shall I then stand up before Thy face
When from Thine eyes repentance shall be hid
　　And utmost Justice stand in Mercy's place:
When every sin I thought or spoke or did
　　Shall meet me at the inexorable bar,

45   And there be no man standing in the mid
          To plead for me; while star fallen after star
       With heaven and earth are like a ripened shock,
          And all time's mighty works and wonders are
       Consumed as in a moment; when no rock
50   Remains to fall on me, no tree to hide,
       But I stand all creation's gazing-stock,
          Exposed and comfortless on every side,
       Placed trembling in the final balances
          Whose poise this hour, this moment, must be tried?—
55   Ah Love of God, if greater love than this
          Hath no man, that a man die for his friend,
       And if such love of love Thine Own Love is,
          Plead with Thyself, with me, before the end;
       Redeem me from the irrevocable past;
60   Pitch Thou Thy Presence round me to defend;
       Yea seek with piercèd feet, yea hold me fast
          With piercèd hands whose wounds were made by love;
       Not what I am, remember what Thou wast
          When darkness hid from Thee Thy heavens above,
65   And sin Thy Father's Face, while Thou didst drink
          The bitter cup of death, didst taste thereof
       For every man; while Thou wast nigh to sink
          Beneath the intense intolerable rod,
       Grown sick of love; not what I am, but think
70   Thy Life then ransomed mine, my God, my God.

GOOD FRIDAY.

Am I a stone and not a sheep
   That I can stand, O Christ, beneath Thy Cross,
   To number drop by drop Thy Blood's slow loss,
And yet not weep?

5   Not so those women loved
        Who with exceeding grief lamented Thee;
        Not so fallen Peter weeping bitterly;
    Not so the thief was moved;

    Not so the Sun and Moon
10   Which hid their faces in a starless sky,
    A horror of great darkness at broad noon—
        I, only I.

    Yet give not o'er,
        But seek Thy sheep, true Shepherd of the flock;
15 Greater than Moses, turn and look once more
        And smite a rock.

THE LOWEST PLACE.

    Give me the lowest place: not that I dare
        Ask for that lowest place, but Thou hast died
    That I might live and share
        Thy glory by Thy side.

5   Give me the lowest place: or if for me
        That lowest place too high, make one more low
    Where I may sit and see
        My God and love Thee so.

III Poems Added in Goblin Market, The Prince's Progress and Other Poems

(1875)

BY THE SEA.

Why does the sea moan evermore?
    Shut out from heaven it makes its moan,
It frets against the boundary shore;
    All earth's full rivers cannot fill
5   The sea, that drinking thirsteth still.

Sheer miracles of loveliness
    Lie hid in its unlooked-on bed:
Anemones, salt, passionless,
    Blow flower-like; just enough alive
10   To blow and multiply and thrive.

Shells quaint with curve, or spot, or spike,
    Encrusted live things argus-eyed,
All fair alike, yet all unlike,
    Are born without a pang, and die
15   Without a pang, and so pass by.

FROM SUNSET TO STAR RISE.

Go from me, summer friends, and tarry not:
    I am no summer friend, but wintry cold,
    A silly sheep benighted from the fold,
A sluggard with a thorn-choked garden plot.
5 Take counsel, sever from my lot your lot,
    Dwell in your pleasant places, hoard your gold;
    Lest you with me should shiver on the wold,
Athirst and hungering on a barren spot.

For I have hedged me with a thorny hedge,
10   I live alone, I look to die alone:
Yet sometimes when a wind sighs through the sedge
    Ghosts of my buried years and friends come back,
My heart goes sighing after swallows flown
    On sometime summer's unreturning track.

DAYS OF VANITY.

        A dream that waketh,
        Bubble that breaketh,
    Song whose burden sigheth,
        A passing breath,
5   Smoke that vanisheth,—
    Such is life that dieth.

        A flower that fadeth,
        Fruit the tree sheddeth,
    Trackless bird that flieth,
10   Summer time brief,
        Falling of the leaf,—
    Such is life that dieth.

        A scent exhaling,
        Snow waters failing,
15 Morning dew that drieth,
        A windy blast,
        Lengthening shadows cast,—
    Such is life that dieth.

        A scanty measure,
20   Rust-eaten treasure,
    Spending that nought buyeth,
        Moth on the wing,
        Toil unprofiting,—
    Such is life that dieth.

25   Morrow by morrow
      Sorrow breeds sorrow,
    For this my song sigheth;
      From day to night
      We lapse out of sight,—
30   Such is life that dieth.

ONCE FOR ALL.
(MARGARET.)

I said: This is a beautiful fresh rose.
    I said: I will delight me with its scent;
    Will watch its lovely curve of languishment,
Will watch its leaves unclose, its heart unclose.
5   I said: Old earth has put away her snows,
    All living things make merry to their bent,
    A flower is come for every flower that went
In autumn, the sun glows, the south wind blows.
So walking in a garden of delight
10   I came upon one sheltered shadowed nook
Where broad leaf shadows veiled the day with night,
    And there lay snow unmelted by the sun:—
I answered: Take who will the path I took,
    Winter nips once for all; love is but one.

ENRICA, 1865.

She came among us from the South
    And made the North her home awhile;
    Our dimness brightened in her smile,
Our tongue grew sweeter in her mouth.

5   We chilled beside her liberal glow,
         She dwarfed us by her ampler scale,
         Her full-blown blossom made us pale,
     She summer-like and we like snow.

     We Englishwomen, trim, correct,
10   All minted in the selfsame mould,
         Warm-hearted but of semblance cold,
     All-courteous out of self-respect.

     She woman in her natural grace,
         Less trammelled she by lore of school,
15   Courteous by nature not by rule,
     Warm-hearted and of cordial face.

     So for awhile she made her home
         Among us in the rigid North,
         She who from Italy came forth
20   And scaled the Alps and crossed the foam.

     But if she found us like our sea,
         Of aspect colourless and chill,
         Rock-girt; like it she found us still
     Deep at our deepest, strong and free.

AUTUMN VIOLETS.

     Keep love for youth, and violets for the spring:
         Or if these bloom when worn-out autumn grieves,
         Let them lie hid in double shade of leaves,
     Their own, and others dropped down withering;
5   For violets suit when home birds build and sing,
         Not when the outbound bird a passage cleaves;
         Not with dry stubble of mown harvest sheaves,
     But when the green world buds to blossoming.
     Keep violets for the spring, and love for youth,
10   Love that should dwell with beauty, mirth, and hope:
         Or if a later sadder love be born,

Let this not look for grace beyond its scope,
But give itself, nor plead for answering truth—
A grateful Ruth tho' gleaning scanty corn.

A DIRGE.

Why were you born when the snow was falling?
You should have come to the cuckoo's calling,
Or when grapes are green in the cluster,
Or, at least, when lithe swallows muster
5   For their far off flying
       From summer dying.

Why did you die when the lambs were cropping?
You should have died at the apples' dropping,
When the grasshopper comes to trouble,
10 And the wheat-fields are sodden stubble,
       And all winds go sighing
       For sweet things dying.

"THEY DESIRE A BETTER COUNTRY."

                    I.
I would not if I could undo my past,
    Tho' for its sake my future is a blank;
    My past for which I have myself to thank,
For all its faults and follies first and last.
5 I would not cast anew the lot once cast,
    Or launch a second ship for one that sank,
    Or drug with sweets the bitterness I drank,
Or break by feasting my perpetual fast.
I would not if I could: for much more dear
10   Is one remembrance than a hundred joys,
       More than a thousand hopes in jubilee;

Dearer the music of one tearful voice
     That unforgotten calls and calls to me,
"Follow me here, rise up, and follow here."

II.

15   What seekest thou, far in the unknown land?
         In hope I follow joy gone on before;
         In hope and fear persistent more and more,
     As the dry desert lengthens out its sand.
     Whilst day and night I carry in my hand
20   The golden key to ope the golden door
         Of golden home; yet mine eye weepeth sore,
     For long the journey is that makes no stand.
     And who is this that veiled doth walk with thee?
         Lo, this is Love that walketh at my right;
25   One exile holds us both, and we are bound
     To selfsame home-joys in the land of light.
     Weeping thou walkest with him; weepeth he?—
         Some sobbing weep, some weep and make no sound.

III.

     A dimness of a glory glimmers here
30   Thro' veils and distance from the space remote,
         A faintest far vibration of a note
     Reaches to us and seems to bring us near;
     Causing our face to glow with braver cheer,
         Making the serried mist to stand afloat,
35   Subduing languor with an antidote,
     And strengthening love almost to cast out fear:
     Till for one moment golden city walls
         Rise looming on us, golden walls of home,
     Light of our eyes until the darkness falls;
40   Then thro' the outer darkness burdensome
     I hear again the tender voice that calls,
         "Follow me hither, follow, rise, and come."

A GREEN CORNFIELD.

"And singing still dost soar and
    soaring ever singest."

The earth was green, the sky was blue:
    I saw and heard one sunny morn
A skylark hang between the two,
    A singing speck above the corn;

5   A stage below, in gay accord,
    White butterflies danced on the wing,
And still the singing skylark soared
    And silent sank and soared to sing.

The cornfield stretched a tender green
10   To right and left beside my walks;
I knew he had a nest unseen
    Somewhere among the million stalks:

And as I paused to hear his song
    While swift the sunny moments slid,
15   Perhaps his mate sat listening long,
    And listened longer than I did.

A BRIDE SONG.

Thro' the vales to my love!
    To the happy small nest of home
Green from basement to roof;
    Where the honey-bees come
5   To the window-sill flowers,
    And dive from above,
Safe from the spider that weaves
    Her warp and her woof
In some outermost leaves.

10   Thro' the vales to my love!
           In sweet April hours
           All rainbows and showers,
       While dove answers dove,—
           In beautiful May,
15   When the orchards are tender
           And frothing with flowers,—
           In opulent June,
       When the wheat stands up slender
           By sweet-smelling hay,
20   And half the sun's splendour
           Descends to the moon.

       Thro' the vales to my love!
           Where the turf is so soft to the feet
           And the thyme makes it sweet,
25   And the stately foxglove
           Hangs silent its exquisite bells;
           And where water wells
       The greenness grows greener,
           And bulrushes stand
30   Round a lily to screen her.

       Nevertheless, if this land,
           Like a garden to smell and to sight,
       Were turned to a desert of sand;
           Stripped bare of delight,
35   All its best gone to worst,
       For my feet no repose,
           No water to comfort my thirst,
       And heaven like a furnace above,—
           The desert would be
40   As gushing of waters to me,
       The wilderness be as a rose,
           If it led me to thee,
           O my love.

CONFLUENTS.

As rivers seek the sea,
   Much more deep than they,
So my soul seeks thee
   Far away:
5 As running rivers moan
On their course alone,
   So I moan
   Left alone.

As the delicate rose
10   To the sun's sweet strength
Doth herself unclose,
   Breadth and length;
So spreads my heart to thee
Unveiled utterly,
15   I to thee
   Utterly.

As morning dew exhales
   Sunwards pure and free,
So my spirit fails
20   After thee:
As dew leaves not a trace
On the green earth's face;
   I, no trace
   On thy face.

25 Its goal the river knows,
   Dewdrops find a way,
Sunlight cheers the rose
   In her day:
Shall I, lone sorrow past,
30 Find thee at the last?
   Sorrow past,
   Thee at last?

THE LOWEST ROOM.

Like flowers sequestered from the sun
   And wind of summer, day by day
I dwindled paler, whilst my hair
   Showed the first tinge of grey.

5   "Oh what is life, that we should live?
   Or what is death, that we must die?
A bursting bubble is our life:
   I also, what am I?"

"What is your grief? now tell me, sweet,
10   That I may grieve," my sister said;
And stayed a white embroidering hand
   And raised a golden head:

Her tresses showed a richer mass,
   Her eyes looked softer than my own,
15   Her figure had a statelier height,
   Her voice a tenderer tone.

"Some must be second and not first;
   All cannot be the first of all:
Is not this, too, but vanity?
20   I stumble like to fall.

"So yesterday I read the acts
   Of Hector and each clangorous king
With wrathful great Aeacides:—
   Old Homer leaves a sting."

25   The comely face looked up again,
   The deft hand lingered on the thread:
"Sweet, tell me what is Homer's sting,
   Old Homer's sting?" she said.

"He stirs my sluggish pulse like wine,
30   He melts me like the wind of spice,
Strong as strong Ajax' red right hand,
   And grand like Juno's eyes.

"I cannot melt the sons of men,
   I cannot fire and tempest-toss:—
35 Besides, those days were golden days,
    Whilst these are days of dross."

She laughed a feminine low laugh,
   Yet did not stay her dexterous hand:
"Now tell me of those days," she said,
40   "When time ran golden sand."

"Then men were men of might and right,
   Sheer might, at least, and weighty swords;
Then men in open blood and fire
    Bore witness to their words,

45 "Crest-rearing kings with whistling spears;
   But if these shivered in the shock
They wrenched up hundred-rooted trees,
    Or hurled the effacing rock.

"Then hand to hand, then foot to foot,
   Stern to the death-grip grappling then,
Who ever thought of gunpowder
    Amongst these men of men?

"They knew whose hand struck home the death,
   They knew who broke but would not bend,
55 Could venerate an equal foe
    And scorn a laggard friend.

"Calm in the utmost stress of doom,
   Devout toward adverse powers above,
They hated with intenser hate
60   And loved with fuller love.

"Then heavenly beauty could allay
   As heavenly beauty stirred the strife:
By them a slave was worshipped more
    Than is by us a wife."

65 She laughed again, my sister laughed;
   Made answer o'er the laboured cloth:
"I rather would be one of us
    Than wife, or slave, or both."

"Oh better then be slave or wife
70   Than fritter now blank life away:
Then night had holiness of night,
    And day was sacred day.

"The princess laboured at her loom,
    Mistress and handmaiden alike;
75 Beneath their needles grew the field
    With warriors armed to strike.

"Or, look again, dim Dian's face
    Gleamed perfect thro' the attendant night;
Were such not better than those holes
80   Amid that waste of white?

"A shame it is, our aimless life:
    I rather from my heart would feed
From silver dish in gilded stall
    With wheat and wine the steed—

85 "The faithful steed that bore my lord
    In safety thro' the hostile land,
The faithful steed that arched his neck
    To fondle with my hand."

Her needle erred; a moment's pause,
90   A moment's patience, all was well.
Then she: "But just suppose the horse,
    Suppose the rider fell?

"Then captive in an alien house,
    Hungering on exile's bitter bread,—
95 They happy, they who won the lot
    Of sacrifice," she said.

Speaking she faltered, while her look
    Showed forth her passion like a glass:
With hand suspended, kindling eye,
100   Flushed cheek, how fair she was!

"Ah well, be those the days of dross;
    This, if you will, the age of gold:
Yet had those days a spark of warmth,
    While these are somewhat cold—

105 "Are somewhat mean and cold and slow,
    Are stunted from heroic growth:
We gain but little when we prove
    The worthlessness of both."

"But life is in our hands," she said:
110   "In our own hands for gain or loss:
Shall not the Sevenfold Sacred Fire
    Suffice to purge our dross?

"Too short a century of dreams,
    One day of work sufficient length:
115 Why should not you, why should not I
    Attain heroic strength?

"Our life is given us as a blank;
    Ourselves must make it blest or curst:
Who dooms me I shall only be
120   The second, not the first?

"Learn from old Homer, if you will,
    Such wisdom as his books have said:
In one the acts of Ajax shine,
    In one of Diomed.

125 "Honoured all heroes whose high deeds
    Thro' life, thro' death, enlarge their span:
Only Achilles in his rage
    And sloth is less than man."

"Achilles only less than man?
130   He less than man who, half a god,
Discomfited all Greece with rest,
    Cowed Ilion with a nod?

"He offered vengeance, lifelong grief
    To one dear ghost, uncounted price:
135 Beasts, Trojans, adverse gods, himself,
    Heaped up the sacrifice.

"Self-immolated to his friend,
    Shrined in world's wonder, Homer's page,
Is this the man, the less than men
140   Of this degenerate age?"

"Gross from his acorns, tusky boar
Does memorable acts like his;
So for her snared offended young
Bleeds the swart lioness."

145 But here she paused; our eyes had met,
And I was whitening with the jeer;
She rose: "I went too far," she said;
Spoke low: "Forgive me, dear.

"To me our days seem pleasant days,
150 Our home a haven of pure content;
Forgive me if I said too much,
So much more than I meant.

"Homer, tho' greater than his gods,
With rough-hewn virtues was sufficed
155 And rough-hewn men: but what are such
To us who learn of Christ?"

The much-moved pathos of her voice,
Her almost tearful eyes, her cheek
Grown pale, confessed the strength of love
160 Which only made her speak:

For mild she was, of few soft words,
Most gentle, easy to be led,
Content to listen when I spoke
And reverence what I said;

165 I elder sister by six years;
Not half so glad, or wise, or good:
Her words rebuked my secret self
And shamed me where I stood.

She never guessed her words reproved
170 A silent envy nursed within,
A selfish, souring discontent
Pride-born, the devil's sin.

I smiled, half bitter, half in jest:
"The wisest man of all the wise
175 Left for his summary of life
'Vanity of vanities.'

"Beneath the sun there's nothing new:
　　Men flow, men ebb, mankind flows on:
If I am wearied of my life,
180　　Why so was Solomon.

"Vanity of vanities he preached
　　Of all he found, of all he sought:
Vanity of vanities, the gist
　　Of all the words he taught.

185 "This in the wisdom of the world,
　　In Homer's page, in all, we find:
As the sea is not filled, so yearns
　　Man's universal mind.

"This Homer felt, who gave his men
190　　With glory but a transient state:
His very Jove could not reverse
　　Irrevocable fate.

"Uncertain all their lot save this—
　　Who wins must lose, who lives must die:
195 All trodden out into the dark
　　Alike, all vanity."

She scarcely answered when I paused,
　　But rather to herself said: "One
Is here," low-voiced and loving, "Yea,
200　　Greater than Solomon."

So both were silent, she and I:
　　She laid her work aside, and went
Into the garden-walks, like spring,
　　All gracious with content;

205 A little graver than her wont,
　　Because her words had fretted me;
Not warbling quite her merriest tune
　　Bird-like from tree to tree.

I chose a book to read and dream:
210　　Yet half the while with furtive eyes
Marked how she made her choice of flowers
　　Intuitively wise,

And ranged them with instinctive taste
   Which all my books had failed to teach;
215 Fresh rose herself, and daintier
   Than blossom of the peach.

By birthright higher than myself,
   Tho' nestling of the selfsame nest:
No fault of hers, no fault of mine,
220   But stubborn to digest.

I watched her, till my book unmarked
   Slid noiseless to the velvet floor;
Till all the opulent summer-world
   Looked poorer than before.

225 Just then her busy fingers ceased,
   Her fluttered colour went and came;
I knew whose step was on the walk,
   Whose voice would name her name.

*   *   *   *   *

Well, twenty years have passed since then:
230   My sister now, a stately wife
Still fair, looks back in peace and sees
   The longer half of life—

The longer half of prosperous life,
   With little grief, or fear, or fret:
235 She, loved and loving long ago,
   Is loved and loving yet.

A husband honourable, brave,
   Is her main wealth in all the world:
And next to him one like herself,
240   One daughter golden-curled;

Fair image of her own fair youth,
   As beautiful and as serene,
With almost such another love
   As her own love has been.

245 Yet, tho' of world-wide charity,
        And in her home most tender dove,
    Her treasure and her heart are stored
        In the home-land of love:

    She thrives, God's blessed husbandry;
250   Most like a vine which full of fruit
    Doth cling and lean and climb toward heaven
        While earth still binds its root.

    I sit and watch my sister's face:
        How little altered since the hours
255 When she, a kind, light-hearted girl,
        Gathered her garden flowers;

    Her song just mellowed by regret
        For having teased me with her talk;
    Then all-forgetful as she heard
260   One step upon the walk.

    While I? I sat alone and watched;
        My lot in life, to live alone
    In mine own world of interests,
        Much felt but little shown.

265 Not to be first: how hard to learn
        That lifelong lesson of the past;
    Line graven on line and stroke on stroke;
        But, thank God, learned at last.

    So now in patience I possess
270   My soul year after tedious year,
    Content to take the lowest place,
        The place assigned me here.

    Yet sometimes, when I feel my strength
        Most weak, and life most burdensome,
275 I lift mine eyes up to the hills
        From whence my help shall come:

    Yea, sometimes still I lift my heart
        To the Archangelic trumpet-burst,
    When all deep secrets shall be shown,
280   And many last be first.

DEAD HOPE.

Hope new born one pleasant morn
   Died at even;
Hope dead lives nevermore,
   No, not in heaven.

5   If his shroud were but a cloud
   To weep itself away;
Or were he buried underground
   To sprout some day!
But dead and gone is dead and gone
10   Vainly wept upon.

Nought we place above his face
   To mark the spot,
But it shows a barren place
   In our lot.
15 Hope has birth no more on earth
   Morn or even;
Hope dead lives nevermore,
   No, not in heaven.

A DAUGHTER OF EVE.

A fool I was to sleep at noon,
   And wake when night is chilly
Beneath the comfortless cold moon;
A fool to pluck my rose too soon,
5   A fool to snap my lily.

My garden-plot I have not kept;
   Faded and all-forsaken,
I weep as I have never wept:
Oh it was summer when I slept,
10   It's winter now I waken.

Talk what you please of future Spring
   And sun-warmed sweet tomorrow:—
Stripped bare of hope and everything,
No more to laugh, no more to sing,
15   I sit alone with sorrow.

SONG.

Oh what comes over the sea,
   Shoals and quicksands past;
And what comes home to me,
   Sailing slow, sailing fast?

5   A wind comes over the sea
   With a moan in its blast;
But nothing comes home to me,
   Sailing slow, sailing fast.

Let me be, let me be,
10   For my lot is cast:
Land or sea all's one to me,
   And sail it slow or fast.

VENUS'S LOOKING-GLASS.

I marked where lovely Venus and her court
   With song and dance and merry laugh went by;
   Weightless, their wingless feet seemed made to fly,
Bound from the ground and in mid air to sport.
5 Left far behind I heard the dolphins snort,
   Tracking their goddess with a wistful eye,
   Around whose head white doves rose, wheeling high
Or low, and cooed after their tender sort.

All this I saw in Spring. Thro' Summer heat
10   I saw the lovely Queen of Love no more.
      But when flushed Autumn thro' the woodlands went
I spied sweet Venus walk amid the wheat:
    Whom seeing, every harvester gave o'er
      His toil, and laughed and hoped and was content.

LOVE LIES BLEEDING.

Love that is dead and buried, yesterday
    Out of his grave rose up before my face;
    No recognition in his look, no trace
Of memory in his eyes dust-dimmed and grey.
5   While I, remembering, found no word to say,
    But felt my quickened heart leap in its place;
    Caught afterglow, thrown back from long-set days,
Caught echoes of all music passed away.
Was this indeed to meet?—I mind me yet
10   In youth we met when hope and love were quick,
    We parted with hope dead, but love alive:
    I mind me how we parted then heart-sick,
    Remembering, loving, hopeless, weak to strive:—
Was this to meet? Not so, we have not met.

BIRD RAPTURES.

The sunrise wakes the lark to sing,
    The moonrise wakes the nightingale.
Come darkness, moonrise, everything
    That is so silent, sweet, and pale,
5   Come, so ye wake the nightingale.

Make haste to mount, thou wistful moon,
   Make haste to wake the nightingale:
Let silence set the world in tune
   To hearken to that wordless tale
10   Which warbles from the nightingale.

O herald skylark, stay thy flight
   One moment, for a nightingale
Floods us with sorrow and delight.
   Tomorrow thou shalt hoist the sail;
15 Leave us tonight the nightingale.

MY FRIEND.

Two days ago with dancing glancing hair,
   With living lips and eyes:
   Now pale, dumb, blind, she lies;
So pale, yet still so fair.

5 We have not left her yet, not yet alone;
   But soon must leave her where
   She will not miss our care,
Bone of our bone.

Weep not; O friends, we should not weep:
10   Our friend of friends lies full of rest;
   No sorrow rankles in her breast,
Fallen fast asleep.

She sleeps below,
   She wakes and laughs above:
15   Today, as she walked, let us walk in love;
Tomorrow follow so.

TWILIGHT NIGHT.

I

We met, hand to hand,
   We clasped hands close and fast,
As close as oak and ivy stand;
   But it is past:
5   Come day, come night, day comes at last.

We loosed hand from hand,
   We parted face from face;
Each went his way to his own land
   At his own pace,
10   Each went to fill his separate place.

If we should meet one day,
   If both should not forget,
We shall clasp hands the accustomed way,
   As when we met
15   So long ago, as I remember yet.

II

Where my heart is (wherever that may be)
   Might I but follow!
If you fly thither over heath and lea,
O honey-seeking bee,
20   O careless swallow,
Bid some for whom I watch keep watch for me.

Alas! that we must dwell, my heart and I,
   So far asunder.
Hours wax to days, and days and days creep by;
25   I watch with wistful eye,
   I wait and wonder:
When will that day draw nigh—that hour draw nigh?

Not yesterday, and not, I think, today;
   Perhaps tomorrow.
30   Day after day "tomorrow" thus I say:
I watched so yesterday
   In hope and sorrow,
Again today I watch the accustomed way.

A BIRD SONG.

It's a year almost that I have not seen her:
Oh last summer green things were greener,
Brambles fewer, the blue sky bluer.

It's surely summer, for there's a swallow:
5 Come one swallow, his mate will follow,
The bird-race quicken and wheel and thicken.

Oh happy swallow whose mate will follow
O'er height, o'er hollow! I'd be a swallow
To build this weather one nest together.

A SMILE AND A SIGH.

A smile because the nights are short!
  And every morning brings such pleasure
Of sweet love-making, harmless sport:
  Love that makes and finds its treasure;
5   Love, treasure without measure.

A sigh because the days are long!
  Long long these days that pass in sighing,
A burden saddens every song:
  While time lags which should be flying,
10   We live who would be dying.

AMOR MUNDI.

"Oh where are you going with your love-locks flowing
  On the west wind blowing along this valley track?"
"The downhill path is easy, come with me an it please ye,
  We shall escape the uphill by never turning back."

5   So they two went together in glowing August weather,
       The honey-breathing heather lay to their left and right;
     And dear she was to doat on, her swift feet seemed to float on
       The air like soft twin pigeons too sportive to alight.

     "Oh what is that in heaven where grey cloud-flakes are seven,
10   Where blackest clouds hang riven just at the rainy skirt?"
     "Oh that's a meteor sent us, a message dumb, portentous,
       An undeciphered solemn signal of help or hurt."

     "Oh what is that glides quickly where velvet flowers grow
         thickly,
       Their scent comes rich and sickly?"—"A scaled and hooded
         worm."
15   "Oh what's that in the hollow, so pale I quake to follow?"
       "Oh that's a thin dead body which waits the eternal term."

     "Turn again, O my sweetest,—turn again, false and fleetest:
       This beaten way thou beatest I fear is hell's own track."
     "Nay, too steep for hill-mounting; nay, too late for
         cost-counting:
20   This downhill path is easy, but there's no turning back."

     THE GERMAN-FRENCH CAMPAIGN.
     1870–1871.

       These two pieces, written during the suspense
     of a great nation's agony, aim at expressing
     human sympathy, not political bias.

                    1.
           "THY BROTHER'S BLOOD CRIETH."
     All her corn-fields rippled in the sunshine,
       All her lovely vines, sweets-laden, bowed;
     Yet some weeks to harvest and to vintage:
       When, as one man's hand, a cloud
5   Rose and spread, and, blackening, burst asunder
       In rain and fire and thunder.

Is there nought to reap in the day of harvest?
   Hath the vine in her day no fruit to yield?
Yea, men tread the press, but not for sweetness,
10   And they reap a red crop from the field.
Build barns, ye reapers, garner all aright,
   Tho' your souls be called tonight.

A cry of tears goes up from blackened homesteads,
   A cry of blood goes up from reeking earth:
15 Tears and blood have a cry that pierces Heaven
   Thro' all its Hallelujah swells of mirth;
God hears their cry, and tho' He tarry, yet
   He doth not forget.

Mournful Mother, prone in dust weeping
20   Who shall comfort thee for those who are not?
As thou didst, men do to thee; and heap the measure,
   And heat the furnace sevenfold hot:
As thou once, now these to thee—who pitieth thee
   From sea to sea?

25 O thou King, terrible in strength, and building
   Thy strong future on thy past!
Tho' he drink the last, the King of Sheshach,
   Yet he shall drink at the last.
Art thou greater than great Babylon,
30   Which lies overthrown?

Take heed, ye unwise among the people;
   O ye fools, when will ye understand?—
He that planted the ear shall He not hear,
   Nor He smite who formed the hand?
35 "Vengeance is Mine, is Mine," thus saith the Lord:—
   O Man, put up thy sword.

2.
"TODAY FOR ME."
She sitteth still who used to dance,
She weepeth sore and more and more:—
Let us sit with thee weeping sore,
40   O fair France.

She trembleth as the days advance
Who used to be so light of heart:—
We in thy trembling bear a part,
    Sister France.

45   Her eyes shine tearful as they glance:
"Who shall give back my slaughtered sons?
"Bind up," she saith, "my wounded ones."—
    Alas, France!

She struggles in a deathly trance,
50   As in a dream her pulses stir,
She hears the nations calling her,
    "France, France, France."

Thou people of the lifted lance,
Forbear her tears, forbear her blood:
55   Roll back, roll back, thy whelming flood,
    Back from France.

Eye not her loveliness askance,
Forge not for her a galling chain;
Leave her at peace to bloom again,
60   Vine-clad France.

A time there is for change and chance,
A time for passing of the cup:
And One abides can yet bind up
    Broken France.

65   A time there is for change and chance:
Who next shall drink the trembling cup,
Wring out its dregs and suck them up
    After France?

A CHRISTMAS CAROL.

In the bleak mid-winter
    Frosty wind made moan,

    Earth stood hard as iron,
      Water like a stone;
5   Snow had fallen, snow on snow,
      Snow on snow,
    In the bleak mid-winter
      Long ago.

    Our God, Heaven cannot hold Him
10   Nor earth sustain;
    Heaven and earth shall flee away
      When He comes to reign:
    In the bleak mid-winter
      A stable-place sufficed
15   The Lord God Almighty
      Jesus Christ.

    Enough for Him whom cherubim
      Worship night and day,
    A breastful of milk
20   And a mangerful of hay;
    Enough for Him whom angels
      Fall down before,
    The ox and ass and camel
      Which adore.

25   Angels and archangels
      May have gathered there,
    Cherubim and seraphim
      Throng'd the air,
    But only His mother
30   In her maiden bliss
    Worshipped the Beloved
      With a kiss.

    What can I give Him,
      Poor as I am?
35   If I were a shepherd
      I would bring a lamb,
    If I were a wise man
      I would do my part,—
    Yet what I can I give Him,
40   Give my heart.

CONSIDER.

      Consider
The lilies of the field whose bloom is brief:—
      We are as they;
      Like them we fade away,
5 As doth a leaf.

      Consider
The sparrows of the air of small account:
      Our God doth view
Whether they fall or mount,—
10   He guards us too.

      Consider
The lilies that do neither spin nor toil,
      Yet are most fair:—
      What profits all this care
15 And all this coil?

      Consider
The birds that have no barn nor harvest-weeks;
      God gives them food:—
Much more our Father seeks
20   To do us good.

BY THE WATERS OF BABYLON.
B.C. 570.

Here, where I dwell, I waste to skin and bone;
    The curse is come upon me, and I waste
    In penal torment powerless to atone.
The curse is come on me, which makes no haste
5   And doth not tarry, crushing both the proud
    Hard man and him the sinner double-faced.
Look not upon me, for my soul is bowed
    Within me, as my body in this mire;
    My soul crawls dumb-struck, sore bestead and cowed.

10 As Sodom and Gomorrah scourged by fire,
  As Jericho before God's trumpet-peal,
  So we the elect ones perish in His ire.
  Vainly we gird on sackcloth, vainly kneel
    With famished faces toward Jerusalem:
15   His heart is shut against us not to feel,
  His ears against our cry He shutteth them,
    His hand He shorteneth that He will not save,
    His law is loud against us to condemn:
  And we, as unclean bodies in the grave
20   Inheriting corruption and the dark,
    Are outcast from His presence which we crave.
  Our Mercy hath departed from His Ark,
    Our Glory hath departed from His rest,
    Our Shield hath left us naked as a mark
25 Unto all pitiless eyes made manifest.
    Our very Father hath forsaken us,
    Our God hath cast us from Him: we oppress'd
  Unto our foes are even marvellous,
    A hissing and a butt for pointing hands,
30   Whilst God Almighty hunts and grinds us thus;
  For He hath scattered us in alien lands,
    Our priests, our princes, our anointed king,
    And bound us hand and foot with brazen bands.
  Here while I sit my painful heart takes wing
35   Home to the home-land I may see no more,
    Where milk and honey flow, where waters spring
  And fail not, where I dwelt in days of yore
    Under my fig-tree and my fruitful vine,
    There where my parents dwelt at ease before:
40 Now strangers press the olives that are mine,
    Reap all the corners of my harvest-field,
    And make their fat hearts wanton with my wine;
  To them my trees, to them my gardens yield
    Their sweets and spices and their tender green,
45   O'er them in noontide heat outspread their shield.
  Yet these are they whose fathers had not been
    Housed with my dogs, whom hip and thigh we smote
    And with their blood washed their pollutions clean,

Purging the land which spewed them from its throat;
50   Their daughters took we for a pleasant prey,
            Choice tender ones on whom the fathers doat.
Now they in turn have led our own away;
            Our daughters and our sisters and our wives
            Sore weeping as they weep who curse the day,
55 To live, remote from help, dishonoured lives,
            Soothing their drunken masters with a song,
            Or dancing in their golden tinkling gyves:
Accurst if they remember thro' the long
            Estrangement of their exile, twice accursed
60   If they forget and join the accursèd throng.
How doth my heart that is so wrung not burst
            When I remember that my way was plain,
            And that God's candle lit me at the first,
Whilst now I grope in darkness, grope in vain,
65   Desiring but to find Him Who is lost,
            To find Him once again, but once again!
His wrath came on us to the uttermost,
            His covenanted and most righteous wrath:
            Yet this is He of Whom we made our boast,
70 Who lit the Fiery Pillar in our path,
            Who swept the Red Sea dry before our feet,
            Who in His jealousy smote kings, and hath
Sworn once to David: One shall fill thy seat
            Born of thy body, as the sun and moon
75   'Stablished for aye in sovereignty complete.
O Lord, remember David, and that soon.
            The Glory hath departed, Ichabod!
            Yet now, before our sun grow dark at noon,
Before we come to nought beneath Thy rod,
80   Before we go down quick into the pit,
            Remember us for good, O God, our God:—
Thy Name will I remember, praising it,
            Tho' Thou forget me, tho' Thou hide Thy face,
            And blot me from the Book which Thou hast writ;
85 Thy Name will I remember in my praise
            And call to mind Thy faithfulness of old,
Tho' as a weaver Thou cut off my days
            And end me as a tale ends that is told.

PARADISE.

Once in a dream I saw the flowers
    That bud and bloom in Paradise;
    More fair they are than waking eyes
Have seen in all this world of ours.
5   And faint the perfume-bearing rose,
    And faint the lily on its stem,
And faint the perfect violet
    Compared with them.

I heard the songs of Paradise:
10   Each bird sat singing in his place;
    A tender song so full of grace
It soared like incense to the skies.
Each bird sat singing to his mate
    Soft cooing notes among the trees:
15   The nightingale herself were cold
    To such as these.

I saw the fourfold River flow,
    And deep it was, with golden sand;
    It flowed between a mossy land
20   With murmured music grave and low.
It hath refreshment for all thirst,
    For fainting spirits strength and rest;
Earth holds not such a draught as this
    From east to west.

25   The Tree of Life stood budding there,
    Abundant with its twelvefold fruits;
    Eternal sap sustains its roots,
Its shadowing branches fill the air.
Its leaves are healing for the world,
30   Its fruit the hungry world can feed,
Sweeter than honey to the taste
    And balm indeed.

I saw the gate called Beautiful;
    And looked, but scarce could look within;
35   I saw the golden streets begin,
And outskirts of the glassy pool.

Oh harps, oh crowns of plenteous stars,
   Oh green palm branches many-leaved—
Eye hath not seen, nor ear hath heard,
40   Nor heart conceived.

I hope to see these things again,
   But not as once in dreams by night;
   To see them with my very sight,
And touch and handle and attain:
45   To have all Heaven beneath my feet
   For narrow way that once they trod;
To have my part with all the saints,
   And with my God.

MOTHER COUNTRY.

Oh what is that country
   And where can it be,
Not mine own country,
   But dearer far to me?
5   Yet mine own country,
   If I one day may see
Its spices and cedars,
   Its gold and ivory.

As I lie dreaming
10   It rises, that land;
There rises before me
   Its green golden strand,
With the bowing cedars
   And the shining sand;
15 It sparkles and flashes
   Like a shaken brand.

Do angels lean nearer
   While I lie and long?
I see their soft plumage
20   And catch their windy song,

Like the rise of a high tide
    Sweeping full and strong;
I mark the outskirts
    Of their reverend throng.

25 Oh what is a king here,
    Or what is a boor?
Here all starve together,
    All dwarfed and poor;
Here Death's hand knocketh
30   At door after door,
He thins the dancers
    From the festal floor.

Oh what is a handmaid,
    Or what is a queen?
35 All must lie down together
    Where the turf is green,
The foulest face hidden,
    The fairest not seen;
Gone as if never
40   They had breathed or been.

Gone from sweet sunshine
    Underneath the sod,
Turned from warm flesh and blood
    To senseless clod,
45 Gone as if never
    They had toiled or trod,
Gone out of sight of all
    Except our God.

Shut into silence
50   From the accustomed song,
Shut into solitude
    From all earth's throng,
Run down tho' swift of foot,
    Thrust down tho' strong;
55 Life made an end of
    Seemed it short or long.

Life made an end of,
   Life but just begun,
Life finished yesterday,
60   Its last sand run;
Life new-born with the morrow,
   Fresh as the sun:
While done is done for ever;
   Undone, undone.

65 And if that life is life,
   This is but a breath,
The passage of a dream
   And the shadow of death;
But a vain shadow
70   If one considereth;
Vanity of vanities,
   As the Preacher saith.

"I WILL LIFT UP MINE EYES UNTO THE HILLS."

I am pale with sick desire,
   For my heart is far away
From this world's fitful fire
   And this world's waning day;
5 In a dream it overleaps
   A world of tedious ills
To where the sunshine sleeps
   On the everlasting hills.—
Say the Saints: There Angels ease us
10   Glorified and white.
They say: We rest in Jesus,
   Where is not day nor night.

My soul saith: I have sought
   For a home that is not gained,
15 I have spent yet nothing bought,
   Have laboured but not attained;

My pride strove to mount and grow,
   And hath but dwindled down;
My love sought love, and lo!
20   Hath not attained its crown.—
   Say the Saints: Fresh souls increase us,
     None languish or recede.
   They say: We love our Jesus,
     And He loves us indeed.

25   I cannot rise above,
     I cannot rest beneath,
I cannot find out love,
   Or escape from death;
Dear hopes and joys gone by
30   Still mock me with a name;
My best beloved die
   And I cannot die with them.—
   Say the Saints: No deaths decrease us,
     Where our rest is glorious.
35   They say: We live in Jesus,
     Who once died for us.

O my soul, she beats her wings
   And pants to fly away
Up to immortal things
40   In the heavenly day:
Yet she flags and almost faints;
   Can such be meant for me?—
Come and see, say the Saints.
   Saith Jesus: Come and see.
45   Say the Saints: His pleasures please us
     Before God and the Lamb.
   Come and taste My sweets, saith Jesus:
     Be with Me where I am.

"THE MASTER IS COME, AND CALLETH FOR THEE."

Who calleth?—Thy Father calleth,
   Run, O Daughter, to wait on Him:
He Who chasteneth but for a season
   Trims thy lamp that it burn not dim.

5 Who calleth?—Thy Master calleth,
   Sit, Disciple, and learn of Him:
He Who teacheth wisdom of Angels
   Makes thee wise as the Cherubim.

Who calleth?—Thy Monarch calleth,
10   Rise, O Subject, and follow Him:
He is stronger than Death or Devil,
   Fear not thou if the foe be grim.

Who calleth?—Thy Lord God calleth,
   Fall, O Creature, adoring Him:
15 He is jealous, thy God Almighty,
   Count not dear to thee life or limb.

Who calleth?—Thy Bridegroom calleth,
   Soar, O Bride, with the Seraphim:
He Who loves thee as no man loveth,
20   Bids thee give up thy heart to Him.

WHO SHALL DELIVER ME?

God strengthen me to bear myself;
That heaviest weight of all to bear,
Inalienable weight of care.

All others are outside myself;
5 I lock my door and bar them out,
The turmoil, tedium, gad-about.

I lock my door upon myself,
And bar them out; but who shall wall
Self from myself, most loathed of all?

10 If I could once lay down myself,
    And start self-purged upon the race
    That all must run! Death runs apace.

    If I could set aside myself,
    And start with lightened heart upon
15 The road by all men overgone!

    God harden me against myself,
    This coward with pathetic voice
    Who craves for ease, and rest, and joys:

    Myself, arch-traitor to myself;
20 My hollowest friend, my deadliest foe,
    My clog whatever road I go.

    Yet One there is can curb myself,
    Can roll the strangling load from me,
    Break off the yoke and set me free.

"WHEN MY HEART IS VEXED, I WILL COMPLAIN."

    "O Lord, how canst Thou say Thou lovest me?
        Me whom Thou settest in a barren land,
        Hungry and thirsty on the burning sand,
    Hungry and thirsty where no waters be
5   Nor shadows of date-bearing tree:—
        O Lord, how canst Thou say Thou lovest me?"

    "I came from Edom by as parched a track,
        As rough a track beneath My bleeding feet.
        I came from Edom seeking thee, and sweet
10 I counted bitterness; I turned not back
        But counted life as death, and trod
        The winepress all alone: and I am God."

    "Yet, Lord, how canst Thou say Thou lovest me?
        For Thou art strong to comfort: and could I
15   But comfort one I love, who, like to die,

Lifts feeble hands and eyes that fail to see
In one last prayer for comfort—nay,
I could not stand aside or turn away."

"Alas! thou knowest that for thee I died,
20   For thee I thirsted with the dying thirst;
     I, Blessed, for thy sake was counted cursed,
In sight of men and angels crucified:
All this and more I bore to prove
My love, and wilt thou yet mistrust My love?"

25   "Lord, I am fain to think Thou lovest me,
     For Thou art all in all and I am Thine,
     And lo! Thy love is better than new wine,
And I am sick of love in loving Thee.
But dost Thou love me? speak and save,
30   For jealousy is cruel as the grave."

"Nay, if thy love is not an empty breath
     My love is as thine own, deep answers deep.
     Peace, peace: I give to My beloved sleep,
Not death but sleep, for love is strong as death:
35   Take patience; sweet thy sleep shall be,
Yea, thou shalt wake in Paradise with Me."

AFTER COMMUNION.

Why should I call Thee Lord, Who art my God?
     Why should I call Thee Friend, Who art my Love?
     Or King, Who art my very Spouse above?
Or call Thy Sceptre on my heart Thy rod?
5   Lo, now Thy banner over me is love,
All heaven flies open to me at Thy nod:
For Thou hast lit Thy flame in me a clod,
     Made me a nest for dwelling of Thy Dove.
     What wilt Thou call me in our home above,
10   Who now hast called me friend? how will it be
     When Thou for good wine settest forth the best?

Now Thou dost bid me come and sup with Thee,
   Now Thou dost make me lean upon Thy breast:
How will it be with me in time of love?

SAINTS AND ANGELS.

It's oh in Paradise that I fain would be,
   Away from earth and weariness and all beside:
Earth is too full of loss with its dividing sea,
   But Paradise upbuilds the bower for the bride.

5   Where flowers are yet in bud while the boughs are green,
   I would get quit of earth and get robed for heaven;
Putting on my raiment white within the screen,
   Putting on my crown of gold whose gems are seven.

Fair is the fourfold river that maketh no moan,
10   Fair are the trees fruit-bearing of the wood,
Fair are the gold and bdellium and the onyx stone,
   And I know the gold of that land is good.

O my love, my dove, lift up your eyes
   Toward the eastern gate like an opening rose;
15   You and I who parted will meet in Paradise,
   Pass within and sing when the gates unclose.

This life is but the passage of a day,
   This life is but a pang and all is over,
But in the life to come which fades not away
20   Every love shall abide and every lover.

He who wore out pleasure and mastered all lore,
   Solomon wrote "Vanity of vanities:"
Down to death, of all that went before
   In his mighty long life, the record is this.

25   With loves by the hundred, wealth beyond measure,
   Is this he who wrote "Vanity of vanities"?
Yea, "Vanity of vanities" he saith of pleasure,
   And of all he learned set his seal to this.

Yet we love and faint not, for our love is one,
30   And we hope and flag not, for our hope is sure,
Altho' there be nothing new beneath the sun
        And no help for life and for death no cure.

The road to death is life, the gate of life is death,
        We who wake shall sleep, we shall wax who wane;
35 Let us not vex our souls for stoppage of a breath,
        The fall of a river that turneth not again.

Be the road short, and be the gate near,—
        Shall a short road tire, a strait gate appal?
The loves that meet in Paradise shall cast out fear,
40   And Paradise hath room for you and me and all.

A ROSE PLANT IN JERICHO.

At morn I plucked a rose and gave it Thee,
        A rose of joy and happy love and peace,
                A rose with scarce a thorn:
                But in the chillness of a second morn
5   My rose bush drooped, and all its gay increase
Was but one thorn that wounded me.

I plucked the thorn and offered it to Thee;
        And for my thorn Thou gavest love and peace,
                Not joy this mortal morn:
10   If Thou hast given much treasure for a thorn,
        Wilt Thou not give me for my rose increase
Of gladness, and all sweets to me?

My thorny rose, my love and pain, to Thee
        I offer; and I set my heart in peace,
15   And rest upon my thorn:
                For verily I think tomorrow morn
        Shall bring me Paradise, my gift's increase,
Yea, give Thy very Self to me.

Introduction to Textual Notes

The variant readings given in the textual notes are taken from three kinds of sources: the extant manuscripts of Christina's poems, the private printing or publication of individual poems before they were incorporated into her published collections, and all of the English and American editions of her poems through William Michael Rossetti's *The Poetical Works of Christina Georgina Rossetti* (1904). I have not recorded the textual variants from publications of individual poems after they were included in one of her collections, because these texts were usually copied directly from the texts in the published collections.

William Michael Rossetti's 1896 and 1904 editions are to some extent unreliable. Many of his spelling, paragraphing, and punctuation variants are not in Christina's extant manuscripts or her editions (that is, editions published during her lifetime); moreover, he rarely explains the sources of his texts. Nevertheless, I have included his readings in the textual notes because as her brother he had access to materials no longer available.

The American texts likewise contain some nonauthorial editing of spelling and punctuation, but they also reflect many of the changes Christina made in the collections after they were published. In one case she added new poems to the Roberts Brothers edition before adding them to the Macmillan edition.[1] Her evident interest in the American texts warrants their inclusion in the variant notes.

At the beginning of the textual notes for each poem is a headnote listing the manuscripts and editions in which the poem occurs

---

1. *Poems* (2 vols.; Boston: Roberts Brothers, 1888), II, contains seventeen new poems not seen earlier in Christina's collections; the new poems are at the end of the collection entitled "A Pageant and Other Poems." Two years later they were added to the English edition of *Poems* (London: Macmillan, 1890) in the section entitled "The Second Series."

and any separate publications of the poem before it became part of the collection. The basic text (or copy-text), taken from the first English edition that includes the poem, appears in italics. Reprints are not listed in the headnotes or cited in the variant notes unless they show a new variant. Editions and reprints are identified by date of publication rather than by title; the titles are given in the table of editions and reprints. An *a* after the date of publication indicates an American edition, and parentheses enclose the dates of reprints. The variants designated 1862p (p = page proof) and 1896s (s = special edition) are recorded only if they differ from the first editions published in those years.

In the textual notes, Am. eds. refers to all the American editions in which the poem appears. Matter in roman type within square brackets [thus] is supplied by the editor. Italic print within square brackets [*thus*] indicates words or letters deleted, erased, or written over in the manuscripts. Angle brackets <thus> enclose words or letters written in the manuscripts as additions or as replacements for deletions and erasures. Words added in the manuscripts and then deleted are in italic print enclosed in angle brackets and square brackets [<*thus*>]. A solidus represents a line break. The abbreviation for *manuscript* is MS.

A variant within the line is preceded by a pickup word and is followed by a drop word and any punctuation immediately after the drop word.[2] A capitalized variant with no pickup word indicates the beginning of a line.[3] A variant at the end of the line is accompanied by a pickup word and the end-of-line punctuation.[4] If the variation is in the end line punctuation itself, a pickup word precedes it.[5] When a capitalized pickup word occurs within the line, it is accompanied by the preceding word.[6] When a pickup word appears more than once in the line, it is accompanied by the preceding word.[7] If a text contains several variants within the same line, they are presented together in one reading; where the variants are separated by more than two words in the line, empty angle

2. For example, see the manuscript variant for line 16 of "Goblin Market."
3. For example, see the manuscript variant for line 33 of "Goblin Market."
4. For example, see the variant in the American editions for line 39 of "Goblin Market."
5. For example, see the manuscript variant for line 45 of "Goblin Market."
6. For example, see the manuscript variant for line 147 of "Goblin Market."
7. For example, see the manuscript variant for line 197 of "Goblin Market."

brackets represent the word or words omitted between the variants.[8]

All of the manuscripts and manuscript revisions cited are in ink and in Christina's handwriting unless otherwise indicated. Christina's later pencil changes, her brothers' markings in her manuscripts, and the manuscripts not in her own hand are noted as such.

The following kinds of variants are not registered because they do not seem to perceptibly affect the sound or sense of the poem. I have not recorded the false starts and obvious slips of the pen that were immediately corrected in the manuscripts. In some of her manuscripts Christina preceded every line of a quotation with quotation marks, but I have followed the practice in her later manuscripts and in all her editions of inserting only the opening and closing sets of quotation marks. In the manuscript titles only the first letter of a word is capitalized, but in the printed titles and in this edition all of the letters are capitals. Titles are centered in Christina's manuscripts and editions, but they are aligned at the left margin in this edition. I have eliminated the house practices (noted earlier) imposed upon Christina's paragraphing, namely, of setting the first word of the poem in capital letters and indenting the first line of each new paragraph in the longer narrative poems. In cases where the printed spelling consistently differs from that in the manuscripts, I have emended the text to the manuscript spelling; thus I have changed the house spellings *to-day, to-night,* and *to-morrow* to the manuscript spellings *today, tonight,* and *tomorrow* and ignored such American spellings as *labor* or *neighbor*. The American texts leave a space before the apostrophe in contractions and sometimes place the punctuation outside the quotation marks, but I have followed the practice in the manuscripts and English editions of eliminating the space before the apostrophe and placing the punctuation inside the quotation marks. The 1896 and 1904 editions omit the period after the title, but I have retained it because it is in the manuscripts and all her editions. The 1904 edition uses single rather than double quotation marks, but since almost all the manuscripts and all her editions use double quotation marks, I have followed her usual practice. I have not recorded the occurrence of partially printed or missing end-of-line punctuation due to faulty inking, which I found in collating copies of the editions

8. For example, see the manuscript variant for line 116 of "Goblin Market."

and reprints.[9] All variants in words, paragraphing, spelling, and punctuation other than the kinds described above are recorded in the textual notes.

GOBLIN MARKET.

[Composed April 27, 1859. Editions: *1862*, 1865, 1866a, 1875, 1876a, 1893, 1904. The notebook MS is owned by Mrs. Geoffrey Dennis.]

Title. MS: [*A Peep at the Goblins.*] <Goblin-Market.> / [*To M. F. R.*] [The deletion of *To M. F. R.* is marked in pencil. In a copy of *Goblin Market* (1893) Christina wrote the following note, dated December 7, 1893: "'Goblin Market' first published in 1862 was written (subject of course to subsequent revision) as long ago as April 27. 1859, and in M.S. was inscribed to my dear only sister Maria Francesca Rossetti herself long afterwards the author of 'A Shadow of Dante.' In the first instance I named it 'A Peep at the Goblins' in imitation of my cousin Mrs. Bray's 'A Peep at the Pixies,' but my brother Dante Gabriel Rossetti substituted the greatly improved title as it now stands. And here I like to acknowledge the general indebtedness of my first and second volumes to his suggestive wit and revising hand. Christina G. Rossetti" (inscribed copy, in Iowa State Department of History and Archives, Des Moines).]

2. 1893: cry
4. MS: buy:—
14. MS: strawberries,—
16. MS: In Summer weather,
24. MS: bilberries,—
25. MS: try:—
29. MS: the south,
30. MS: eye,
32. MS: [*Morning and*] <Evening by> evening
33. MS: Amongst the
34. MS: hear
35. MS: blushes;
38. MS: lips

39. Am. eds.: and finger-tips.
40. MS: said
45. MS: roots?"—
46. MS: buy," [*cry*] <call> the
47. MS: glen.—
48. Am. eds.: "O," cried
49. MS: men."—
50. MS: Lizzie hid her eyes with hands
51. MS: [illegible erasure] <That showed like> curds or cream;
52. MS: Laura [*raised*] <reared> her [*golden*] <glossy> head
53. MS: And spoke like music of the stream:
54. MS: "Look Lizzie, look Lizzie,
55. MS: men:
57. MS: One [*lugs*] <bears> a
58. MS: One [*bears*] <lugs> a
59. Am. eds., 1904: many pounds' weight.
61. MS: That swung those grapes luscious;
63. MS: bushes."—
64. Am. eds.: said Lizzie, "no, no,
66. MS: us."—
70. MS: each [*goblin*] <merchant> man.
76. Am. eds.: tumbled hurry-scurry.
78. MS: together;
81. MS: neck,
82. MS: a rush-innested swan,
84. MS: a silver poplar branch/ Which the moonshine dwells upon, 1893: branch.
88. MS: men
89. MS: cry:

9. For exact copies, see table of editions and reprints herein.

90. MS: buy."—
92. MS: moss
93. MS: other
94. MS: with quaint brother,
95. MS: other
98. MS: plate,
100. MS: brown
 Am. eds., 1875, 1893, 1904: leaves, and
101. MS: town,)
104. MS: cry.—
106. 1904: money.
107. 1866a: taste,
109. MS, 1866a: cat-faced purred,
113. MS: for "Pretty Polly,"—
 1904: for 'Pretty Polly';
116. MS: folk I <> coin,
 1875, 1893, 1904: "Good Folk, I
122. MS: heather."—
124. Am. eds.: answered altogether:
125. MS: curl."—
127. MS: pearl;
128. MS: their fruit-globes fair
 1904: red.
132. MS: before;
136. MS: sore,
137. Am. eds.: away,
138. MS: kernel-stone
 1865, Am. eds., 1875, 1904: one kernel stone,
147. MS: remember Jeanie
152. MS: Where Summer ripens
156. 1875, 1876a, 1893, 1904: more, but
162. MS: so."—
163. MS: "Nay hush,"
164. MS: "Nay hush,
165. MS: fill
166. 1904: still:
168. MS: her.
 Am. eds.: more,"—and <> her.
 1875, 1893: more;" and
 1904: more; and <> her.
169. MS: sorrow:
170. MS: [*tomorrow,*] <tomorrow>
175. MS: melons icy cold
180. MS: be that mead
181. MS: grow, those waters clear they drink
 Am. eds.: drink,
183. MS: sap."—
187. MS: They laid down

189. MS, Am. eds.: of new-fallen snow,
192. MS: stars [*peered*] <gazed> in
194. 1875, 1904: owls forebore to
196. 1904: their nest:
197. MS: to breast,
205. MS: wheat
206. MS: eat;
213. MS: One songful for
219. 1904: deep.
220. MS: flags;
221. Am. eds., 1875, 1893, 1904: turning homeward said:
222. MS: Those farthest loftiest crags,
223. MS: Come Laura not
 1875, 1904: lags.
225. MS: asleep."—
226. 1904: rushes,
229. MS, Am. eds.: not fallen, the
 1875, 1893, 1904: chill;
231. MS: cry
235. 1866a: Nor for
237. 1904: hobbling—
241. MS: Of [*quaint*] <brisk> fruit-merchant [Christina's revision is in pencil.]
242. MS: urged: "O Laura come;
 Am. eds.: urged: "O
243. 1875, 1876a, 1893, 1904: fruit-call, but
244. MS: brook,
247. MS: winks his spark,
 Am. eds., 1904: Each glow-worm winks
248. Am. eds.: dark;
250. MS: is Summer weather,
252. MS: do?"—
255. MS: cry:
256. MS: buy."—
257. 1862, 1865, 1866a: dainty fruits?
258. MS: more [*the*] <that> succous <> find
 1862: more that succous
261. MS: ache
 1904: ache:
262. MS: the [*darkness,*] <dimness,> nought
263. MS: home her
266. MS: yearning
267. MS: for hope deferred and
270. Am. eds.: vain,
272. MS: never heard again
 1904: cry,

273. MS: buy:"—
279. Am. eds.: decay, and
283. 1893: root.
284. MS: shoot;
285. 1904: none.
291. MS: trees
300. 1876a, 1904: care,
305. Am. eds.: buy."
309. MS: hear:
310. MS: her
312. MS: grave
313. MS: bride,
316. MS: her glad prime,
317. MS: time
Am. eds.: earliest winter-time,
1904: earliest winter time,
318. MS: rime
319. Am. eds.: crisp winter-time.
1904: crisp winter time.
320. Am. eds.: Till Laura, dwindling,
321. MS: at death's door:
1904: door.
323. MS, Am. eds.: worse,
326. MS: brook,
Am. eds.: brook;
338. MS: Pulling queer faces
341. Am. eds.: Ratel and
344. Am. eds.: Helter-skelter,
hurry-skurry,
347. MS: fishes,
348. 1865, 1875, 1893, 1904: kissed
her:
Am. eds.: kissed her;
349. MS: her,
Am. eds.: her;
350. MS: dishes
351. MS, Am. eds.: Panniers and
355. MS: peaches
360. MS: twigs,
361. 1904: them,—
362. Am. eds., 1904: figs.'
363. MS: said Lizzie
364. Am. eds.: of Jeanie,
365. Am. eds.: many";—
1904: many:'
366. 1875, 1893: [line indented two
spaces]
371. 1893: beginning,
373. 1893: and dew pearly,
379. MS: by:
382. Am. eds.: us."

383. Am. eds.: said Lizzie; "but one
385. MS: parleying
Am. eds.: So, without
389. Am. eds.: fee."
390. MS: pates;
408. MS: stood
409. MS: flood,
411. MS: obstreperously,
413. MS: sea
414. MS: golden [*flame*] <fire>
415. MS: fruit-crowned orange tree
417. MS: bee,
423. MS: drink:—
428. MS: Pulled and
429. MS: Kicked and
430. MS: word:
432. MS: in,
Am. eds.: in;
434. MS: face
1904: that syruped all
435. MS: chin
437. 1875, 1876a, 1893, 1904: people,
438. 1875, 1876a, 1893, 1904:
resistance,
441. Am. eds.: shoot.
445. 1866a: sound
452. 1866a: jingle,
453. 1862p: purse,
1862, 1865, Am. eds., 1875, 1893,
1904: purse,—
457. MS: with mock or
459. MS: after
464. MS: [*cried*:] <cried> "Laura,"
1875, 1893, 1904: cried, "Laura,"
466. MS: me;
470. MS: dew;
472. 1875, 1893, 1904: me;
474. MS: men."—
480. MS: your [*life*] <light> like
481. MS: Your sweet life
482. 1875, 1893, 1904: undoing,
484. Am. eds.: goblin-ridden?"
488. MS: her horny eyes
490. MS: In long-drawn Summer
drouth:
491. MS: fear and pain
1862p: with [*anguish*,] ⟨aguish⟩
fear [The correction is in pencil
in Christina's handwriting.]
497. MS: robe and
498. MS: haste

500. MS: Her [*hair*] <locks> streamed
503. MS: when [*he*] <she> stems
     [Christina's revision is in pencil]
506. MS: [*run / And scream for fright.*]
     <run.>
511. MS: Ah, fool,
     1904: Ah fool,
512. MS: care.
516. MS: lightning-stricken [*tree,*]
     <mast,>
519. MS, Am. eds.: foam-topped
     water-spout
522. MS: anguish past;
523. MS: life?—
526. MS: pulse's lagging stir,
528. MS: lips and
529. 1904: leaves.
530. MS: about [*the*] <their> eaves
532. MS: sheaves

534. MS: morning wind so <> pass
536. MS: of flags and lilies
540. (1890), (1891), 1893: grey
541. Am. eds., 1904: as May,
543. 1862: years,
553. MS, 1904: wicked quaint
554. Am. eds.: throat,
555. 1904: blood
556. MS: Men <> town:
     Am. eds.: town;)
     1875, 1893, 1904: town):
558. MS: good
561. 1904: together,—
562. MS: For
     Am. eds.: sister,
563. MS: In sunshine or foul weather;
     Am. eds.: weather,
567. MS: stands.

IN THE ROUND TOWER AT JHANSI, JUNE 8, 1857.

[Composed in September, 1857. Editions: *1862*, 1865, 1866a, 1875, 1876a, 1904. No MS known.]

Title. 1866a: June, 8,
     1904: JHANSI / 8 JUNE 1857
  3. Am. eds.: swarming, howling
  5. 1904: wife.
  6. 1904: come.'
  7. 1904: life,
 14. 1904: both.'—
 16. 1866a: not loath."

20. Am. eds.: "Good by."—"Good by."
     1875, 1904: "Good-bye."—
     "Good-bye."
Note. 1862, 1865, 1866a: [No note fol-
     lows the poem.]
     1876a: Note.—I
     1904: [The note is quoted in the
     annotations.]

DREAM-LAND.

[Composed in April, 1849. Editions: *1862*, 1865, 1866a, 1875, 1876a, 1904. The notebook MS is in the Bodleian Library. The poem was printed in *The Germ: Thoughts Towards Nature in Poetry, Literature, and Art*, I (January, 1850), 20.]

Title. 1862, 1865, 1875, 1904:
     DREAM LAND.
  3. 1850: a charmed sleep;
  5. MS: star
  6. 1850: far,
 11. 1850: lorn,
 12. MS, 1850: And water-springs.
 13. MS: sleep as <> veil
 15. 1850: nightingale,
 17. 1850: perfect rest,

19. 1875: west
22. 1904: plain,
25. Am. eds.: Rest, rest, forevermore
26. MS: shore:
     1850: shore,
27. MS: Rest, rest that shall endure
     1850: Rest, rest, that shall endure,
28. 1850: cease;—
29. 1850, 1862, 1865, Am. eds.: wake,
30. 1862, 1865, 1875: break

AT HOME.

[Composed June 29, 1858. Editions: *1862*, 1865, 1866a, 1875, 1876a, 1904. The first page of the notebook MS is in the British Library; the second page was separated from the notebook and is now in the Huntington Library. In the printed texts the last line of each stanza is indented two spaces instead of four.]

Title. MS: [*After the Pic-nic.*] [The title is deleted in pencil but no alternate title is added.]
1. MS: dead my
2. Am. eds., 1875: the much-frequented house: 1904: the much-frequented house.
3. MS: door and
4. Am. eds., 1904: green orange-boughs;
6. MS: peach,
7. MS: sang they jested and <> laughed
9. 1904: chat.
11. Am. eds., 1875, 1904: sands,
12. MS: sea."—
14. MS: the [illegible erasure] <eyrie-seat."—>

16. MS: Today but <> sweet."—
17. MS: they strong <> hope
19. MS: all
    Am. eds.: they, one
21. MS: noon,
22. MS: I only I had
23. MS: cried:
26. Am. eds.: the table-cloth;
27. MS, 1876a: I, all-forgotten, shivered,
    1866a: I, all forgotten, shivered,
28. MS: how loath:
    1866a: stay, and <> how loath:
    1876a: stay, and
29. MS: room
30. MS: away

A TRIAD.

[Composed December 18, 1856. Editions: *1862*, 1865, 1866a, 1896, 1904. The notebook MS is in the British Library.]

Title. MS: A Trio.
    1862, 1865, 1866a: A TRIAD. / SONNET.
3. MS, Am. eds., 1896, 1904: and finger-tips;
4. Am. eds.: who, soft <> snow,
7. MS: a harp-string snapped

Am. eds.: Who, like a harp-string snapped, rang
10. MS: love a placid wife;
11. MS: love:—thus two
    Am. eds.: famished, died
13. MS: bee:—

LOVE FROM THE NORTH.

[Composed December 19, 1856. Editions: *1862*, 1865, 1866a, 1875, 1876a, 1904. The notebook MS is in the British Library.]

Title. MS: In the days of the Sea Kings. Kings.
2. MS: in May:
4. MS: nay;
8. MS: My *yea* his yea, my *nay* his
8. MS: [After stanza 2 is the following stanza:]

The hour was come, the guests were come,
    Was donned my bridal rich array,
The priest stood waiting in the church
    To take our *yea* that cancels nay;
9. MS: We thronged along the shaded aisles

10. MS: All flushed
11. Am. eds.: thoughts,—
12. MS: It's <> nay.—
    1862: 'It's <> nay.'—
14. MS: answered *yea*, —
    1862: answered 'yea:'
16. MS: resounding *nay*.
    1862: resounding 'nay'.
19. MS: And <> answer *yea*, fair

20. MS: with *nay*?—
22. MS: Light-locked with
    1862, 1865, Am. eds.: dangerous
    gray:
23. MS: Put *yea* by
24. MS: nay.—
27. MS: morass and hair-breadth pass,
    Am. eds.: and hair-breadth pass,
30. MS: stay,

WINTER RAIN.

[Composed January 31, 1859. Editions: *1862*, 1865, 1866a, 1875, 1876a, 1904. The notebook MS is in the British Library.]

1. MS: drinks
2. 1875, 1904: hollow;
3. MS: and sinks
5. 1866a: weeks,
   1904: weeks—
7. MS: Wool-coat glue-coat spots or
   streaks
8. MS: hedges:
16. MS: showers,

18. MS: rocking tree tops,
20. MS: the lea crops.
22. MS: the sunbright leas
27. Am. eds.: waving meadow-grass
28. MS: with broad eyed daisies:
29. MS: sand
30. 1904: daughter;
31. MS: land

COUSIN KATE.

[Composed November 18, 1859. Editions: *1862*, 1865, 1866a, 1896, 1904. The notebook MS is owned by Mrs. Geoffrey Dennis.]

Title. MS: [*Up and Down.*] <Cousin
    Kate> [Dante Gabriel Rossetti de-
    leted the original title and added
    the alternate reading in pencil.]
1. 1896, 1904: a cottage-maiden
3. 1896, 1904: my cottage-mates,
5. MS, 1896, 1904: out
9. 1896, 1904: his palace-home—
11. MS: life
13. MS, 1896, 1904: a golden knot,
14. MS, 1896, 1904: glove:
15. MS, 1896, 1904: moan an <>
    thing
17. MS, 1896, 1904: my Cousin Kate,
18. MS: than I;

19. MS: your Father's gate,
20. MS, 1896, 1904: you and
22. MS: Your sport among
    1896, 1904: Your sport among <>
    rye:
33. MS, 1896, 1904: O Cousin Kate,
37. MS, 1896, 1904: He had not won
38. 1896, 1904: land:
41. MS, 1896, 1904: got
43. MS: and wedding ring
45. MS: My fair haired son,
46. MS: Cling closer closer
47. MS, 1896, 1904: Your sire would
    give broad lands

NOBLE SISTERS.

[Composed probably after November 18, 1859, and before March 27, 1860. Editions: *1862*, 1865, 1866a, 1875, 1876a, 1904. The notebook MS is owned by Mrs.

Geoffrey Dennis. In the MS the last page, which contains the last stanza of the poem and the date of composition, is missing. The MS version contains no quotation marks.]

5. MS: With golden bells about his neck:
6. MS: beneath his wing?
10. MS: day;
12. MS: I frayed him away.—
16. MS: Or couched by
17. MS: a golden collar on his
21. Am. eds.: hound, high-born sister,
22. MS: moon;
26. 1904: gate?
27. Am. eds.: whistling, whistling
28. MS: late?
29. MS: cap
30. MS: glove:
    1904: glove.
31. MS: out
34. MS: red;
35. MS, (1890), (1891), 1904: you
37. Am. eds.: "O patience,
    1904: sister! Did

40. MS: to chastise the wrong?
41. MS: the barren sea
42. MS: wife;
43. MS: locked
46. MS: Hard by your chamber door;
    1862, 1865, 1866a: Hard by your chamber door:
47. MS: said your husband loves you much,
    1865: [end comma imperfectly printed]
    1866a, 1875, 1876a: much.
    1904: much
48. MS: yet you love him
50. 1876a: wicked lie;
    1904: wicked lie!
60. 1862, 1865, 1866a: you."—

SPRING.

[Composed August 17, 1859. Editions: *1862*, 1865, 1866a, 1875, 1876a, 1904. The notebook MS is owned by Mrs. Geoffrey Dennis.]

1. MS: the Winter
2. MS: Seeds and roots and <> fruits
6. MS: Leaf or blade or
12. MS: the waxing sun:
13. MS: plain,
14. MS: trees,
15. MS: Seeds and roots and <> fruits
16. MS: shoots,
    Am. eds.: sap, put
    1904: Swoln with

17. MS: lane,
19. MS: like Spring
20. MS: everything:
    1866a: everything,—
23. Am. eds.: track,—
24. MS: wing
25. MS, 1862: lack—,
31. MS: die:
35. MS: [*Hedged*] <Fledged> on
38. MS: born and

THE LAMBS OF GRASMERE, 1860.

[Composed July 24, 1860. Editions: *1862*, 1865, 1866a, 1875, 1876a, 1904. The notebook MS is owned by Mrs. Geoffrey Dennis.]

Title. MS: of Westmoreland. 1860.
3. MS: them
10. MS: went
11. 1875, 1904: mouths,
15. MS: hand

17. MS: Then as <> weeks
20. MS: lea;
21. MS, 1875, 1904: tender trustful
29. MS: years
31. MS: flooded Spring

A BIRTHDAY.

[Composed November 18, 1857. Editions: *1862*, 1865, 1866a, 1875, 1876a, 1904. The notebook MS is in the British Library. The poem was published in *Macmillan's Magazine*, III (April, 1861), 498.]

2. MS: shoot,
 1904: shoot:
3. 1861, Am. eds., 1875, 1904: an apple-tree
 1862, 1865: an appletree
4. MS: fruit,
 Am. eds.: with thick-set fruit;
6. MS: sea,
7. 1861: these,
8. 1861: love has come

9. MS, 1861: down,
10. MS, 1861: dyes,
11. MS: [*Carves*] <Carve> it <>
 pomegranates
 1862, 1865, 1866a: doves, and
12. MS, 1861: eyes,
13. MS: grapes
14. MS: silver fleurs de lys,
 1861: fleurs-de-lys,
 1862, 1865, 1866a: leaves, and

REMEMBER.

[Composed July 25, 1849. Editions: *1862*, 1865, 1866a, 1875, 1876a, 1904. The notebook MS is in the Bodleian Library.]

Title. 1862, 1865, Am. eds., 1875:
 REMEMBER. / SONNET.
4. MS: go, yet
5. Am. eds.: more, day by day,
6. MS: you can tell me our <>

planned,
 1904: you plann'd:
10. MS: grieve;
12. MS: [line not indented]
14. MS: [line not indented]

AFTER DEATH.

[Composed April 28, 1849. Editions: *1862*, 1865, 1866a, 1875, 1876a, 1904. The notebook MS is in the Bodleian Library. In the MS no lines are indented.]

Title. 1862, 1865, Am. eds., 1875:
 AFTER DEATH. / SONNET.
2. MS: rushes; rosemary
4. MS: lattice ivy shadows crept.
6. 1904: say,

7. MS: "Poor child, poor child," and
8. MS: silence and
11. MS: head.
12. MS: living: but
13. MS: me: and

AN END.

[Composed March 5, 1849. Editions: *1862*, 1865, 1866a, 1875, 1876a, 1904. The notebook MS is in the Bodleian Library. The poem was printed in *The Germ: Thoughts Towards Nature in Poetry, Literature, and Art*, I (January, 1850), 48. It was also published in William Allingham [Giraldis] (ed.), *Nightingale Valley, A Collection of Choice Lyrics and Short Poems*, (London: Bell and Daldy, 1859). In *The Germ*, lines 3, 7, 10-12, 14, 16, and 20 are indented two spaces.]

1. MS: Love strong
 1850: as death, is
 1875: dead,

8. 1850, 1875, 1904: the spring,
9. MS, 1850: harvesting.

10. 1850, 1862, 1865, Am. eds., 1875,
    1904: warm summer day
11. MS: us, he
    1850: us;—he
12. 1850, 1875, 1904: For autumn
    twilight <> and grey.
    1862, 1865: and grey.
    Am. eds.: twilight, cold

13. MS, 1850: grave and
14. 1866a: [no stanza break after line
    14]
15. 1850: chords, and sad, and low,
16. 1850: so.
17. MS, 1850: grass,
18. MS, 1850: Shadow-veiled, as

MY DREAM.

[Composed March 9, 1855. Editions: *1862*, 1865, 1866a, 1875, 1876a, 1904. The notebook MS is in the Bodleian Library.]

Title. MS: My dream.
 4. 1904: youth.
 5. 1862, 1865, 1866a, 1904: sight;
 7. MS: crocodiles a <> crew
 8. MS: Fresh hatched perhaps <>
    dew.—
 9. 1862, 1865: friend
10. MS: untrue,
    Am. eds., 1875, 1904: friend, would
11. MS: untold:—
12. MS, 1862: why hear
14. MS: and costly stones
    Am. eds.: stones, that
18. MS: All [illegible deletion]
    <gleamed> compact
19. Am. eds.: mail,
21. MS: brethren shook before <> tail
22. MS: flail;
23. MS: kin.—
24. MS: woes?—
26. MS: them, [*scrunched*]
    <crunched> and <> in,
28. MS, 1904: jaw.

29. MS: fat [illegible erasure]
    <distilled upon his chin,>
31. MS: maw,
32. MS: every [illegible deletion]
    <minor> crocodile
    1904: Till, every
34. MS: claw.—
    1904: [stanza break after line 34]
35. MS: saw—
    Am. eds.: O marvel
    1904: saw!
36. MS: size
38. MS: a winged vessel
39. MS: flame;
42. MS: [illegible erasure] <It
    levelled> strong
44. MS: force,
45. MS, 1904: beat.
46. MS: [illegible erasure] <Lo as>
    the <> sands
47. 1904: feet,
49. MS: ask; I
50. MS: echo What?—

SONG. ["OH ROSES FOR THE FLUSH OF YOUTH"]

[Composed February 6, 1849. Editions: *1862*, 1865, 1866a, 1875, 1876a, 1904. The notebook MS is in the Bodleian Library. The poem was printed in *The Germ: Thoughts Towards Nature in Poetry, Literature, and Art,* II (February, 1850), 64. In the printed texts the last line of each stanza is indented two spaces instead of four.]

Title. MS: A Song in a Song.
 1. MS: [The following stanzas pre-
    cede the two published stanzas:]

    They told me that she would not live,
      But how could I believe their word?

Her cheeks were redder than a rose,
  And smoother than a curd.

Her eyes were full of a deep light,
  Steady, unmoved by hope and fear:
And though indeed her voice was low,
  It was so sweet and clear.

But now that she is gone before,
  I trust I too shall follow fast:
And so I sit and sing her song,
  And muse upon the past.
1. 1850: Oh! roses
   Am. eds.: O roses

2. MS: prime,
3. 1850: an ivy-branch for me,
5. 1850: Oh! violets
   Am. eds.: O violets
6. MS: prime,
8. 1850: the olden time.

THE HOUR AND THE GHOST.

[Composed September 11, 1856. Editions: *1862*, 1865, 1866a, 1875, 1876a, 1904. The notebook MS is in the British Library. In the 1904 text no period follows the speakers' names.]

1. MS: O love love hold
   Am. eds.: fast,—
2. MS: thee,
3. MS: And I <> blast
4. 1866a: sea;
6. MS: pines,
9. MS: near,
12. MS: our home come home;
15. MS: When I wooed leaned and said
    1862, Am. eds.: When I wooed, and
16. MS: 'Come our <> made'—
    1862, 1865: 'Come, <> made'—
    Am. eds.: made,"—
18. 1904: longer!
19. MS: past;
20. 1904: stronger;
22. MS: heart
23. MS: withhold;
26. MS: old.
    Am. eds.: O bitter
27. MS: eyes;
28. MS: ourselves earth <> skies
32. MS: Come for <> stay;

33. MS: Come for
34. MS: Ah sure <> house
    1904: Ah sure
35. MS: death;
    1904: death,
36. MS: breath:—
    1904: breath!
37. MS: Come crown
38. MS: word
39. MS: still
42. 1904: friend, forsake
43. MS: forgot;
44. MS: me
45. MS: thy [illegible erasure] <faith> true <> bright,
48. MS: darling, peace;
    Am. eds.: Nay, peace,
52. MS: in:
54. MS: cold,
    (1891), 1904: cold:
56. MS: old.
59. 1875: bear:
    1904: bear;
60. 1875, 1904: together,
61. 1875, 1904: weather,

A SUMMER WISH.

[Composed June 21, 1851. Editions: *1862*, 1865, 1866a, 1875, 1876a, 1904. The notebook MS is in the Bodleian Library. In the MS the second, fifth, sixth, and seventh lines of each stanza are indented two spaces.]

1. MS: thro'
2. MS: Sweet Rose, dew sprent;
3. MS: down thy evening
   1904: dew,
6. MS: thou wert [illegible erasure] <meant>

8. MS: sky
9. MS: soaring [*bird*;] <Bird;>
13. 1904: heard,
15. Am. eds.: O that
16. 1904: flower!
17. MS: tree,

18. MS: bee,
20. MS: bloom my hour,
    1904: hour,
22. MS: my [illegible erasure] <work>
    were
    Am. eds.: O that

24. MS: the Sun.
25. MS: my [illegible erasure] <time>
    is [illegible erasure] <run>

AN APPLE-GATHERING.

[Composed November 23, 1857. Editions: *1862,* 1865, 1866a, 1875, 1876a, 1904. The notebook MS is in the British Library. The poem was published in *Macmillan's Magazine,* IV (August, 1861), 329. In the *Macmillan's* text, only the last line of each stanza is indented.]

Title. 1862, 1865, Am. eds., 1875, 1904: AN APPLE GATHERING.

1. 1861, Am. eds.: mine apple-tree,
   1875, 1904: mine apple-tree
2. 1861: hair;
3. 1861: Then, in <> season, when <> see,
5. 1861: grass,
6. MS: I [illegible deletion] <had> come
   1861: come, I <> track;
9. 1861: by;
10. MS: Their [*piled-up*] <heaped-up> basket
    1861, Am. eds.: basket teased me

11. MS: sky
    1861: sky;
13. 1861: full;
17. MS: Ah Willie Willie, [*is*] <was> my
    1861: Ah! Willie,
    Am. eds.: Ah, Willie,
21. 1861: talk,
22. 1875, 1904: lane;
24. MS: again!—
26. MS: chill
    1861: groups: the
27. 1861: hastened; but <> loitered; while
    1904: loitered; while
28. 1861: fast, I

SONG. ["TWO DOVES UPON THE SELFSAME BRANCH"]

[Date of composition unknown. Editions: *1862,* 1865, 1866a, 1875, 1876a, 1904. No MS known.]

4. Am. eds.: O happy
   1904: them!

7. 1904: in hand,

MAUDE CLARE.

[Composed probably after December 8, 1857, and before April 14, 1858. Editions: *1862,* 1865, 1866a, 1875, 1876a, 1904. The notebook MS is in the British Library. The poem was printed in *Once A Week,* I (November 5, 1859), 381–82. The last page of the MS is missing from the notebook, and the last two stanzas of the published version are not in the MS as it now stands. In the MS single quotation marks are used and each line of a quotation begins with a quotation mark. In the *Once A Week* text, the second line in each stanza is indented two spaces and the fourth line is indented four spaces.]

1. MS: [The following stanzas begin the poem:]

The fields were white with lily buds,
  White gleamed the lilied beck,
Each mated pigeon plumed the pomp
  Of his metallic neck;

A lark sat brooding in the corn,
  Her mate sang in the height,
From heaven he sent clear notes to her
  Of love and full delight.—

'Is it a wedding you're going to,
  'Maude Clare, that you're so fine?'—
'Oh its the wedding I'm going to
  'Of a prosperous friend of mine.

'I'll break no bread, I'll eat no salt,
  'I'll pledge no toast in wine,
'For its the wedding I'm going to
  'Of a false false love of mine.'—

Her gown was in a glow with gold,
  Her cheeks were pale like pearls,
Her breast was in a glow with gold
  With clustering golden curls;

There were sparkling jewels in her hair
  And her necklace sparkled bright,
But never a sparkle in her eyes
  That had wept the yesternight.

She followed his new love to the Church
  His new love frank and fair,
Yet who lacked the witching winning grace
  Of his old love pale Maude Clare:

1. 1859: [The following stanza begins the poem:]

The fields were white with lily-buds,
  White gleamed the lilied beck;
Each mated pigeon plumed the pomp
  Of his metallic neck.

1. MS: She followed his bride into the Church
   1859: She follow'd his bride into the church,
2. MS: mien,
3. MS: And his bride <> maid
4. MS: And Maude
4. MS: [After line 4 are the following stanzas:]

Lord Thomas shook when he met her face,
  He flushed when he met her eye,
He stepped towards her a single step
  And smothered a single sigh;

He cared not to meet her eyes again
  And he dared not touch her hand,
For Maude Clare for all she was so fair
  Had never an inch of land.

The priest asked 'Wilt thou?' of the man
  And 'Yea' the bridegroom said;
The priest asked 'Wilt thou?' of the maid
  And she blushing bowed her head:

Never a word said pale Maude Clare
  But she stood up rigid then,
She sang no praise, she prayed no prayer,
  And she uttered no amen.

When bride and bridegroom left the Church
  Arm in arm they went;
Lady Maude glittered in their train
  Like a star of the firmament:

No eyes were fixed upon the bride
  Or on the bridegroom more,
All eyes were fixed on grand Maude Clare
  While she looked straight before.

The bridegroom whispered to the bride:
  'You are pale, sweet Nell, you sigh.'—
She answered with a woful look:
  'You are paler far than I.'—

The bridegroom whispered to his bride:
  'Do you tremble in my hold?'—
She answered in a woful voice:
  'You are trembling with the cold. '—

Along the blossomed streets they
  [illegible deletion]
  <trooped,>
The bells rang marriage chimes,
While some were thinking of today
  But some of other times:

Along the blossomed streets they trooped
  And up the blossomed stair,
The bride and bridegroom paced before
  And after them Maude Clare.

The minstrels made loud marriage din,
  Each guest sat in his place
To eat and drink and wish good luck
  To do the wedding grace:

To eat and drink and wish good luck,
  To sing and laugh and jest;
One only neither ate nor drank
  Nor clapped her hands nor blessed.

4. 1859: [After line 4 are the follow-
ing stanzas:]

The minstrels made loud marriage din;
　　Each guest sat in his place,
To eat and drink, and wish good luck,
　　To do the wedding grace;

To eat and drink, and wish good luck,
　　To sing, and laugh, and jest:
One only neither ate nor drank,
　　Nor clapp'd her hands, nor bless'd.

5. MS: 'Son Thomas' his <> said
6. MS: smiles almost
   1859: tears,
9. 1859: father, thirty <> ago,
11. MS: you
12. MS: as Nell.'—
12. MS: [After line 12 are the follow-
ing stanzas:]

A whispered 'Hark' ran thro' the room
And then a whispered 'Hush':
He bowed to kiss his mother's hand
Bowed low but did not flush.

Then one stood up to pledge the bride
With hint and waggish smile,
Yet tho' his words were for the bride
He glanced at Maude the while:

'Health to the bride, and length of days
'And hopes fulfilled and wealth':—
Lord Thomas turned to young Maude
　　Clare
Before he drank the health;

13. MS: strife
14. MS: pride,
16. 1859: he kiss'd the
16. MS: [After line 16 are the follow-
ing stanzas:]

The songs were sung, the dreamlike
　　songs,
The wedding feast was done,
From the fair presence in the hall
The guests went one by one;

They left warm blessings, kind good
　　will,
They left of gifts a store,
A heap of gear of gems and gold
Heaped on the rushy floor.

The guests went out guest after guest
Until the last was gone,
Until Lord Thomas and young Nell
And Maude were left alone.

She faced the bridegroom and the
　　bride,—
But oh her heart must ache—
With steady eyes and steady voice
And hand that would not shake.

16. 1859: [After line 16 is the follow-
ing stanza:]

No eyes were fix'd upon the bride,
　　Or on the bridegroom more,
All eyes were fix'd on grand Maude Clare,
　　While she look'd straight before.

17. MS: gift my Lord
18. MS: said,
    1859: said—
19. 1859: To
20. MS: the marriage bed.
22. MS: neck
23. MS: waded ancle deep
    1859, 1862: waded ancle-deep
24. 1904: beck.
26. MS: bough
    1859: We pluck'd from
27. MS: leaves,
    1859, Am. eds.: the lily-leaves,—
28. MS: now.'—
28. MS: [After line 28 is the following
stanza:]

No memory shook her ringing voice
Or dimmed her taunting eye,
Tho' boy and girl they used to play
Among the corn breast high.

30. 1859: He falter'd in
31. MS: 'Lady,' he said, 'Maude <>
said,
    1859: "Lady," he said,—"Maude
Clare," he said,
32. MS: 'Maude Clare,' and
    1859: "Maude Clare,"—and
33. MS: She turned to Nell: 'My Lady
Nell
    Am. eds., 1904: She turned to
34. MS, 1859: you,
35. MS: fruit the <> gone
36. MS: Or were <> flowers the
38. MS: love;
39. 1859: Take it, or leave it, as
40. MS: thereof.
40. MS: [After line 40 are the follow-
ing stanzas:]

'For you have purchased him with gold,'—
　　Her words cut sharp and slow:
'For its your gold he took you for,'—
　　She said and turned to go.

But 'Fie for shame, [My] <my> Lady
　　Maude,'
Nell cried with kindling cheek:
'It's shame on me who hear the words,
'It's shame on you who speak.

'I never guessed you loved my Lord,
'I never heard your wrong;
'You should have spoken before the
    priest
'Had made our tie so strong;
'You should have stood up in the
    Church
'To claim your rights before;
'You should have parted us in the
    Church
'Or kept silence evermore.

41. MS: [The remainder of the MS is
    missing from the notebook.]
42. 1859: spurn I'll wear,
    1904: spurn I'll
45. 1904: 'Yea though
46. 1904: fair,
47. 1859, 1904: best—
48. 1859: all, Maude Clare!"

ECHO.

[Composed December 18, 1854. Editions: *1862,* 1866a, 1875, 1876a, 1904.
The notebook MS is in the Bodleian Library.]

1. MS: night,
3. MS: cheeks, and
6. MS: [After line 6 are the following
    stanzas:]

Come with the voice whose musical low
    tone
    My heart still hears tho' I must hear
        no more:
Come to me in my weakness left alone:
    Come back, not as before
        In smiles but pale,
But soft with love that loves without
    avail.
Dearer than daylight on an unknown
    sea,
    Or oasis in a far desert place,
Dearer than hope and life, come back to
    me,
    Full of a tender grace,
        Not changed except
For trace of weary tears thou too hast
    wept.
Come back that I may gaze my soul
    away
    And from thy presence pass into my
        rest;

My soul as a tired bird at close of day
    Pants toward the accustomed nest;
        Come back, come back,
Set my life free that faints upon the
    rack.

7. Am. eds., 1875, 1904: O dream
8. MS: in Paradise
9. MS: souls brim full of <> meet,
    Am. eds.: souls brimful of
14. MS: death;
16. MS: for breath;
18. 1862, 1865, Am. eds.: ago!
18. MS: [After line 18 is the following
    stanza:]

So may I dream to death, the languid
    lull
    Of death, unnoticed, trenching on
        my sleep,
Sealing the sentence change cannot
    annul;
        No vigils more to keep,
            No death to die,
Only to watch for thee as days go by.

WINTER: MY SECRET

[Composed November 23, 1857. Editions: *1862,* 1865, 1866a, 1875, 1876a, 1904.
The notebook MS is in the British Library. In Christina Rossetti's English and
American editions the first line of every stanza except the first is indented two
spaces.]

Title. MS: Nonsense.
    1862, 1865, 1866a: MY SECRET.
1. MS: secret? no indeed not

2. MS: day—who knows?—
3. MS: froze and blows and snows:
4. MS: fie.

6. MS: Only my <> mine and
6. MS: [no stanza break after line 6]
7. MS: Or after all perhaps <> none;
8. MS: all
10. MS: biting day,
11. MS: shawl
12. MS: veil a cloak and
13. MS: taps
14. MS: hall,
15. MS: me
16. MS: buffeting astounding me
18. MS: warmth: whoever shows

20. MS: blows?—
21. Am. eds.: for good-will,
26. MS: even May whose
27. MS: may [illegible deletion]
    <wither> [*through*] <thro' the>
    sunless
28. MS: day
29. MS: and less
30. MS: excess
31. MS: cloud
33. MS: say

ANOTHER SPRING.

[Composed September 15, 1857. Editions: *1862*, 1865, 1866a, 1875, 1876a, 1904. The notebook MS is in the British Library. In the printed texts the last line of each stanza is indented only two spaces instead of four.]

Title. MS: [*When Harvest failed.*]
    <Another Spring > [The original
    title is deleted in pencil. The later
    title is in pencil in William Michael
    Rossetti's handwriting.]
    1. MS: If I [*could*] <might> see
    another spring
    1904: another Spring,
5. MS: snowdrops, sweeter yet
    1875: chill-veined snow-drops,
    choicer
8. MS, 1862, 1865, Am. eds.: once
    not

9. MS: another spring
    1904: another Spring,
11. MS: sing
17. MS: another spring—
18. Am. eds.: O stinging
19. MS: in 'if'—
20. MS: another spring
22. MS: anything;
    Am. eds.: [line indented two
    spaces]
23. MS: last

A PEAL OF BELLS.

[Composed July 7, 1857. Editions: *1862*, 1865, 1866a, 1875, 1876a, 1904. The notebook MS is in the Bodleian Library.]

2. MS: well,
5. MS: oil
6. MS: trees
    Am. eds., 1875, 1904: laden
    orange-trees,
9. MS: fruit
10. MS: fruit ablush and ripe,
11. MS: pipe,
12. MS: hours,
    Am. eds.: hours;
13. MS: lute,
    Am. eds.: lute;

14. MS: thinking shut <> pain
    1875, 1904: [line not indented]
15. 1875, 1904: [line not indented]
18. MS: bed
19. MS: asleep.
20. MS: head
21. MS: feet,
    Am. eds.: feet,—
22. MS: him.—
23. MS: a [*sham,*] <show,> my [The
    deletion and revision are in pencil
    in Christina's handwriting.]

24. MS: sweet:
25. MS: him,
    1904: him.
26. MS: done,
    1875, 1904: done:
28. MS: [line indented two spaces]

29. MS: [line indented two spaces] My
    [*blood's achill,*] <blood is chill,> his
    <> cold, [The revision is in pencil
    in Christina's handwriting.]
30. MS: full and

FATA MORGANA.

[Composed April 18, 1857. Editions: *1862*, 1865, 1866a, 1875, 1876a, 1904. The notebook MS is in the British Library. In the printed texts the last line of each stanza is indented two spaces instead of four.]

2. MS: laughing leaping
3. MS: evermore
5. MS, Am. eds.: on bound;

9. MS: laugh it
10. MS: before I

"NO, THANK YOU, JOHN."

[Composed March 27, 1860. Editions: *1862*, 1865, 1866a, 1875, 1876a, 1904. The notebook MS is owned by Mrs. Geoffrey Dennis. The first page of the MS (lines 1-13) is missing from the notebook.]

Title. 1862: "NO THANK
1. 1904: John;
2. 1866a: me, day
    1875: you tease me
    1876a: you tease me, day
4. 1862, 1865: "pray?"

19. 1875: answer "No," to
20. 1875: answer "Yes," to
22. MS: youth;
23. 1862, 1904: before;
30. 1904: on.
32. MS, 1862: No thank

MAY.

[Composed November 20, 1855. Editions: *1862*, 1865, 1866a, 1875, 1876a, 1904. The notebook MS is in the Bodleian Library.]

2. 1904: pass—
4. MS: young—ah pleasant May.
    1862, 1865, Am. eds., 1875: ah,
    pleasant
    1904: young, ah
6. MS: corn,
7. MS: yet

8. 1875, 1904: bird forgone its
9. 1862, 1865, Am. eds.: [line indented two spaces]
10. MS: pass.—
12. MS: away
13. MS: old and cold and

A PAUSE OF THOUGHT.

[Composed February 14, 1848. Editions: *1862*, 1865, 1866a, 1875, 1876a, 1904. There are two notebook MSS of the poem, both in the Bodleian Library. The earlier notebook MS is referred to here as MS1 and the later as MS2. The poem was printed in *The Germ: Thoughts Towards Nature in Poetry, Literature, and Art,* II (February, 1850), 57. In MS1, only the last line of each stanza is indented.]

Title. MS1: Lines / In memory of
    Schiller's "Der Pilgrim."
    MS2: Three Stages./ 1.
1. 1904: THREE STAGES / 1.—A
    PAUSE OF THOUGHT
2. MS1, MS2: truth;
    1850: sick, in truth;
    Am. eds.: truth
3. MS1: But [*h*] <years> must
6. 1850: And, tho' the
7. MS1, MS2: for; ever, day by day,
    1850: ever, day by day,
9. MS1, MS2: more:
    1850: said,—"This
    1904: said: 'This

10. 1850: wearies, and
11. MS1: now, and <> peace:—
    MS2: peace:—
    1850: now, and <> peace:"—
    1904: peace':
13. 1850: said,—"It
    1904: said: 'It
15. MSI: The [*joy*] <peace> of
    1850, 1904: live?"—
17. 1850: Alas! thou <> one,—alike
    1904: Alas thou
18. MS1, MS2: pain;
    1850: pain,

TWILIGHT CALM.

[Composed February 7, 1850. Editions: *1862,* 1865, 1866a, 1875, 1876a, 1904. The notebook MS is in the Bodleian Library. The poem was printed in Mary Howitt (ed.), *The Dusseldorf Artist's Album,* (Dusseldorf, Germany: Arnz and Comp, 1854), 7–8. In the MS no lines are indented.]

Title: MS: Twilight calm.
    1854: A Summer Evening.
1. 1862, 1865, 1875: Oh, pleasant
    Am. eds.: O pleasant
3. 1875, 1876a, 1904: greyer, hiding
4. MS, 1854: birds their <> done
8. 1854: The merry squirrel
9. 1854: But, lazily, pauses and <>
    now,
11. MS, 1854: close;
19. 1854: fill, he
22. 1854: home;
23. 1875: [line indented two spaces]
24. MS: sea
25. MS: loud now
28. MS, 1854: opes his broad eyes
29. MS: prey: the <> the shelless
    snail
    1854: wakes, and the shelless snail
30. MS, 1854, 1862: forth clammy
31. 1854: nightingale
32. Am. eds., 1875, 1904: the
    self-same tale
33. MS: when the ancient <> young;
    1854: when the ancient

35. MS, 1854: first woody vale.
36. 1854: pain,
    1866a: pain,—
    1904: pain.
37. 1854: strain,
38. 1854: know,
39. MS: not rather be joy
40. MS, 1854: vein?—
43. MS: fawn;
45. MS, 1854: sleep forgetting
46. MS, 1854, 1862: lies
47. MS: eyes:
48. MS, 1854: cluck;
51. MS: Singly each little star
    1854: Slowly each
52. MS, 1854: out, until they
53. MS, 1854, 1904: brightly. How the
54. MS, 1854: While on the earth the
    <> lights his lamp
    1862, 1865: the glowworm lights
    1875, 1904: lamp.
55. MS, 1854: Faint twinkling from
    afar.—
56. MS, 1854: done,

58. MS: the east;
    1854: Day-giving, had <> the east:
    Am. eds.: the east:
    1904: the East—
59. MS: come: and
    1854: night is here; and <> ceased;
60. MS: [After line 60 is the following stanza:]

Yet deeper calm there is,
Yea better calm than this;
When for the last time weary eyelids drop
O'er weary eyes, when the blood cools, and stop
The aching heart-pulses.

WIFE TO HUSBAND.

[Composed June 8, 1861. Editions: *1862*, 1865, 1866a, 1875, 1876a, 1904. The notebook MS is in the British Library.]

Title. MS: to [*husband.*[<Husband.>
 1. 1862p: the [*fault,*] <faults> in [The correction is in pencil in Christina's handwriting.]
 3. 1865: Good-by.
    Am. eds.: Good by.
    1875, 1904: Good-bye.
 8. MS: wine and eat;
 9. MS: Good bye:
    1865: Good-by.
    Am. eds.: Good by.
    1875, 1904: Good-bye.
10. MS: run
11. MS: feet;
13. MS: upon;
15. 1865: Good-by.
    Am. eds.: Good by.
    1875, 1904: Good-bye.
16. MS: Whilst you <> must begone,
    1862: Whilst you
21. 1865: Good-by:—
    Am. eds.: Good by:—
    1875, 1904: Good-bye:—
26. MS: kiss;
27. MS: Good bye:
    1865: Good-by.
    Am. eds.: Good by.
    1875, 1904: Good-bye.

THREE SEASONS.

[Composed November 9, 1853. Editions: *1862*, 1865, 1866a, 1875, 1876a, 1904. The notebook MS (MS1) is in the Bodleian Library and a fair copy (MS2) is in the University of Texas Library.]

Title. MS1: Three seasons.
    MS2: Three Seasons
 1. MS1: hope,"—she
    MS2: said
 2. MS1: the [illegible erasure] <bloom was old:>
    MS2: old
    1904: old;
 4. MS2: her mouths richer
 5. MS1: love,"—how
    MS2: low
 6. MS1: words; [illegible erasure] <and> all
    MS2: words; & all
 7. MS1: smile,
 9. MS1: memory;"—
10. MS1: alone,
    MS2: alone
11. MS2: up & moan
13. MS1: love:—
14. MS2: morn, & love <> day

MIRAGE.

[Composed June 12, 1860. Editions: *1862*, 1865, 1866a, 1875, 1876a, 1904. The notebook MS is owned by Mrs. Geoffrey Dennis. In the published texts the last line of each stanza is indented two spaces instead of four.]

  2. MS: dream, and
     1904: wake,
  3. MS: comfortless and worn and old
  6. MS: lake:

  9. MS: Lie still, lie still my <> heart,
 10. MS: heart lie
 11. MS: Life and <> world and <>
     self are

SHUT OUT.

[Composed January 21, 1856. Editions: *1862*, 1865, 1866a, 1875, 1876a, 1904. The notebook MS is in the Bodleian Library.]

Title. MS: What happened to me.
  4. MS: flowers, bedewed <> green.
     1904: green.
  5. MS: the song birds crost;
  6. 1904: bees:
  9. MS: gate
 11. MS: said: Let
     1875, 1904: I, peering through,
     said; "Let
 12. MS: state.
 13. MS: not.—Or <> me then
 16. MS: again.
 17. MS: silent: but

 18. MS: and bricks to
 20. MS, 1904: look.
 21. 1904: alone,
 24. MS: my delightsome land
 25. MS: near
 26. MS: made his nest:
     1904: nest;
 28. MS: [After line 28 is the following
     stanza, deleted in pencil:]

     [*Oh thought of solace gone before,*
        Faint thought of love no love could save,
        By pathway of the narrow grave
     At least shall I reach home once more.]

SOUND SLEEP.

[Composed August 13, 1849. Editions: *1862*, 1865, 1866a, 1875, 1876a, 1904. The notebook MS is in the Bodleian Library.]

  1. MS: weeping,
  3. MS: are [*creeping;*] <peeping;>
     [The revision is in pencil in Christ-
     ina's handwriting.]
  3. MS: [After line 3 are the following
     lines, deleted in pencil:]

     [*There the timid deer are peeping,*
        And the grasshoppers are leaping;]

  4. MS: heaping heaping
  5. MS: [After line 5 is the following
     line, deleted and revised in pencil,
     in Christina's handwriting:]

     [*And hard by a stream is* [*sweeping*]
        <*creeping*>.]

  6. Am. eds.: the cornfields ripe
     1875, 1904: the corn-fields ripe
  6. MS: [After line 6 is a stanza break
     and then the following lines, de-
     leted in pencil:]

     [*Pleasant stream that runs and gushes,*
        Full of flags and reeds and rushes;]

  7. MS: lilies; and [*there*] <deep>
     blushes [The revision is in pencil in
     Christina's handwriting.]
  8. MS: [*The deep*] [<*Of the deep*>] <Of
     deep> rose; and [The revisions
     are in pencil in Christina's hand-
     writing.]
  9. MS: Sing, until the sunlight

10. MS: The broad west; and the wind
11. MS: leaves, till evening
12. MS: is [*winging*] <singing> [The revision is in pencil in Christina's handwriting.]
13. MS: springing:
14. MS: is swinging
14. [After line 14 is the following line, deleted in pencil:]
    [*And the nightingale is singing:*]
15. Am. eds.: There forever winds

16. MS: Far off chimes of Church bells ringing.
18. MS: with heaven.
18. MS: [After line 18 are the following lines, deleted in pencil:]
    [*The long strife at length is striven; The long errors are forgiven,*]
20. MS: her grave bands shall
    1862, 1865, Am. eds.: riven
21. MS: portion, given

SONG. ["SHE SAT AND SANG ALWAY"]

[Composed November 26, 1848. Editions: *1862*, 1865, 1866a, 1875, 1876a, 1904. The notebook MS (MS1) is in the Bodleian Library; the version in Christina's notebook MS of *Maude: Prose and Verse* (MS2) is in the Huntington Library; and a fair copy (MS3) is in the University of Texas Library. The poem was printed in *Maude: Prose & Verse, by Christina Rossetti; 1850* (Chicago: Herbert S. Stone and Company, 1897), 40. In MS1 the first line of each stanza is indented one space and the fourth line of each stanza is indented two spaces. In MS2 the first line of each stanza is indented four spaces and the last line of each stanza is indented six spaces. In MS3 lines 4, 8, 10, and 11 are indented two spaces and line 12 is indented four spaces. In the 1897 text the first and last lines of each stanza are indented four spaces.]

Title. MS2: [no title]
1. MS3: sat & sang
2. MS3: stream
3. MS3: leap & play
4. MS1: glad sun beam.
   MS2: glad sun-beam.
   MS3: sunbeam
5. MS3: sat & wept

6. MS3: the moons most <> beam
7. MS1, MS2: the may
8. MS3: stream
9. MS3, 1862: memory:
10. MS1, MS2: fair;—
    MS3: fair
    1875: fair;
11. MS3: swallowed in the sea

SONG. ["WHEN I AM DEAD, MY DEAREST"]

[Composed December 12, 1848. Editions: *1862*, 1865, 1866a, 1875, 1876a, 1904. The notebook MS is in the Pierpont Morgan Library.]

2. MS: me:
4. Am. eds.: shady cypress-tree:
6. MS: and dew drops wet:
   1904: wet:
8. MS: [no stanza break after line 8]
9. MS: shadows:

10. MS: rain:
12. MS, 1904: on as
14. MS: doth nor rise
15. MS: Haply, I
16. MS: haply, may

DEAD BEFORE DEATH.

[Composed December 2, 1854. Editions: *1862,* 1865, 1866a, 1875, 1876a, 1904.
The notebook MS is in the Bodleian Library.]

Title. MS: Dead before death.
   1862, 1865, Am. eds., 1875: DEAD
   BEFORE DEATH. / SONNET.
  1. MS: Ah changed <> very cold.
   1862, 1865, 1866a: very cold,
   1904: Ah changed <> very cold,
  2. MS: eyes;
   1904: eyes!

  3. MS: Changed yet <> same, vanity
   of vanities,
   1904: wise,—
  4. MS: This was <> old.
  6. MS: Grown steadfast in
 11. MS: All lost all lost the
 12. MS, 1875: death shut to the

BITTER FOR SWEET.

[Composed December 1, 1848. Editions: *1862,* 1865, 1866a, 1875, 1876a, 1904.
The notebook MS is in the Bodleian Library.]

  3. MS: warm [illegible erasure]
   <air> and <> showers:—
  6. MS: colder:
   1862, 1865, Am. eds., 1875: And
   winter comes
  7. MS: hoar-frost waxeth bolder,
   1862, 1865, Am. eds.: bolder
  8. MS: [After line 8 are the following
   stanzas; the last three stanzas are
   deleted in pencil; the revisions in
   the last two stanzas are in pencil in
   Christina's handwriting.]

    The birds are silent all; but ever
     Low winds sing melancholy dirges,
    And with their sound the weary
     surges
    Join in of the dark river.

Listen, their voices have a meaning:—
 They mourn and utter lamentation
For fulness turned to desolation,
 Harvests that left no gleaning.

[*They sorrow for the past and present;*
 And for the future look with terror,
When comes the reckoning for that error
 Which at the time was pleasant.]

[*Oh sweet as honey in the doing,*
 But bitterness to think on after!
We [forget] <*know not*> *tears must pay*
 for laughter
When flushed in the pursuing.]

[*We [forget]* <*know not*> *how the sure*
 death nears us
While we suck out the poison juices;
And hug the may bloom which produces
 A strong sharp thorn to pierce us.]

SISTER MAUDE.

[Date of composition unknown. Editions: *1862,* 1865, 1866a, 1875, 1876a, 1896,
1904. No MS known.]

  3. 1866a: O who
  4. 1896: [line indented four spaces]
   1896s: [line indented two spaces]
 12. 1896: [line indented four spaces]
   1896s: [line indented two spaces]

 21. 1866a, 1896, 1904: sister Maude,
   O sister

REST.

[Composed May 15, 1849. Editions: *1862*, 1865, 1866a, 1875, 1876a, 1904. The notebook MS is in the Bodleian Library.]

Title: 1862, 1865, Am. eds., 1875:
REST. / SONNET.
1. MS: O Earth lie <> eyes:
1862, 1865, Am. eds., 1875: O
earth, lie
2. MS: watching, Earth:

6. Am. eds., 1875, 1904: a blessed
dearth
9. 1862, 1865: than noon-day holdeth
Am. eds., 1875, 1904: than
noonday holdeth
11. MS: stir.

THE FIRST SPRING DAY.

[Composed March 1, 1855. Editions: *1862*, 1865, 1866a, 1875, 1876a, 1904. The notebook MS is in the Bodleian Library.]

Title. MS: The first Spring day.
4. MS: one.—
5. 1876a: robin, sing!
6. MS: concerning spring.
7. Am. eds.: the spring-tide of
1904: the Springtide of
8. MS: another spring both
9. MS: their spring,
10. MS: sing.—

11. MS: me,
1876a: me!
15. MS: So spring must <> bloom
16. MS: this world or <> come.
1904: this world or
17. MS: Sing, promise-voice,
1876a: of Spring!
18. MS: too bud and blossom and
rejoice.

THE CONVENT THRESHOLD.

[Composed July 9, 1858. Editions: *1862*, 1865, 1866a, 1875, 1876a, 1904. The notebook MS is in the British Library.]

Title. MS: From the Convent
Threshold.
1. MS: us, love my
2. MS: brother's blood,
3. 1904: pass.
4. MS: above
5. MS: skyward stair
1904: golden sky-ward stair,
7. MS: mud
11. MS: Alas my
12. MS: heart this <> there:—
Am. eds.: this self-same stain
14. MS: snare:
15. MS: higher;
16. MS: me mount
17. MS: up:—
18. MS: the far off city
20. MS: the gulph a
24. 1904: and Seraphim.

28. MS: unfurled
30. MS: see you—
1862, 1865, 1866a: earthward
what
31. 1862, 1865, 1866a: Milk-white
wine-flushed
36. MS: [illegible erasure] <Love>
music warbling
40. Am. eds.: flee: the
45. Am. eds.: sudden bluebirds nest
47. 1875, 1876a, 1904: Today,
while <> called today,
49. MS: short tomorrow nigh,
51. MS: sin,
52. MS: me for
53. MS: unlearn,
54. MS: went
55. MS: return.
56. MS: begin

61. MS: eyes
62. MS: more:—
    Am. eds.: more,—
63. MS: for joys that
64. MS: For vanity of vanities!—
    1904: love that dies!
65. MS: you
66. MS: cry, Repent.—
    1876a, 1904: cry, Repent!
67. Am. eds., 1875, 1904: O weary life,
    O weary
68. Am. eds., 1904: O weary <> few!
    1875: O weary
69. MS: in paradise
70. Am. eds.: of Heaven alone?
    1875: alone
71. 1904: love,
72. 1876a: throne?
    1904: throne,
74. MS: thereof—
    1866a: thereof?
    1904: thereof.
75. MS: eyes
77. MS: [*heaven,*] <heaven.>
    1866a: O save <> in Heaven.
    1876a: O save <> in Heaven!
    1904: heaven!
78. MS: gave
79. MS: Repent repent and
    1904: forgiven.
82. MS: No sweeter song
85. MS: night:—
    1904: night.
86. MS: A Spirit with a dulcimer
87. MS: infinite height.
88. MS: pinions stir,
89. MS: Heaven bells rejoicing
90. MS: Heaven air was
91. MS: Worlds loitered on their

92. MS: shrieking: Give <> light.
    1876a: light!"
    1904: shrieking 'Give <> light!'
93. MS: more light,
    1862: was pour'd on
94. MS: Angels Archangels
    Am. eds., 1904: outstripped,
95. MS: might
97. MS: Still Give <> light, he
98. MS: face and
99. MS: slake.—
101. MS: crown,
    Am. eds.: crown,—
102. MS: —His <> snake,—
    Am. eds.: snake,—
104. MS: of Seraph's feet:
107. Am. eds.: Yea, all
110. MS: night:—
    1904: night.
113. 1904: there,
114. MS: And: Do <> me? you [*said,*]
    <said.>
117. MS: My pillow
118. MS: bed;
121. MS: mine.
122. 1875, 1904: while I, like lead,
    1904: hands: while I, like lead,
124. MS: Outside the world reeled
    drunk with mirth,
125. MS: But you reeled drunk with
    tears like wine.
129. 1904: prayed.
131. MS: few,
133. MS: thunder; when this <>
    broke
140. Am. eds., 1875, 1904: in Paradise.
146. MS: grown, our thrones are set;
147. Am. eds., 1875, 1904: met,

UP-HILL.

[Composed June 29, 1858. Editions: *1862*, 1865, 1866a, 1875, 1876a, 1904. The notebook MS (MS1) is in the Huntington Library; a fair copy of the first stanza (MS2) is in the Princeton University Library; another fair copy of the first stanza (MS3) is in the University of Texas Library. The poem was published in *Macmillan's Magazine*, III (February, 1861), 325. In MS2, lines 2 and 4 are indented four spaces.]

Title. MS1: Up-hill.
  1. MS1: the [illegible erasure] <road

wind> up-hill <> way?—
MS3: wind uphill all

4. MS3: my Friend.
5. MS1: But at night is there a resting place?
6. MS1, 1861: A bed for
11. MS1: Must I [*knock or halloo*]

⟨halloo or knock⟩ when
1861: call, when
13. MS1: comfort travel-sore
16. MS1: Yea beds

"THE LOVE OF CHRIST WHICH PASSETH KNOWLEDGE."

[Composed October 15, 1858. Editions: *1862*, 1865, 1866a, 1875, 1876a, 1904. The notebook MS is in the British Library. The first page (lines 1–6) of the MS is missing from the notebook.]

Title. 1904: THE <> KNOWLEDGE
4. 1875, 1904: For three-and-thirty years.
7. MS: not My Flesh I not My Spirit spared:
1862: not my flesh, <> not my spirit
9. MS: drouth
10. MS: frost,
11. MS: to My Mouth
13. MS: on My Shoulders and
15. MS: cross, and <> hungry-voiced
17. MS: upon My Hands, thy

18. MS: between Mine Eyes:
20. MS: I God,
21. MS: upon My Right Hand and My Left,
22. MS: misery;
23. MS: smote My Heart and
24. MS: A Hiding-place for
25. MS: Six hours the
26. MS: dear to Me to stretch
27. MS: kingdom, share
1904: kingdom,—Share My
28. MS: harvest, come
1904: harvest,—Come and

"A BRUISED REED SHALL HE NOT BREAK."

[Composed June 13, 1852. Editions: *1862*, 1865, 1866a, 1875, 1876a, 1904. The notebook MS is in the Bodleian Library.]

Title. MS: "A bruised reed shall He not break.—"
1904: A <> BREAK
1. MS: be;
2. MS: sin;
3. MS: love that
4. MS: after Me.
5. MS: fruitful: blessing
1862, 1865, 1866a only, 1875, 1904: still,
7. MS: part:—
8. MS: will.—
9. MS: soul? yet I
10. MS: soul
Am. eds.: soul;

11. MS: them, turning towards Me: I
12. MS: grieve.
15. MS: and Heaven above:—
16. MS: I [illegible erasure] <cannot> wish, alas.—
17. MS: What neither
18. MS: constrain.
19. MS: the Cross in pain;
21. 1904: love nor hate
22. MS: wish; resign
1904: choose nor <> still,
23. MS: will:—
24. MS: deprecate.—

A BETTER RESURRECTION.

[Composed June 30, 1857. Editions: *1862*, 1865, 1866a, 1875, 1876a, 1904. The notebook MS is in the British Library.]

Title. MS: A better Resurrection.
3. 1904: fears.
5. 1875: but dimned with
7. MS: leaf:—
8. MS: O Jesus quicken
   1862: [line indented six spaces]
   1876a: me!
10. 1875, 1904: husk:
11. MS: life tho' void
12. MS: Is tedious
13. MS: thing
14. MS: see,
    1904: see;

15. MS: shall the <> of spring:—
    Am. eds.: shall,—the
16. MS: O Jesus rise
    1876a: me!
21. 1875, 1904: thing;
22. MS: and re-mould it till
23. MS: my King:—
    1875, 1904: for Him, my
24. MS: O Jesus drink
    1876a: me!

ADVENT.

[Composed May 2, 1858. Editions: *1862*, 1865, 1866a, 1875, 1876a, 1904. The notebook MS is in the British Library. In the MS every line of a quotation begins with quotation marks.]

1. MS: The Advent
2. MS: The Advent <> long,
3. Am. eds.: after year,
5. MS: "Watchman what
   Am. eds., 1904: cry,
6. MS: Heart sick with
12. MS: win:
13. MS: "Watchman what
    1904: night?' But still
16. 1862, 1865: "Nor
17. Am. eds.: speak,
19. Am. eds.: seek,"—
20. MS: rise"—
    1875: All
22. MS: dim,
23. MS: slack
27. MS: goal

28. MS: us, Come up higher"—
30. MS: home:
31. MS: "With Christ"—"They <>
    most sweet
    Am. eds.: With Christ." "They
38. MS: rest
42. Am. eds.: laugh, for
45. Am. eds., 1904: fast Who
46. MS: fast
    Am. eds.: us,—we
49. MS: tonight,
51. Am. eds.: sight,
53. MS: bud and
54. MS: day:
55. MS: say: "Arise My love
56. MS: one come away.

THE THREE ENEMIES.

[Composed June 15, 1851. Editions: *1862*, 1865, 1866a, 1875, 1876a, 1904. The notebook MS is in the Bodleian Library. In the MS the four stanzas from "The World" are in the following order: 1, 4, 2, 3; and every line of a quotation begins with quotation marks. In the printed texts the second line of each stanza is indented approximately twenty-five spaces.]

1. MS: pale:—"
2. MS: see
5. MS: sad:—"
8. MS: "The wine-press of
9. MS: weary:—"
10. MS: so Christ
    1904: so Christ;
11. MS: mighty Love of
12. MS: "For [*strength,*] <Strength,>
    Salvation,
13. MS: art foot-sore:—"
15. MS: "His Feet have bled; yea,
    1875: bled; yea in <> need.
    1904: bled; yea in
17. MS: young:—"
20. MS: the Cross, with
21. MS: fair:—"
23. MS: to bear
24. MS: "A Visage marred
25. MS: riches:—"

27. 1875, 1904: is His: Who, living,
29. MS: sweet:—"
31. MS: "To Him, Whose cup did
33. MS: deep:—"
35. MS: cup;
37. MS: shalt have [*glory:*—"]
    <Glory:—">
39. MS: "Lord Jesus cover, up
41. MS: have [*knowledge:*—"]
    <Knowledge:—">
42. 1862, 1865, 1866a only, 1875,
    1904: dust!
    1862p, (1872a): dust,
43. MS: trust;
    1875, 1904: In thee, O
45. MS: "And Might:—"
    Am. eds.: "And Might."
46. MS: me: Lord,
47. MS: redeemed, and
48. Am. eds.: soul, O keep

ONE CERTAINTY.

[Composed June 2, 1849. Editions: *1862*, 1865, 1866a, 1875, 1876a, 1904. The notebook MS (MS1) is in the Bodleian Library; the version in Christina's notebook MS of *Maude: Prose and Verse* (MS2) is in the Huntington Library. The poem was printed in *Maude: Prose & Verse, by Christina Rossetti; 1850* (Chicago: Herbert S. Stone, 1897), 66–67. In MS1 the poem is in the handwriting of Christina's mother, Frances Mary Lavinia Rossetti; the title is in Christina's handwriting; no lines are indented. In MS2, lines 1, 4, 5, 8, 10, and 13 are indented eight spaces and lines 11 and 12 are indented three spaces. In the 1897 text, lines 1, 4, 5, 8, 10, and 13 are indented two spaces. The indentation of the 1904 text is the same as that of the present edition, except that lines 11 and 12 are indented four spaces.]

Title. MS1: The one Certainty.
    MS2, 1897: [no title]
    1862, 1865, 1866a: THE ONE
    CERTAINTY. / SONNET.
    1875, 1876a: ONE CERTAINTY.
    / SONNET.
2. MS1: eye & ear
3. MS1, MS2, 1897: hear:

4. MS1: dew or
5. MS1, MS2: withereth
11. MS1, MS2, 1897: sun.
12. MS1, MS2, 1897: of time be
13. 1897: stem;
14. MS1, Am. eds.: cold, and
    MS2: grey.—

CHRISTIAN AND JEW. / A DIALOGUE.

[Composed July 9, 1858. Editions: *1862*, 1865, 1866a, 1875, 1876a, 1904. The notebook MS is in the British Library. In the MS no lines are indented and no quotation marks are used, except in line 20.]

Title. MS: and Jew: / a dialogue.
    1. Am. eds.: "O happy

4. MS: sight,
5. 1862: hand."

6. MS: wind they
8. MS: glory star
9. 1904: far;
10. 1862, 1865, Am. eds.: [line indented two spaces]
11. MS: White winged the Cherubim
12. MS: whiter Seraphim
14. MS: dim,
15. MS: above
17. MS: Angels Archangels
20. MS: One 'Holy Holy Holy'
    Am. eds.: One 'Holy, Holy, Holy,'
    to
22. MS, 1862, 1865, 1866a: "At one side Paradise
    1904: thee, Paradise,
23. MS, 1862, 1865, 1866a: Is curtained from the rest,
26. MS: Of mother dove clad

31. Am. eds.: praise,
33. Am. eds., 1904: the Living Vine,
36. Am. eds., 1904: the Royal Vine, it
39. MS: flesh sing;
40. 1862: For he hath
41. MS, 1862, Am. eds., 1904: nor scorned our
45. 1904: Lo she
54. MS: sum,
57. MS: thy Light is
60. MS: saw them clothed
    1862p: skin,
    1862, 1865, Am. eds., 1875, 1904: skin;
61. MS: The wind
    1862p: in,
    1862, 1865, Am. eds.: in;
    1875, 1904: them, and <> in;
62. MS: rose:

SWEET DEATH.

[Composed February 9, 1849. Editions: *1862*, 1865, 1866a, 1875, 1876a, 1904. The notebook MS is in the Bodleian Library. The poem was printed in *Art and Poetry: Being Thoughts Towards Nature Conducted Principally by Artists,* III (March, 1850), 117. In the MS no lines are indented. In the 1850 text, the first, fifth, sixth, and eighth lines in each stanza are indented four spaces, the third line is indented two spaces, and the second, fourth, and seventh lines are not indented.]

2. MS: that [*passing*] <going> day
3. 1850, Am. eds.: the church to
4. MS, 1850: green church-yard thoughtfully,
6. MS, 1850: showers;
10. 1850: die, and fall and
11. MS, 1850: birth.
12. MS: life: but
    1850: life: but <> by,
13. MS: been.—
    1850: as tho' it <> been.
14. MS: green:
    1850: All colors turn <> green:

15. 1850: vanish, and <> fly;
    1875, 1904: vanish, and
18. MS: it O
    1850: my God, thou God <> truth.
    1866a only: truth
    1875, 1904: of Truth:
20. 1850: Are saints and angels, a <> company:
21. MS: And Thou O

SYMBOLS.

[Composed January 7, 1849. Editions: *1862*, 1865, 1866a, 1875, 1876a, 1904. The notebook MS (MS1) is in the Bodleian Library; the version in Christina's notebook MS of *Maude: Prose and Verse* (MS2) is in the Huntington Library; a fair copy (MS3) is in the Yale University Library. The poem was printed in *Maude: Prose &*

Verse, by Christina Rossetti; 1850 (Chicago: Herbert S. Stone, 1897), 112–13. In MS3 the last line of each stanza is indented six to eight spaces; in all of the printed texts except the 1897 version the last line of each stanza is not indented.]

Title. MS2, 1897: [no title]
1. MS1: a rose-bud very long,
   MS3: long,
4. 1897: Then when
5. MS1: hour,
6. Am. eds.: at even-song.
8. MS1, MS3: shade
   MS2, 1897: nest, full
9. MS1, MS2, MS3, 1897: three little
   eggs
11. MS2, 1897: afraid,
14. MS1, MS2, 1897: tended with such
    care,
    MS3: tended with such care
15. MS2, 1897: air:
17. MS1, MS3: fair;—
    MS2, 1897: fair:—
24. MS2: rod?—

"CONSIDER THE LILIES OF THE FIELD."

[Composed October 21, 1853. Editions: *1862*, 1865, 1866a, 1875, 1876a, 1904. The notebook MS is in the Bodleian Library. In the 1904 text, quotation marks enclose the quotations that constitute lines 3–5, 7–10, 11–12, and 15–17.]

Title. MS: "Consider the lilies of the
   field."
   1904: CONSIDER <> FIELD
2. 1876a: morn,
21. MS: weed
22. MS: love Who sends

THE WORLD.

[Composed June 27, 1854. Editions: *1862*, 1865, 1866a, 1875, 1876a, 1904. The notebook MS is in the Bodleian Library.]

Title. 1862, 1865, Am. eds., 1875:
   THE WORLD. / SONNET.
1. 1875, 1904: she woos me,
3. MS, Am. eds., 1904: leprosy,
5. 1875, 1904: she woos me
7. 1875: [line not indented] <>
   night, a
9. MS: lie; by
   Am. eds.: stands,
10. MS, Am. eds., 1904: truth,
11. MS: horns, and <> hands:
12. MS, 1904: indeed, that
14. MS: hell?—

A TESTIMONY.

[Composed August 31, 1849. Editions: *1862*, 1865, 1866a, 1875, 1876a, 1904. The notebook MS is in the Bodleian Library. The poem was printed in *The Germ: Thoughts Towards Nature in Poetry, Literature, and Art,* II (February, 1850), 73–75. The notebook MS is in the handwriting of Christina's sister, Maria Francesca Rossetti.]

1. MS, 1850: laughter: It is vain;—
   Am. eds.: laughter, it
2. MS, 1850: said: What profits it?—
   Am. eds.: said, what
3. MS: book, [illegible deletion]
   <and> writ
4. MS, 1850: Therein, how
5. MS: sickness, everyone

9. 1850, Am. eds.: again.
   1865: again
   1875, 1904: again;
10. MS: sea
11. 1850: source:
12. 1850: winds, too, turn
13. 1850: treasures, moth <> corrupt;
14. 1850: steal; or
16. MS: supped
    1850: he supp'd,
17. 1850: dim,
19. Am. eds.: sand,
20. 1850: withoutside, and
22. MS, 1850, Am. eds.: stand;
24. MS: Rotten at the foundation
    stone.
    1850: Loose at the hidden
    basement
25. Am. eds.: said,—
26. Am. eds.: Yea, vanity
27. Am. eds.: poor dies;
29. MS: lackest keep
    1850: Whatso thou <> trust:—
30. MS, 1850: dust.

32. MS, 1850: share.
34. MS, 1850: weary are at
37. 1862, 1865, 1866a: leaf
39. 1850: Or, as <> stay,
    Am. eds.: Or, as
40. MS: brief;
41. 1850: Yet doth man hope
42. MS: he doth die:—oh
    Am. eds.: dead:—O foolish
44. 1850: seeing; nor <> be fill'd
45. 1850: build,
46. 1850: buy, and <> wide:
51. 1850: Our labor is
52. 1904: lies.
60. 1850: renewed, and
62. 1850: cease;
64. MS: [illegible erasure] <And> her
    <> not numbered;
    1850: not numbered;
65. MS: green and
70. MS, 1850: And weary is
73. 1850: A king dwelt in Jerusalem:
76. 1850: them:
78. 1850: vanity,

SLEEP AT SEA.

[Composed October 17, 1853. Editions: *1862*, 1865, 1866a, 1875, 1876a, 1904.
The notebook MS (MS1) is in the Bodleian Library; a fair copy (MS2) is in the Yale
University Library.]

Title. MS1: Something like [*truth.*]
       <Truth.>
       MS2: Something like Truth.
  3. 1862p: plummet
     1862, 1865, Am. eds., 1875, 1904:
     plummet,
  6. MS1: steep:
     1862p: steep,
 10. MS1, MS2: mast,
 12. MS1, MS2: fast.
 13. 1904: ahead
 17. 1862p: Oh soft
     1862, 1865, 1875: Oh, soft
     Am. eds.: O, soft
 22. MS1, MS2: Love hidden from
 24. MS1, MS2: Love music fills.
 28. MS1, MS2: face.
 29. 1875, 1904: is driving,—driving,—
 30. MS1, MS2: apace,—

31. MS1: smile and
40. MS1, MS2: arise?—
41. MS1, MS2: Wake, call <>
    spirits;—
42. 1862, 1865, 1875, 1904: ears:
    1866a only: ears
49. MS1, MS2: Wake, call <> again;—
52. MS1: them [*wake.*] <awake.>
54. 1904: sake:
57. MS1, MS2: slowly—
58. 1862p: slow,
    1862, 1865, Am. eds., 1875: Ah,
    how <> slow!
    1904: slow!
61. Am. eds., 1904: spirits,
62. Am. eds.: White,—as
    1875, 1904: White, as
63. MS1, MS2: spirits wailing
71. Am. eds.: flitting,

72. MS2: hope deferr'd.
74. MS1, MS2: amain;
76. MS1, MS2: again:
78. MS1, MS2: slain:

83. MS1, MS2: death, in
    1862, 1865, 1866a only: dreaming,
84. MS1, MS2: days.—

FROM HOUSE TO HOME.

[Composed November 19, 1858. Editions: *1862,* 1865, 1866a, 1875, 1876a, 1904. The notebook MS is in the British Library. In the MS every line of a quotation begins with quotation marks. In the printed texts the second and fourth lines of each stanza are indented two spaces.]

Title. MS: "Sorrow not as those who
    have no hope."
  1. MS: heat;
  2. MS, 1904: swoon
  5. MS: friend: "what <> where?"—
  6. MS: soul,
11. MS: Why build the false fair
    fabric to
13. MS: My [*palace*] <mansion>
    stood [The revision is in pencil in
    Dante Gabriel Rossetti's hand-
    writing.]
17. MS: green
19. Am. eds.: between,
21. MS: the pasture took <> ease
23. MS: All singing birds rejoicing
25. 1862p: Wood pigeons cooed <>
    nestled there,
    1862, 1865, 1875: Woodpigeons
    cooed <> nestled there;
    Am. eds.: Wood-pigeons cooed
    there, stock-doves nestled there;
26. MS, 1904: fruit;
27. Am. eds.: air,
29. MS: off where
30. MS: gone,
32. Am. eds., 1875, 1904: But
    nowhere dwelt
33. MS: hop and plod
34. MS: peace an
35. MS: rustling [*not*] <nod>
37. MS: rule
40. 1862p: night;
    1862, 1865, Am. eds., 1875,
    1904: night.
42. 1866a: to year:
45. MS: Oft'times one <> me

    1862, 1865: Oft times one
    1904: Oft-times one
46. MS: like subtle fire,
    1904: fire
47. MS, 1904: sea,
48. MS: desire.
54. 1862p: delight.
57. MS: walked
58. MS: sealed,
    1904: sealed:
59. MS: talked
60. MS: revealed.
61. MS: tell that
65. MS: smiles:—
    1904: smiles.
66. MS: dumb.—
    1904: To-night,' he <> gravely;
    and
69. 1875, 1904: sweet:
70. MS: days:"—
74. 1904: hand,
75. MS: from punishment,
76. 1862p: land."—
    1862, 1865, Am. eds., 1875,
    1904: land."
77. MS: avalanche,
    1865: an alvalanche;
80. 1862p: below;
    1862, 1865, Am. eds., 1875,
    1904: below,—
86. 1862p: fallen but
    1862, 1865, Am. eds., 1875,
    1904: fallen, but
89. MS: muttered stunned <> pain;
    1862, 1865: muttered stunned
90. MS: hand:
92. MS: land."—

93. MS: arose;
97. MS: after night—
99. MS: wailed, "no more": and <>
    light
    Am. eds.: wailed, "no more"; and
100. MS: pray;
    Am. eds.: gnashed, but
103. MS: stroke:
104. MS: farewell."—
105. MS: me; and
107. 1862p: long"—
    1862, 1865, Am. eds., 1875,
    1904: long."—
108. 1862p: see"—
    1862, 1865, Am. eds., 1875,
    see."—
    1904: see."
109. MS: pain
    1862, 1865, 1875, 1904: cried:
    "Oh blessèd she
    Am. eds.: cried: "O blessed
110. 1862p: receive"—
    1862, 1865, Am. eds., 1875,
    1904: receive."—
111. MS: so; she
112. MS: live."—
113. Am. eds.: So, while <>
    entranced, a
114. MS: face,
    1904: face:
115. MS: beamed,
118. MS: and clear morning
119. MS: Most singularly pale and
    passing fair
122. MS: stars and
126. MS: flowers,
130. MS: thorn [illegible erasure]
    <shot upright from its sands>
131. MS: feet: hoarse
135. MS: length
136. MS: breadth and depth and
139. MS: wind and storm
    1875: wind and
142. MS: suffer and
    1862p: attain."
    1862, 1865, Am. eds., 1875,
    1904: attain."—

143. MS: the tempest-shock:
    1904: shock—
144. MS: again."—
146. 1865, 1875, 1904: Brimfull of
    Am. eds.: Brimful of
148. MS: depth, nor make
149. MS: Yet as
150. MS: honey, making
151. MS: First bitter sweet, then
154. MS: want"—
    Am. eds.: want";
    1904: sang 'My
155. MS: sung
158. MS: rose"—
    1862, 1865, Am. eds., 1875,
    1904: rose."—
160. MS: goes."—
162. 1862p: Time and [*space change,
    and*] <space, change and> death,
    [The correction is in pencil in
    Christina's handwriting.]
163. 1876a, 1904: whole:
165. MS: Multitudes multitudes stood
169. MS: a song a <> height
170. MS: and True;
    1904: to Him who is strong and
    true:
172. 1904: Lo all
173. 1904: they rose and rose and
    rose,
185. 1862, 1865, 1875, 1904: each
    blessèd head,
191. MS: All loving loved
194. MS: cup:
197. 1862, 1865, 1875, 1904: the
    blessèd noon,
205. MS: soul,
206. MS: face
207. MS: whole
214. MS: I precious <> than
    seven-times molten
221. MS, 1862, 1865: pain
222. MS: doth His Blood nourish <>
    root;
223. Am. eds.: again,

OLD AND NEW YEAR DITTIES. / 1.

[Composed December 13, 1856. Editions: *1862*, 1865, 1866a, 1875, 1876a, 1904. The notebook MS is in the British Library.]

Title. MS: The End of the Year.
 1. MS: sad;
 4. MS: desired:—
 5. MS: [illegible erasure] <Yet> farther
    Am. eds., 1904: to-day,

 7. 1904: apace,
 9. 1904: scathe or
10. MS, 1904: honest face,
11. MS: me:—

OLD AND NEW YEAR DITTIES. / 2.

[Composed December 31, 1858. Editions: *1862*, 1865, 1866a, 1875, 1876a, 1904. The notebook MS is in the British Library. In the MS the poem is divided into stanzas of three lines each.]

Title. MS: New Year's Eve.
 1. MS: men women and
 4. MS: business some
    1862, 1865, Am. eds.: their pleasure-scheme;
 6. MS: apart.—
 7. 1862, 1865: me blessèd spirits
    1875: me, blessèd spirits,

11. MS: this Eve of Resurrection slow,
12. MS: cry "How <> strong.—
    1904: cry 'How
13. 1862, 1865: me Jesus,
16. MS: this vigil-night;
18. Am. eds.: am Thine; Thou, Lord, my

OLD AND NEW YEAR DITTIES. / 3.

[Composed December 31, 1860. Editions: *1862*, 1865, 1866a, 1875, 1876a, 1904. The notebook MS (MS1) is owned by Mrs. Geoffrey Dennis; a fair copy of the first stanza (MS2) is owned by the Historical Society of Pennsylvania.]

Title. MS1: The Knell of the Year.
    MS2: [no title]

 1. MS1: Passing away, [*saith the World,*] <(saith the World)> passing
 2. 1904: beauty, and youth, sapped
 8. MS1: aye.—
 9. MS1: answered: Yea.—
10. MS1: Passing away (saith my Soul) passing
    1862p: my soul, passing
11. MS1: hope of <> play
    (1890), (1891), 1904: play,
14. MS1: bud, thy strength must

15. MS1: midnight, at cock crow, at
    Am. eds.: midnight, at cock-crow, at
16. 1862, 1865, Am. eds., 1875: Lo, the
    1904: delay;
17. MS1: pray.—
18. MS1: answered: Yea.—
19. MS1: Passing away (saith my God) passing
23. MS1, 1862, 1865: tarry wait
    1904: pray:
24. Am. eds.: past, and
25. MS1: spouse; thou <> say.—
26. MS1: answered: Yea.—

AMEN.

[Composed April 20, 1856. Editions: *1862*, 1865, 1866a, 1875, 1876a, 1904. The notebook MS is in the Bodleian Library.]

1. MS: It is over—what is
2. MS: Nay how
   1862p: truly:
   1862, 1865, Am. eds.: truly!—
   1875, 1904: Nay, now much <> truly!—

6. MS: It is finished—what is
8. MS: finished, time
11. MS: It suffices—what suffices?
15. MS: the sun shine hotly brightly,

THE PRINCE'S PROGRESS.

[Lines 481–540 composed October 11, 1861; lines 1–480 composed January, 1865. Editions: *1866*, 1866a, 1875, 1876a, 1904. The notebook MS, now in the British Library, comprises only lines 481–540 of the final version. Lines 481–540 were published in *Macmillan's Magazine,* VIII (May, 1863), 36. In the MS and the 1863 version no quotation marks are used.]

Title. MS: The Prince who arrived too late.
    1863: THE FAIRY PRINCE WHO ARRIVED TOO LATE.
3. 1904: go;
8. Am. eds.: time,"
9. Am. eds.: Her women say. "There 's a
   1904: say): 'there's
10. 1875: ford, sleep, dream and sleep;
    1904: and sleep;
11. Am. eds.: Sleep," they say: "we've
    1904: chime;
14. 1904: mat;
16. 1875: youth."
17. 1904: that;
26. Am. eds.: droop,—will
28. 1875, 1904: rare:
31. 1904: feet.
33. 1875, 1904: bud-coats, hairy
34. Am. eds.: swell; one
35. Am. eds.: sweet,—
    1875: their death cups drowsy
    1904: their death cups drowsy <> sweet:—
46. 1904: strength:
47. Am. eds.: limb, if
50. 1866, 1866a: Crossing green
51. 1866, 1866a: born;
53. 1904: worn

80. 1904: me,
85. 1866, Am. eds.: stay, but to
89. Am. eds.: Ahead, too, the
93. Am. eds.: braid,
94. 1866, 1866a: it shining in serpent-coils,
95. 1866, 1866a, 1904: day and a night
98. 1866: play
108. Am. eds.: the west.
110. Am. eds.: réveillée: "Hearken, O hark!
    1904: réveillée; 'Hearken,
129. Am. eds.: trickled, its
146. 1904: crust,
147. 1875, 1904: dust,
156. Am. eds.: [line indented two spaces]
167. 1866, 1866a: he espied a
177. 1875, 1904: hot:
185. 1866, 1866a: His blinking eyes
188. 1904: ado;
206. Am. eds.: see,—
207. Am. eds.: be,—
226. 1875: wire
243. 1904: slipped:—
253. Am. eds.: the Prince. "This
254. 1866, 1866a: Forth I start with
257. 1875: of life when my bride is
    1904: of life, when my bride is won,
283. 1904: o'er.

293. 1875, 1904: Loitered a while for a deep stream bath,
297. 1875, 1904: still leaves and
298. Am. eds.: It's O for
304. Am. eds.: its bank-side bare;
305. Am. eds.: hill-reserve,—
307. 1904: above and
309. 1875, 1904: Like hill torrents after
311. 1875, 1904: sweeping to
314. Am. eds.: whirl,—which
317. Am. eds.: grim,—
320. Am. eds.: "This way,—this
322. Am. eds.: He catches,— misses,—catches
325. 1875, 1904: breath—
327. Am. eds.: shadoweth,—
333. Am. eds.: hands,"—"and I,"— "and you
340. 1866, 1866a: one held his drooping head breast-high,
343. 1866, 1875: Oh, a
     Am. eds.: O, a
345. 1866, 1866a: voice that says:
346. Am. eds.: sea,—
347. Am. eds.: ways,—
351. Am. eds.: us,"—some <> word,—
357. 1866a: can,—
358. Am. eds.: [line not indented] <> way,—
364. Am. eds.: one,—
367. Am. eds.: Come, gone,—gone forever,—
368. Am. eds.: river,—
369. Am. eds.: liver,—
370. Am. eds.: fall,—
371. Am. eds.: never,—
374. 1904: and last last
375. Am. eds.: away,—
385. 1904: live!—does
391. 1904: word, the
417. Am. eds.: back,—
418. 1875: past,
     1904: past:
419. 1875: slack
     1904: slack—
439-44. 1866, 1866a: [lines not in text]
445. 1876a: the portion of
452. 1904: fanned.
457. Am. eds.: gate,—

458. Am. eds.: late,—
464. 1904: promised Bride:
467. Am. eds.: pride,—
480. 1904: flame:—
482. MS: Too late, too late:
486. MS: mate,
     1866, Am. eds.: [line indented four spaces]
488. MS: died behind <> grate:
     1863: Slept—died behind
490. 1866, Am. eds.: [line indented four spaces]
493. MS: time
494. MS: slow:
     1863: slow.
494. MS: [In the outside margin at right angle to lines 488-94, Christina wrote the following lines in pencil:]

     <Even then tho' [*golden*] [<*pauseless*>]
          <shelving> sands of time
     [*Had*] Swift sands had [*run so*]
          <dwindled> low—>

495-96. MS, 1863: [lines not in text]
498. MS: gone one to
499. MS: The soft south
500. MS: snow,/ And life have been a cordial yes/ Instead of dreary no.
     1863: snow,/ And life have been a cordial "Yes,"/ Instead of dreary "No."
     1866, Am. eds.: [line indented four spaces]
502. MS: fair,
503. MS, 1863: king
504. MS: With gold dust on
505. MS: Now those are lilies in
     1863: Now those are
506. MS: Dead lilies she
507. MS: to hide her
510. 1866, Am. eds.: [line indented four spaces]
511. MS: smile,
513. MS: to her
516. MS: Kirtle, or lace, or
521. MS: haste,
     1904: haste;
522. MS, 1863: sweet
528. MS: feet:
529. MS: her
531. MS: yesterday

532. MS: [*Writhing*] <Wasting> upon
     <> bed,
535. MS: today
     1863: So, we
     1904: Lo we

537. MS: these lilies that
539. MS: these lilies, not

MAIDEN-SONG.

[Composed July 6, 1863. Editions: *1866*, 1866a, 1875, 1876a, 1904. The MS is in
the British Library. In the MS every line of a quotation begins with quotation
marks.]

1. MS, 1904: and long ago
3. 1866a: maidens,
7. MS: fair Margaret
10. MS: rose
    1904: When Meggan pluckt the
11. MS, 1866: the briar,
12. MS: would [*stop*] <swoop> to see,
    [The revision is in pencil in Chris-
    tina's handwriting.]
13. MS: nigher,
    1904: beasts drew nigher,
14. MS: the [*sea*] <streams> [The re-
    vision is in pencil in Christina's
    handwriting.]
15. MS: Would bob up
    1904: admire.
16. MS: a [*bluebell*] <flag flower>
    [The revision is in pencil in Chris-
    tina's handwriting.]
    1904: But, when Margaret pluckt
    a flag-flower
17. MS: poppy hot-aflame,
21. MS: and [*may-dew*] <May-dew>
23. MS: and [*may-dew*] <May-dew>
25. MS: leaves;"
    Am. eds.: for strawberry-leaves,"
28. 1904: me, May:
29. MS: down the hill
30. Am. eds.: way,
34. MS: again
39. MS: In heaven's high serene,
42. MS: an [illegible erasure] <ivy>
    bough
51. MS: [*Singing*] <Warbling> out
52. MS: [*Singing singing*] <Warbling
    warbling> still
    Am. eds.: Warbling, warbling
55. MS: spot
58. MS: rest
61. MS: away

66. MS: there:
67. MS: note
68. MS: A [illegible deletion]
    <fitful> wayward
    Am. eds.: fitful, wayward
    (1890), (1891), 1904: lay
69. MS: While [*free*] <shrill> as [The
    vision is in pencil in Christina's
    handwriting.]
72. MS: vale
73. 1904: flame;
74. MS, 1866, Am. eds.: see
75. MS: came:
76. MS: south
79. MS: As love bird on <> nest;
81. MS: [illegible erasure] <With>
    trouble
83. MS: breast;
86. MS: tongue:
97. 1904: him
98. MS: sits
100. MS: sits
102. MS: love
106. MS: where calves and kidlings
     grow."
108. MS: look;
109. MS: White
110. MS: crook:
112. MS: south
116. MS: parching [illegible erasure]
     <hill-side> drouth;
     Am. eds.: parching hillside
     drouth;
121. MS: Pauses, [illegible erasure]
     <cadences:>
125. MS: trees,
     1866a, 1904: through forest-trees:
127. MS: herself [illegible erasure]
     <for love>
128. MS: safe

129. 1875, 1904: But coos and coos thereof:
135. MS, 1866, Am. eds.: hands
138. MS: lambs, which
141. MS: Your [illegible erasure] <sweet> song
146. 1866, Am. eds.: sun,
150. MS: At cock-crow we were sister maids,
151. MS: noon."—
152. MS: Said Meggan "Yes;"—May <> not, "No."
     1904: Said Meggan "Yes";
153. MS: home:
     1904: home;
155. MS: silent; then
     1904: thought
159. MS: herself:
161. MS: rose and <> door
164. MS: mate.
165. MS: the garden-slope she
170. MS: the [*haloes*] <haloed> moon

173. MS: Most awful-pure to sight:
183. MS: sang
185. MS: sang:
     1904: sang;
187. MS: when spring's ablow.
188. 1904: country,
193. MS: Squire and knight and peer.
     1904: Squire and knight and
197. MS: Lord-King of <> land
199. 1875: fish,
204. Am. eds.: shepherd, May,
206. Am. eds.: the hillside way;
208. MS: grey:
211. MS: their marriage-mirth;
212. MS: Sang [*wild*] <free> birds [The revision is in pencil in Christina's handwriting.]
214. MS: the [*sea,*] <deep;> Am. eds.: deep,—
215. 1904: move—
228. MS: brief May-tide

JESSIE CAMERON.

[Composed October, 1864. Editions: *1866,* 1866a, 1875, 1876a, 1904. The MS is in the British Library.]

6. 1904: sea:
10. MS: true"—
13. MS: careless fearless girl
    1904: careless fearless
14. Am. eds.: plain;
16. Am. eds.: Kind-hearted in
17. Am. eds.: tongue,
21. 1866, 1875: "Oh, long
    Am. eds.: "O, long
25. 1904: foam,
29. 1866, 1875: "Oh, can't
    Am. eds.: "O, can't
39. MS: speech
41. 1866, 1875, 1904: "Oh, say
    Am. eds.: "O, say
42. MS: Jessie, Jessie Cameron"—
45. MS: head
47. MS: foot which <> fled
    1904: fled
49. Am. eds.: had gypsy blood,
58. MS: night
59. MS: hear a [*hellish*] <unked> strain [The revision is in pencil in Christina's handwriting.]

60. MS: see a [*hellish*] <unked> sight. [The revision is in pencil in Christina's handwriting.]
61. MS: for Jessie Cameron,— 1866, Am. eds., 1875: Alas, for
62. MS: crept moaning moaning
    1904: nigher;
63. Am. eds.: to be gone,—
64. 1904: her:—
66. 1904: fire,—
67. MS: foam
68. MS: The sea foam sweeping higher.— Am. eds.: sea-foam, sweeping
69. MS: O Mother linger <> door
70. 1866, 1866a, 1875: plain,
74. Am. eds.: only, each
78. MS: startled sea gull screech,
91. 1904: be;
92. MS: Sea winds that
93. MS: Sea birds that
94. MS: Sea waves swelling,
98. 1904: flow
102. MS: [*Bandying words*] <With

words flung > to [The revisions
are in pencil in Christina's hand-
writing.]
103. MS: past;
107. Am. eds.: sea, for <> stir,
110. Am. eds.: pray,

111. Am. eds.: replying,
114. MS: away
118. MS: a gold gleam <> there
120. MS: be [*golden*] <drifting> hair.
[The revision is in pencil in Chris-
tina's handwriting.]

SPRING QUIET

[Composed in 1847. Editions: *1866,* 1866a, 1875, 1876a, 1904. The notebook MS
(MS1), copied by Christina's sister, Maria Francesca Rossetti, is in the Bodleian
Library; a fair copy (MS2) is in the Princeton University Library. The poem was
published in *Macmillan's Magazine,* XI (April, 1865), 460. In MS1 and MS2 the
stanzas are in the following order: 1, 2, 6, 3, 4, 5. The *Macmillan's* text is divided
into three sections: the first section comprises stanzas 1, 2, 3, and 6 of the present
poem; in each stanza the second, fourth, and fifth lines are indented two spaces.
The second and third sections constitute a separate poem entitled "Today and
Tomorrow" in Christina's notebook manuscript. All of the revisions in MS1 are in
pencil in Christina's handwriting. In MS2 every new line of a quotation begins
with quotation marks.]

Title. MS1: The Spring-quiet.
    MS2: "Solitude"
    1865: SPRING FANCIES. / I.

1. 1865: the winter,
2. 1865: the spring,
3. MS1: to the green-wood
    MS2: to the forest
4. MS1: sing:/ <Ding a ding
    dingading> [last line indented two
    spaces]
    MS2: sing/ Ding ding, ding a ding.
    1865: sing/ Ding-ding, ding-a-ding.
    1875: sing.
5. MS1: the [*myrtles*] <whitethorn>
    Am. eds.: the white-thorn
6. MS1: Singeth [*the*] <a> thrush;
    1865: Singeth the thrush,
7. MS1: Where [*the*] <a> robin
    1865: And the robin
8. MS1: holly-bush;/ <With his breast
    ablush> [last line indented two
    spaces]
    MS2, 1865: the holly bush/ With
    his breast ablush. [last line indented
    two spaces]
9. MS1: of [*sweet*] <fresh> scents
10. MS1: the [*leafy*] <budding>
    boughs

    MS2: the leafy boughs,
    1865, Am. eds.: boughs,
11. MS1, MS2: [*Framing*] <Arching>
    high
12. MS1: house./ [illegible deletion]
    <Where doves coo the arouse>
    [last line indented two spaces]
    MS2: house/ Where doves coo the
    arouse. [last line indented two
    spaces]
    1865: house,/ Where doves coo the
    arouse.
    1904: house;
13. MS1: scents
    MS2: of fresh scents,
13–20. 1865: [not in text]
15. MS1, MS2: That sayeth
16. MS1: snare;/ <Here or anywhere>
    [last line indented two spaces]
    MS2: snare/ "Here or anywhere.
    [last line indented two spaces]
20. MS1: stone."/ <Here make your
    sad moan.> [last line indented two
    spaces]
    MS2: stone:/ "Here make your sad
    moan. [last line indented three
    spaces]
21. MS1, MS2: Where the
    1865: There the

23. MS1: [*Where is heard the murmur*]
    <& scarce sounds [<*the tumult*>]
    an echo>
    MS2: And is
    1865: There sounds an
24. MS1: sea.

25. MS1: [illegible deletion] <Though
    far off it be.>
    MS2: be. [line indented three
    spaces]
    1865: be.

THE POOR GHOST.

[Composed July 25, 1863. Editions: *1866*, 1866a, 1875, 1876a, 1904. The
notebook MS (MS1) is in the British Library; a fair copy (MS2) is in the Princeton
University Library. In MS2 there are no quotation marks. The speaker is indi-
cated by *He* or *She* written above the stanzas at the left margin.]

Title. MS1: [*"Alas, poor Ghost!"*] <The
ghosts Petition> [The revision is in
pencil in Christina's handwriting.]
MS2: A Return./ Alas, poor Ghost!
1. MS2: *He.*/ Oh
   Am. eds.: "O whence
4. MS2: sea?—
5. MS2: *She.*/ From
   1904: you:
6. MS1, MS2: with the dropping
   drenching
   Am. eds.: dripping, drenching
8. MS2: too.—
9. MS2: *He.*/ Oh
   Am. eds.: "O, not
10. MS1, MS2: tomorrow too
    Am. eds.: "O, not
12. MS2: day.—
12. MS1: [After line 12 are the follow-
    ing stanzas:]

    "Your body to die or your soul to live
    It is not mine to withhold or to give.
    You must depart when sentence you
        receive:
    You must come home to me, and will
        you grieve?"

    "Alas, my lost love and still my dear,
    I knew you here and I loved you well
        here:
    But now my flesh creeps to feel you so
        near,
    And if I do not shun I needs must fear."

    MS2: [The stanzas are also in MS2,
    with the following variations:]
    1. *She.*/ Your   4. grieve?—
    5. *He.*/ Alas,   8. fear.—
13. MS2: *She.*/ Am

14. MS1, MS2: fright;
15. Am. eds.: right,
16. MS1, MS2: sight?
16. MS1: [After line 16 is the following
    stanza:]

    "Am I so [illegible erasure] <soiled>
        with the damp and the dust
    That my love loathes me as a leprous
        crust?
    Not decay has yet touched me, tho'
        touch it must;
    The nails hold hard, tho' they're 'filed
        with rust."

    MS2: [The stanza is also in MS2,
    with the following variations:]
    1. Am <> so soiled with
    4. rust.—
17. MS1: friend;
    MS2: *He.*/ Indeed <> friend;
18. MS1, MS2: end.
19. Am. eds.: tend;
21. 1875, 1904: yet,
23. MS1, MS2: a blue violet
    1904: violet,
24. MS1, MS2: wet.
24. MS1: [After line 24 is the following
    stanza:]

    "Wait for me there on the green hill
        side;
    Watch for me all my brief life-tide;
    Watch where the daisies blow
        hundred-eyed;
    I will come to you at last, O promised
        bride."

    MS2: [The stanza is also in MS2,
    with the following variations:]
    1. Wait   4. bride.—

25. MS1: too is gone;
    MS2: *She./* Life <> too is gone:
26. MS1, MS2: upon.
29. MS1: "I will go <> my own bed,
    MS2: I will go <> my own bed,

33. MS2: But
36. MS1: the Judgement Day."
    MS2: the Judgment Day.

A PORTRAIT.

[Part I composed November 21, 1850; Part II composed February 24, 1847. Editions: *1866*, 1866a, 1875, 1876a, 1904. The notebook MS of Part I (MS1) and the notebook MS of Part II (MS2) are in the Bodleian Library. MS2 is in the handwriting of Christina's sister, Maria Francesca Rossetti. Part II is included in *Verses: Dedicated to Her Mother* (London: privately printed by G. Polidori, 1847), 54. In the 1847 text, only lines 15, 19, 23, and 26 are indented.]

Title: MS1: Saint Elizabeth of Hungary.
       MS2: Sonnet./ On Lady Isabella.
       1847: SONNET. / LADY
       ISABELLA.
2. MS1: ways:
3. MS1: eyes, lest
7. MS1: days.
   1866a: days
8. MS1, Am. eds.: uncouth,
9. MS1: the [*sick*] <poor> and [*needy*]
   <stricken> she [The revisions are
   in pencil in Christina's handwriting.]
10. MS1: [*Her dwelling; till*] <A home
    until> the [The revision is in pencil in Christina's handwriting.]
11. MS1: wants: her
13. MS1: the Cross,
    ·Am. eds.: cross,
16. 1866: lay
    Am. eds., 1904: lay.
    1875: lay,
18. MS2: [*Shone in upon her, casting rosy
    red*] <Shone through upon her,
    warming into red> [The revision

is in pencil in Christina's handwriting.]
19. MS2: On the [*white*] <shady>
    curtains. [The revision is in pencil in Christina's handwriting.]
20. MS2: Heaven opens, I leave [*all*]
    <these> and [The revision is in pencil in Christina's handwriting.]
    Am. eds.: away:
21. MS2: calls, and shall [*I wish*] <the
    B seek> to stay?— [The revision is in pencil in Christina's handwriting.]
    1847: The bridegroom calls,—
    shall the bride seek
22. MS2: head.—
23. MS2: O [*lily*] <Lily> flower, O
    [*gem*] <Gem> of
    Am. eds.: O lily-flower, O
24. MS2: O [*dove*] <Dove> with
25. MS2: fruitful [*vine*] <Vine> amid
26. 1847: purities
27. MS2: with [*Saints*] <friends> on
    1847: earth,
28. MS2: the Saints in

DREAM-LOVE.

[Composed May 19, 1854. Editions: *1866*, 1866a, 1875, 1876a, 1904. The notebook MS (MS1) is in the Bodleian Library; a fair copy (MS2) is in the Yale University Library. The poem was published in *A Welcome: Original Contributions in Poetry and Prose* (London: Emily Faithfull, 1863), 63–66.]

Title. MS1: The old story.
       MS2: Long enough.
       1863: DREAM LOVE.

1. MS1, MS2: Young love lies
2. MS1, MS2, 1863: In May time of
6. MS1, MS2, 1863: there,

8. MS1, MS2, 1863: The may bushes
   are
9. 1863: pillow,
10. MS1, MS2: oh! a <> cheek,
    1863: oh! a
    Am. eds.: For O, a
    1904: oh a
14. MS1, MS2: speak,
    1863: lulled, and
15. MS1, MS2: There morning lingers
17. MS1, MS2: Young love lies
    dreaming:
    1863: dreaming:
18. MS1, MS2, 1863: dream?—
20. MS1, MS2: Upon the forest
21. MS1: [illegible erasure] <Or>
    perfect
22. MS2: Along a
23. MS1, MS2: silence;
26. MS1, MS2, 1863: air,

28. MS1, MS2; 1863: fro:
29. MS1, MS2: oh! in
    Am. eds.: For O, in waking,
    1904: oh in
33. MS1, MS2: Young love lies
34. MS1, MS2, 1863: gone,
45. 1863: Oh! poor
    1866, 1875: Oh, poor
    Am. eds.: O, poor
48. 1904: palms!
49. MS1, MS2: Young love lies
50. MS1, MS2: death,
54. MS1, MS2, 1904: warm delicious
    1863: warm delicious breath,
56. MS1, MS2: place?—
58. MS1, MS2, 1863: evergreen,
    1904: of branchèd evergreen;
63. MS1, MS2: dove may be
    Am. eds.: dove, maybe,
64. MS1, MS2: Will brood and nestle

TWICE.

[Composed June, 1864. Editions: *1866*, 1866a, 1875, 1876a, 1904. The notebook
MS is in the British Library.]

1. MS, 1904: hand,
2. MS: (O my love, [*o*] <O> my love,)
4. MS: die;
5. Am. eds.: speak
6. MS: (O my love, [*o*] <O> my
   love,)—
   Am. eds.: (O my love, O my love);
7. MS: weak;—
   1876a: weak:
10. MS: smile;
11. MS: scanned;
12. MS: Then [*you*] set [The deletion is
    in pencil.]
14. MS: wait a while;
17. MS: [*In setting*] <As you set> it <>
    broke; [The revision is in pencil in
    Christina's handwriting.]
    Am. eds.: broke,—
24. MS: bird.—
25. MS: hand
26. MS: O my God, [*o*] <O> my
29. MS: written [*in*] <on> sand, [The

revision is in pencil in Christina's
handwriting.]
30. MS: O my God, [*o*] <O> my
    1875, 1904: O my God, O my God:
31. MS: stand,
    Am. eds.: stand,—
32. MS: Yea judge
33. MS: This [*heart,*] contemned [The
    deletion is marked in pencil.]
34. MS: This, marred
    1866a: day
38. MS: away,
    Am. eds.: away,—
39. MS: in Thy hold
    1866, Am. eds., 1875: Yea, hold
41. MS: hand
    Am. eds.: hand,—
42. MS: (I <> die but live),
    Am. eds.: live,—
43. MS: Before Thy Face I stand,
46. 1904: give;
47. MS: sing

SONGS IN A CORNFIELD.

[Composed August 26, 1864. Editions: *1866*, 1866a, 1875, 1876a, 1904. The notebook MS is in the British Library. In the MS no quotation marks are used, and the pattern of indentation is as follows: in lines 1–70 the odd-numbered lines are not indented and the even-numbered lines are indented two spaces; in lines 71–85 the first and third lines of each stanza are indented two spaces and the second, fourth, and fifth lines are not indented; in lines 86–93 the even-numbered lines are not indented and the odd-numbered lines are indented two spaces; in lines 94–109 the last line of each stanza is indented three spaces and the first, second, and third lines are not indented; in the remaining lines of the poem (lines 110–29) the even-numbered lines are not indented and the odd-numbered lines are indented two spaces.]

6. MS: Sing Marian, sing
7. MS: Only Janet cannot
14. MS: hay:
23. 1904: joy,
24. 1875: sorrow
26. 1904: tomorrow;
31. MS: with Marian
34. MS: sang [*altogether:*—] <all together:—> [The revision is in pencil in Christina's handwriting.]
38. 1875: love
46. 1875, 1904: groweth;
47. 1904: winter,
59. MS: dog [*lay down to*] <woke up from> sleep,
60. 1866: coil. [At Christina's request, Macmillan had the period erased by hand, but some copies of the first edition escaped correction.]
61. MS: grass [*grew*] <stood> thickest, bird
  1866: thickest, bird [At Christina's request, Macmillan had the comma changed to a colon by hand, but not all of the copies were so emended.]
  1875, 1876a, 1904: thickest; bird
62. MS: shadows where they
67. MS: ease
68. MS: [*And laid their*] <Their> sickles
69. MS: Marian sang <> strain
71–85. MS: [These lines read as follows:]

  We met hand to hand,
  Clasped hands together close and fast,
    As close as oak and ivy stand:
  But it is past.

Come day, come night, night comes at last.
  We loosed hand from hand,
  We parted face from face,
    Each went his way to his own land
  At his own pace,
  Each went to fill his separate place.

  If we should meet one day,
  If both by chance should not forget,
    We should shake hands the accustomed way
  As when we met
  So long ago, as I remember yet.

71. Am. eds.: swallow,—
73. 1904: swallow, stay,
75. 1904: Look back, swallow, turn back, swallow, stop, swallow.
76. Am. eds.: swallow,—
80. Am. eds.: Good by swallow, 1904: Good-bye, swallow,
85. Am. eds.: follow: good by swallow, 1904: follow; good-bye, swallow,
86. MS: listless Janet raised
103. MS: cold [*as*] <like> snow? [The revision is in pencil in Christina's handwriting.]
  1866, 1875: Oh, but
  Am. eds.: O, but
107. 1866, 1875: Oh, but
  Am. eds.: O, but
  1875: but it is cold
110. 1904: to-day,
112. 1904: to-morrow,
114. 1875, 1904: day,
115. MS: all:
  1904: all—
116. MS: his curly hair,
117. MS: call;
  1904: breast, and

117. MS: [After line 117 are the fol-
      lowing lines:]
  But death will keep her secret,
    Turf will veil her face,
  She will lie at rest at rest
    In her resting place.
  No more reaping
    Wheat thro' the harvest day,

  No more weeping
    False lover gone away:
  It may be sleeping
    As dove sleeps in her nest;
  It may be keeping
    Watch yet at rest.

A YEAR'S WINDFALLS.

[Composed February 26, 1863. Editions: *1866,* 1866a, 1875, 1876a, 1904. An early fair copy (MS1) is in the Brown University Library; the notebook MS (MS2) is in the British Library.]

6. MS1, MS2: comes:
7. MS1, MS2: fire
8. MS1: And give him
   MS2: And [*give*] <toss> him [The
   revision is in pencil in Christina's
   handwriting.]
10. MS1, MS2, Am. eds.: Snow-flakes
    float
13. MS1, MS2: streams
14. MS1, MS2, 1904: sea:
15. MS1, MS2: the Winter ever
    1904: ends,
16. 1904: be!
18. MS1, MS2: down;
22. MS2: way
29. 1866, Am. eds., 1875, 1904:
    Apple-trees and pear-trees
31. 1866, Am. eds., 1875, 1904:
    Plum-trees and peach-trees;
32. MS1: While [*warm*] <sharp>
    showers
34. MS1, MS2: flowers;
42. 1866, Am. eds., 1875, 1904: the
    red rose crop;
43. MS1: day [*new*] <fresh> blossoms
44. MS1, MS2: drop:
45. MS1: White-rose and yellow-rose
46. MS1, 1866, Am. eds.: And
    moss-rose choice
47. MS1, 1866, Am. eds., 1875, 1904:
    Cottage cabbage-rose
50. MS1, MS2: hail;
    1904: hail

51. 1904: lightning-clouds that
52. MS1, MS2: heaven, grown
53. MS1, MS2, 1904: ashore;
57. 1866, Am. eds.: wind,
58. MS1, MS2: head;
    1875, 1904: Corn-fields bow
60. MS1: On [*green*] <low> hills
61. MS1, MS2: down,
62. MS1, MS2: breeze;
63. Am. eds.: First-fruits of
    1875, 1904: First fruits of
68. MS1, MS2: shoots:
70. Am. eds.: streaked
75. MS2: his [illegible deletion]
    <hollow> bed
76. MS1, MS2: rocks:
79. MS1, MS2: sea
    Am. eds.: It's O for
    1904: oh for
80. Am. eds., 1904: home!
81. MS1: In [*raw*] <slack> wind
82. MS1, MS2: shifts:
85–88. MS1: [These lines, inserted in
    the right margin at right angles to
    the text, replace four lines that are
    deleted so thoroughly as to be il-
    legible.]
85. 1904: twigs,
90. MS1, MS2: sands almost run,
92. MS1, MS2: sun:
94. MS1, MS2: low;

THE QUEEN OF HEARTS.

[Composed January 3, 1863. Editions: *1866*, 1866a, 1875, 1876a, 1904. The notebook MS is in the British Library. The poem was published in *Macmillan's Magazine*, VIII (October, 1863), 457.]

1. MS: that whenever
2. MS: invariably
3. MS: parts
4. MS: the [*queen*] <Queen> of
5. 1875: a scrutinising gaze,
6. MS: Striving to
7. MS: But sift <> will
9. MS: and shuffle, shuffle,
11. MS: Vain care, vain <> too,
   Am. eds.: forethought, too;
13. MS: but ere

17. MS: once: I <> private [*mar*] <notch>
   Am. eds.: once: I
18. MS: On Heart Queen's back, <> a keen eyed watch;
   1866a: watch:
20. MS: pack;
22. MS: seemed mine own;
23. MS: notch not <> doing
27. MS: Unless indeed it

ONE DAY.

[Composed June 6, 1857. Editions: *1866*, 1866a, 1875, 1876a, 1904. The notebook MS is in the British Library. The poem was published in *Macmillan's Magazine*, IX (December, 1863), 159. In the MS, lines 2, 4, 7, 10, 12, 14, 18, 20, 22, and 24 are indented two spaces.]

Title. MS: One day.
1. MS: when we met:
2. 1863: of spring;
3. MS: Not a rose had budded yet,
4. MS: Not a young bird proved its wing,
5. MS: and sweet violet
6. MS: set
7. MS: And mating birds began to [*sing.* —] <sing.>
8. MS: [not in text]
9. MS: when we parted:
   1904: parted;
9-10. MS: [These lines were written directly below line 7 and then erased and dropped down a line, making a stanza break after line 7.]

10. MS, (1890), (1891), 1904: brown
   1863: plenteous autumn sheaves
11. MS: Then we parted heavy hearted;
14. MS: Only we had lost our crown;
15. MS: to us those
17. MS: shall we meet?—I <> tell
18. MS: Indeed when we shall
19. MS: But meet we shall in
20. MS: this I wait we wait in
21. 1904: death Love lies
22. MS: today:
23. MS: The Lord shall ask us, Is <> well?
24. MS: And we shall answer, Yea.
   1875, 1904: answer "Yea."

A BIRD'S-EYE VIEW.

[Composed March 4, 1863. Editions: *1866*, 1866a, 1875, 1876a, 1904. The notebook MS is in the British Library. The poem was published in *Macmillan's Magazine*, VIII (July, 1863), 207. In the MS and *Macmillan's* text, every line of a quotation begins with quotation marks.]

2. MS: the [*raven*] <Raven> spoke;
3. MS, 1904: tree,

4. MS, 1863: As black as black could
6. MS: the bridegroom hear

9. MS: Yet: "Croak,
   1904: Yet 'Croak,
10. 1904: oak,
16. MS: the bride mount
17. MS, 1863: land,
18. MS: the [illegible erasure]
    <wave-edged> sand,
22. MS: say, "Now we <> her!"—
    1863: say: "Now we
23. MS: daughter!"—
25. MS: ship [g] <sails> fast
    1866, 1875: Oh, the
    Am. eds.: O, the <> fast,
27. MS: soft:
    1904: soft.
28. MS: aloft.
30. 1875: Croaking, croaking,
    croaking:
    1904: Croaking, croaking,
    croaking.
31. MS: the bridegroom keep watch
    keenly
    1863: the Bridegroom keep watch
    keenly
32. MS: For this choice bride mild and
    queenly.
    1863: For this choice Bride mild
    and queenly.
33. MS: beach
34. MS: the springtide billows
37. MS, 1904: ship that
38. 1904: carries!

44. MS: [S] <Tolled> from
48. MS: too."—
    Am. eds.: knows, too."
50. MS: white,
53. MS: the bride and <> maidens,
    Am. eds.: maidens,—
    1904: maidens—
54. MS: cadence,—
    Am. eds.: Clear <> cadence,—
    1904: Clear
58. MS: dumb,
65. 1866, 1875: Oh, who
    Am. eds.: O, who
    1904: truth?
67. 1866a: down,
68. Am. eds.: crown?
71. MS: An innocent queen and holy
    1863: An innocent queen and holy,
72. MS: To a high throne from a
    lowly?—
    1863: To a high throne from a
    lowly?
    1904: in Heaven.
74. MS: The [jar] <silks> and
81. MS, 1863, 1866, 1866a: and year;
82. 1875, 1904: bridal bell chimes
    clear;
84. MS: The bridegroom is
    1904: gay.
85. 1904: rotten:
86. MS: old bride is
87. MS: ominous ravens only

LIGHT LOVE.

[Composed October 28, 1856. Editions: *1866*, 1866a, 1896, 1904. The notebook MS is in the British Library. The poem was published in *Macmillan's Magazine*, VII (February, 1863), 287. In the 1896 and 1904 texts the fifth and last lines of each stanza are not indented, but the rest of the indentation follows the present text.]

1. 1863: "Oh! sad
   1866a: "O sad
2. 1896, 1904: go,—
3. MS: flame
6. MS, 1896, 1904: gone?
7. MS: rest my
9. 1863: year,
11. 1896, 1904: breast:
13. MS, 1863: lonely rest
18. MS, 1896, 1904: this?
    1866a: this,—
20. MS, 1896, 1904: rest."

21. MS: note my <> dove
    1863: "Oh! sad
    1866, 1875: "Oh, sad
    1866a: "O sad
22. 1896, 1904: cold:
23. 1863: love,
24. MS, 1896, 1904: old
25. MS: gold:
    1896, 1904: gold?
27. MS: away;
    1866a, 1896, 1904: away,—
28. MS, 1896, 1904: flush

30. MS: And <turn> thy
    1896, 1904: day."
31. MS, 1896, 1904: him a word,
32. MS: aside
33. MS, 1896, 1904: Sick with the pain
    of hope deferred
38. MS, 1896, 1904: harms;
39. MS: We two will
    1863: part!
    1896, 1904: We two will <> part:
40. 1863, 1896, 1904: art!"
41. 1866a, 1896, 1904: never tease me,
    1896s: never teaze me,
43. 1863: For, nigh <> hand, there
44. 1896, 1904: morn:
46. 1896, 1904: peach:
47. MS: night;
    1863, 1896s: She woos me
48. 1896, 1904: reach:
49. MS, 1896, 1904: delight,
50. MS: ripens reddens
    1896, 1904: reddens, in
53. MS: thy spiced garden
54. 1896, 1904: bare autumn eves
55. 1896, 1904: of harvest-sheaves?
56. MS: true love, behind,
57. MS, 1896, 1904: true:
58. MS: Go [illegible erasure] <seek>

in haste,—but
1866a: haste; but
1896, 1904: Go seek <> haste,—
but
59. MS, 1896, 1904: for new,
60. MS, 1863, 1896, 1904: enjoy, yea
    trample
    1866a: enjoy,—yea,
61. 1863: Alas! for
62. MS: her like me
    1863: Alas! for
    1896, 1904: her like
63. MS, 1896, 1904: snows."—
    1863: snows!"
64. MS, 1896, 1904: nay not
66. MS, 1896, 1904: ago
    1863: Farewell! and
67. MS: met;
68. MS: slow."—
    1863: Farewell! my
    1896, 1904: Farewell: my <>
    slow."—
70. MS: to Heaven: "Dost [*thou*]
    <Thou> forget?"—
    1863: hard to
    1896, 1904: to Heaven: "Dost
    Thou forget?"

ON THE WING.

[Composed December 17, 1862. Editions: *1866*, 1866a, 1875, 1876a, 1904. The
notebook MS is in the British Library.]

Title. MS: Once in a Dream.
    1866, 1866a: A DREAM./
    SONNET.
    1875, 1876a: ON THE WING./
    SONNET.
1. MS: dream—for <> you—
3. MS: our [*head*] <heads> two [The
    revision is in pencil in Christina's
    handwriting.]
4. MS: view:
    1904: view:—

5. MS: flew
9. Am. eds.: Then, as
12. MS: gone; [*whilst boundary*] <while
    rustling> hedgerow [The revision
    is in pencil in Christina's handwrit-
    ing.]
13. MS: me [*the*] <a> sound [The revi-
    sion is in pencil in Christina's
    handwriting.]

A RING POSY.

[Composed February 20, 1863. Editions: *1866*, 1866a, 1896, 1904. The notebook MS is in the British Library. The 1896 indentation follows the present text except that lines 4 and 20 are indented five spaces and line 17 is indented eight spaces.]

Title. MS, 1896: Jess and Jill.
  6. 1896, 1904: bit—
 17. 1896, 1904: Surely, surely:
 19. MS: <While the sun shines make

their hay—> [The line was added in pencil by Christina.]
1896, 1904: hay—

BEAUTY IS VAIN.

[Composed January 20, 1864. Editions: *1866*, 1866a, 1875, 1876a, 1904. The notebook MS is in the British Library. In the 1904 text all of the lines are indented two spaces except lines 7, 9, and 15, which are not indented.]

Title. MS: "Beauty is vain."
  1. MS: Whilst roses
  2. MS: Whilst lilies

13. MS, 1904: white
15. 1904: her,

MAGGIE A LADY.

[Composed February 23, 1865. Editions: *1866*, 1866a, 1875, 1876a, 1904. The notebook MS is in the British Library.]

Title. MS: My [*lady*] <Lady> of the Manor.
  1866, 1866a: LADY MAGGIE.
  1. MS: me [*dear,*] <Dear,>
  2. MS: For I'm lady of the manor now grand to
  3. MS: babe as one may <> year
  4. 1866, Am. eds.: 'T will be
  5. MS: you my <> cousin Phil
  1866, 1875: Oh, but
  Am. eds.: O, but
  7. MS: mill
  8. MS: you and [*all your*] <ship &> crew [The revision is in pencil in Christina's handwriting.]
  1904: lost.
  9. MS: playfellow when
 10. MS: the [*miller's Nancy said*] <Miller's Nancy told> it
 11. MS: with <the> merry
 12. MS: sea.
 16. MS: you my
 17. Am. eds.: pale,—some <> fair,—

21. MS: gown Philip and
  1904: ring—
23. MS: sing
25. 1866, Am. eds.: roses says
29. MS: "fie" and
  1904: said fie, and <> cried shame,
30. Am. eds.: His high-born ladies
  1904: cried shame from
31. 1904: said fie when
33. MS: fair Philip? Philip did
34. 1875, 1904: girl
35. MS: blue forgetmenots [*grew*] <bloomed> on [The revision is in pencil in Christina's handwriting.]
37. MS: now
  1904: then, sure
38. MS: stand
41. MS: sailor Philip weatherbeaten
44. MS: [*As you coast*] <coasting> along [The revision is in pencil in Christina's handwriting.]
45. MS: bower

WHAT WOULD I GIVE?

[Composed January 28, 1864. Editions: *1866*, 1866a, 1875, 1876a, 1904. The notebook MS is in the British Library.]

Title. MS: What would I give.
    1904: WHAT WOULD I GIVE!
  2. MS: do:
    1904: do!
  4. 1904: come!
  5. 1904: dumb.

  6. MS: friends go
    1866, 1875: Oh, merry
    Am. eds.: O, merry
  7. 1904: for tears! not
  8. MS: clean and <> years;
  9. 1875, 1904: ingrain, and

THE BOURNE.

[Composed February 17, 1854. Editions: *1866*, 1866a, 1875, 1876a, 1904. The notebook MS is in the Bodleian Library. The poem was published in *Macmillan's Magazine*, VII (March, 1863), 382. "The Bourne" comprises the second and fifth stanzas of the MS text.]

Title. MS: "There remaineth therefore a rest."
  1. MS: [The opening stanza is as follows:]

Very cool that bed must be
  Where our last sleep shall be slept:
  There for weary vigils kept,
  There for tears that we have wept,
Is our guerdon certainly.

  3. MS: showers;—
  5. MS: [After line 5 are the following stanzas:]

No more struggling then at length,
  Only slumber everywhere;
  Nothing more to do or bear:
  We shall rest, and resting there
Eagle-like renew our strength.

In the grave will be no space
  For the purple of the proud,
  They must mingle with the crowd;
  In the wrappings of a shroud
Jewels would be out of place.

  7. MS: Courage reckoned <> worth;
    1863: Courage reckoned
  9. MS: Shall hold
 10. MS: [After line 10 are the following stanzas; the revisions are in pencil in Christina's handwriting:]

High and low and rich and poor,
  All will fare alike at last:
  The old promise standeth fast:
  None shall care then if the past
Held more joys for him or fewer.

There no laughter shall be heard,
  Nor the heavy sound of sighs;
  Sleep shall seal the aching eyes;
  All the ancient and the wise
There shall utter not a word.

Yet it may be we shall hear
  How the mounting skylark sings
  And the bell for matins rings;
  Or perhaps the whisperings
Of white Angels sweet and clear.

Sun or moon hath never shone
  In that hidden depth of night;
  But the souls there washed and white
  Are more fair than fairest light
Mortal eye hath looked upon.

The die cast whose throw is life—
  Rest complete; not one in seven—
  Souls love-perfected and shriven
  Waiting at the door of heaven,
Perfected from fear of strife.

What a calm when all is done,
  Wearing vigil, prayer and fast:—
  All [*is full*] <fulfilled> from first to last:—
  All the length of time [*is*] <gone> past
And eternity begun.

[*Bitter cup*] <Fear & hope> and chastening rod
  Urge us on the narrow way:
  Bear we still as best we may
  Heat and burden of the day,
Struggling panting up to God.

SUMMER.

[Composed January 15, 1864. Editions: *1866*, 1866a, 1875, 1876a, 1904. The notebook MS is in the British Library. In the 1904 text, line 4 is indented four spaces, lines 3, 6, 9, 14, 16, and 25 are not indented, and the remaining lines are indented two spaces.]

1. MS: [The following stanza opens the poem:]

    Oh what's the pleasure
      Of a wintry day in spring,
    When early buds are pinched with cold,
      And blackthorn's blossoming,
    And [*robin's*] <Robin's> like to beg
      again
    [*At the window pane?*] <Tapping at the pane?> [The revision is in pencil in Christina's handwriting.]

1. MS: is cold hearted,
3. 1875: a weather-cock
4. MS, 1904: way.
6. MS: When [*leaves are thick on shrub and*] <every leaf is on its> tree; [The revision is in pencil in Christina's handwriting. No stanza break follows this line.]
6. MS: [After line 6 are the following lines:]

    Summer days and nights for me
    When there's enough for beast and bee;

9. MS: hang singing singing singing
10. MS: the wheat fields wide;
10. MS: [After line 10 are the following lines:]

    When the hedges all are green
      Except where maples bide;
    When the hedges all are green
      And the grass fields daisy-pied,
    And poppies [*flaunt*] <sun> their
      pride, [The revision is in pencil in Christina's handwriting.]

11. MS: ride;
12. MS: When the
13. MS: [no stanza break following line 13]
    1904: to side;
14. MS: And [illegible deletion] <blue-black> beetles
17. MS: lost;/ When slim butterflies are alive,
22. 1904: Why one
25. MS: dusty musty lag-last

AUTUMN.

[Composed April 14, 1858. Editions: *1866*, 1866a,1875, 1876a, 1904. The notebook MS is in the British Library. In the MS no lines are indented and no quotation marks are used.]

Title. MS: Ding Dong Bell.

1. MS: I dwell alone, I dwell alone alone,
    Am. eds.: I dwell alone,—I
2. MS: sea
    1904: [line indented six spaces]
3. 1904: [line indented two spaces]
5. MS: O love songs gurgling
6. MS: O love pangs let
8. MS: sea.
9. MS: Slim gleaming <> notes
    1904: Slim gleaming
10. MS: entreating,
    Am. eds.: entreating,—

11. MS:—Ah sweet but
    Am. eds.: fleeting,—
    1904: Ah sweet but
12. MS: shivering snow white sails:
13. MS: Hist, the <> fails,
    Am. eds.: fails,—
14. MS: Hist, they <> strand
    Am. eds.: strand,—
15. MS: strand where
16. MS: land,
    Am. eds.: land,—
18. MS: latest solitary
19. MS: sea: rough autumn tempest tost
    1904: rough autumn-tempest-tost:

20. MS: bird shall
21. MS: Dropt down <> sea
23. MS: it whilst it
28. MS: oaks;
29. Am. eds.: by thunder-strokes,
30. MS, Am. eds.: breeze:
31. MS: trees
32. MS: heads and
33. MS: avenue:
34. MS, 1875: flies
37. MS: sap
38. MS: fair few
39. MS: web
41. MS: It shakes, my <> shake, for
    Am. eds.: It shakes,—my <>
    shake; for
42. MS: housed:—
43. MS, 1904: sail

44. 1904: the water-leaves
45. MS: gale;
46. MS: again
    Am. eds.: again,—
47. MS: maiden whom
50. MS: wane
51. MS: [No stanza break follows the
    line.]
52. MS: grieves
53. MS: Uplifted like <> beacon on
    1904: [line not indented] Uplifted
    like <> beacon on
57. MS: stand
58. MS: in hand,
59. MS: land.—
63. MS: And lonesome very lonesome
    is

THE GHOST'S PETITION.

[Composed April 7, 1864. Editions: *1866*, 1866a, 1875, 1876a, 1904. The notebook MS is in the British Library. In the MS every line of a quotation begins with quotation marks.]

Title. MS: A Return.
  1. MS, Am. eds.: coming: look
     1866: coming: look out, and
  2. MS: calling,
  4. MS: coming: O sister look."—
     1866, Am. eds.: coming: O
  5. MS: dashes,
  9. MS: word and
 11. MS: heaven
 12. MS: word and
 13. MS: sleep my
 14. MS: Sleep the night thro', where
     cold moonlight thro'
 15. MS: Shadeless lattice makes all
     things plain:
 16. MS: awhile and
 18. MS: latch."—
 19. MS: dark and <> light
     1904: dark and
 20. MS: sleeping, and <> weeping
 22. MS: night and <> day
     1904: night and
 23. MS: sleeping, and <> weeping
     Am. eds.: weeping,—
 24. MS: Watching weeping

25. MS: footstep [*mounting*]
    <climbing> the [The revision is in
    pencil in Christina's handwriting.]
27. MS: air,
    Am. eds.: air,—
28. MS: passed:
    1866, Am. eds.: door, and
29. MS: enter? in
30. MS: husband; the
31. MS: "O Robin but <> cold;
    Am. eds.: cold,—
32. MS: the night dew, so lily white
    you
34. MS: O Robin but <> late;
35. MS: near me, sit
    Am. eds.: near me,—sit
36. MS: Blue <> grate.
41. MS: shadow come from [*a*] <the>
    meadow [The revision is in pencil
    in Christina's handwriting.]
42. MS: lie but
43. MS: leaves.
50. MS: weeping,
    Am. eds.: weeping,—
52. MS: Woe's me, woe's me, for

53. MS: sorrow, oh
    1866, 1875: Oh, night <> oh,
    black
    Am. eds.: O, night <>
    sorrow!—O, black
56. MS: least wind, why now
    Am. eds.: least wind,—why,
57. MS: you whom
59. MS: left and brother
60. MS: good.
61. MS: there underground
62. MS: follow:
63. MS: there? what
64. MS: tell,
    Am. eds.: tell;
65. MS: wife content
    Am. eds.: plenty. Kind wife,
    1904: plenty; kind
66. MS: us, it
    Am. eds.: us,—it
68. MS: ended; our
69. MS: pleasure; and
    1904: rest.'
70. MS: ["O] <"Oh> but Robin I'm
    1866: "Oh, but

Am. eds.: "O, but
1875: "Oh, but <> come
71. 1875, 1904: pleasant,
74. MS: tease you who
75. MS: take?
75. MS: [The following stanzas con-
    clude the poem:]

"Yours I was for sorrow or mirth.
  "My heart is broken: give me a token,
"Give me a token from heaven or
      earth."—

"Dry your tears, mine own loving wife;
  "The token given came straight from
      heaven
"That you may bear your most weary
      life:

"Nurse our little baby for God;
  "To sing His praises, when grass and
      daisies
"Cover us both beneath the sod.

"Yet His vineyard its fruit shall yield;
  "Yet our Father will reap and gather
"Sheaf by sheaf all His harvest field.

MEMORY.

[Part I composed November 8, 1857; Part II composed February 17, 1865. Edi-
tions: *1866*, 1866a, 1875, 1876a, 1904. The notebook MS of Part I (MS1) and the
notebook MS of Part II (MS2) are in the British Library.]

Title. MS1: A Blank.
      MS2: A Memory.
  2. MS1: dead:
     1904: dead.
  3. 1904: alone; even
  4. 1904: Alone, and
  6. MS1: stood alone, I
     Am. eds.: stood alone,—I
  7. MS1: of self regard or
  8. MS1: [*Until the whole was*] <Til first
     and last were> shown. [The revi-
     sion is in pencil in Christina's
     handwriting.]
  9. MS1: weighed—
 10. MS1: poise:
 11. MS1: wanting; not <> said

13. MS1: still:
14. MS1: heart
17. MS1: laid it [*dead*] <cold>
18. MS1: Dead in <> live;
19. MS1: by inch:—the <> old
24. 1866, Am. eds., 1875: centres.
25. MS2: goes—[O] <Oh> tedious
    Am. eds.: goes—O tedious
28. MS2: [*In cordial*] <Of lavish>
    summer. [The revision is in pencil
    in Christina's handwriting.]
32. MS2: there:
33. MS2: my [*slow*] <worn> life's [The
    revision is in pencil in Christina's
    handwriting.]
34. MS2: eyes

A ROYAL PRINCESS.

[Composed October 22, 1851. Editions: *1866*, 1866a, 1875, 1876a, 1904. The notebook MS is in the British Library. The poem was published in *Poems: An Offering to Lancashire. Printed and Published for the Art Exhibition for the Relief of Distress in the Cotton Districts.* (London: Emily Faithfull, 1863), 2–10. In the MS and 1863 text, every line of a quotation begins with quotation marks.]

1. MS: king-descended, stuck with
   1863: king-descended, stuck with <> gilded, dressed,
   1875: I a
   1904: I a Princess
   king-descended, deckt with
3. MS: sun and
5. MS: evermore:
6. MS: coo, eagle
   1866: dove, that
   Am. eds.: dove, that <> coo,— eagle, that
6. MS: [After line 6 is the following stanza, which is deleted by a vertical pencil line:]

   [*With blank faces reverential men follow in my train;*
   When I speak they drink my words in, answer not again;
   If I frown they flush or whiten with a pang of pain.]

10. 1863: mirrors whereupon
12. MS, 1863: Selfsame solitary figure, selfsame seeking
14. MS: chair which <> throne:
    1863: my Father's chair, <> throne:
    1904: chair with
16. MS: end:
17. MS: spend;
    1863: My Father and my Mother give <> spend:—
18. MS: father, O <> mother, have <> friend?—
    1863: O my Father, O my Mother, have
19. 1863: my Father is
21. MS: strong [*wh*] <right> hand
    [*world-kingdom's*]
    ⟨world-kingdom's⟩ balances.
22. MS: has [*quarreled*] <quarrelled> with
23. MS: Vassal Counts and Princes follow
24. MS: lords, whom <> knows.
    1863, 1866, 1866a: knows.

27. MS: [After line 27 are the following stanzas, which are deleted with a vertical pencil line:]

    [*Proud to do my bidding, wear my favour, break*
    A stainless lance in tourney for my honourable sake:
    Little guessing they how night by night I lie awake,]

    [*Weeping miserable tears that leave more to weep,*
    Tossing on soft pillows till I cry myself to sleep;
    Loathing daylight, loathing darkness, while the moments creep.]

28. MS: with [*even*] <equal> pen
    [The revision is in pencil in Christina's handwriting.]
    1863: My Father counting
29. 1863: men:
30. MS: slaughter, these for breeding, with <> when:
    1863: slaughter, these for breeding, with <> when
    1866, 1866a: slaughter, these for breeding, with
31. 1863: canals, some
32. MS: beneath [*their*] <sharp> overseers' [The revision is in pencil in Christina's handwriting.]
34. 1875, 1904: heart, and
36. MS, 1863: souls tho'
36. MS: [After line 36 are the following stanzas; the revisions are in pencil in Christina's handwriting; the first, fifth, and sixth stanzas are deleted with a vertical pencil line:]

    [*I smote my hands upon my breast with a passionate force,*
    I cried out in an agony of shame and keen remorse:
    "These are men, are men, I rated lower than dog or horse."—]

    All that day I sat alone, would not eat nor drink,

Sat humiliated down in dust to weep
and think:
My heart grew like a stone, I felt it sink
and sink and sink.
At night my father held a banquet: I
must needs be there,
[*Statue-pale,*] <Statue-cold,> severe,
and stately, if not statue fair.
With hereditary jewels [*wreathed about*]
<clustered in> my hair,
With a fan of rainbow feathers and a
golden chain:
Some bore gusty lights before me, some
bore up my train:
"These are men, are men, are men;"
throbbed my heart and brain.
[*Not then nor ever any man, scaling the
height above,*
*Struck fire, as flint from flint, and kindling
nobly spake thereof:*
*"I love you, do you love me, high princess
and love?"—*]
[*Not then nor ever did I hear that softened
special tone*
*Which whispers faltering in one ear unto
one heart alone,*
*And wins the answer: "Yes, I love: O love,
what is a throne?"—*]

1863: [The MS stanzas above that
are not deleted (the second, third,
and fourth) are in the 1863 text,
with the following variations:]
stanza 2, line 3. stone; I   stanza 3,
line 1. my Father held   line 2.
Statue-cold, severe, <> not
statue-fair;   line 3. jewels
clustered in my   stanza 4, line 1.
chain,   line 3. "These are men,
are men, are men," throbbed
37. 1875, 1904: gay:
38. MS: grey;
    1863: my Mother's graceful
39. MS: father, frowning <> fare,
    seemed
    1863: My Father frowning
42. MS: me I looked old
43. MS: all [*were*] <are> fair [The re-
    vision is in pencil in Christina's
    handwriting.]
45. MS: night: ah <> throne?—
    1863: night: ah
47. MS, 1863: sets; but
48. MS: [After line 48 are the follow-
    ing stanzas, which are deleted
    with a vertical pencil line:]

[*Maskers came and went like ghosts: what
hid beneath the mask?*
*Was the jesting born of mirth, or was it all a
task?—*
*None had dared to answer me even when I
dared to ask.*]
[*At length my mother rose, then rose the king,
I rose the third:*
*Each kissed me on my forehead with a tender
wistful word:*
*I was weak, tears gathered, while a something
in me stirred,*]
[*Struggling blind and dumb, yet crying an
inarticulate cry,*
*For love and nothing else, for love the truth
and not a lie,*
*For love, love, love; but all the while these
eyes gleamed cold and dry.*]
50. MS: chain: meantime
51. MS, 1863: of one that was not
    loosed whether I waked
52. MS: on;
    1863: milk delicately
    1904: on:
53. MS: cinnamon;
54. MS: lit [*my*] <her> shaded <>
    alone.— [The revision is in pencil
    in Christina's handwriting.]
    1863, 1866, Am. eds.: lamp and
55. MS, 1863: week went by; and
    next I
57. 1863: "Men, like <> dogs, are
59. MS: truth ungarnished <> royal
    [illegible erasure] <ear;>
    1863, Am. eds.: Vulgar, naked
60. MS, 1863: for hustling in
61. MS, 1863: truth and mark:—
62. MS: park"—
    1863: park.
    1875, 1904: grazing, like
63. MS: ark."—
    1866, Am. eds.: saved even
64. MS, 1863: laugh; each <> way:
    1904: laugh: each
65. MS, 1863: a pretty lad, in dress
    perhaps too gay:
66. 1866: maid as
67. MS: a [*louder*] <weightier>
    tramp; [The revision is in pencil
    in Christina's handwriting.]
68. MS: said: ["*The*] <"Picked>
    soldiers [The revision is in pencil
    in Christina's handwriting.]
    1866, Am. eds.: camp

69. MS: stamp."—
71. MS: coach, well-aimed and <> thrown"—
72. MS: mown."—
    Am. eds.: work, then, for
73. MS, 1863: fool, with
75. MS: he fell; when <> dead."—
77. MS: staff"—
    1863: life they <> staff."—
    1875, 1904: life they
78. MS: loaf [illegible deletion] <they're> welcome <> chaff. — 1863: chaff."—
78. MS: [After line 78 is the following stanza, which is deleted with a vertical pencil line:]
    [These also passed; the silence settled round
        me as before:
    Could these be men who mocked at men, and
        galled the quivering sore?—
    Another step: my father hard as steel stood at
        the door.]
79. MS: [*Tender-voiced to me, with a forced most tender*] <These passed. The king: stand up, said my F with a> smile: [The revision is in pencil in Christina's handwriting.]
    1863: passed. The King: stand <> my Father with
    1866, Am. eds.: passed. The king: stand
    1904: king": stand
80. MS: awhile:
    1863: your Mother comes
    1904: awhile;
81. MS: beguile?"—
    1863: to-day; and
    Am. eds.: sad to day, and
82. MS: [*So he*] <He too> left <> now whilst I wait; [The revision is in pencil in Christina's handwriting.]
    1863: now whilst I
    1876a: wait
83. MS:—I <> gate—
    1863: I <> gate—
    1866: gate—)
    1866a: gate,—)
    1876a: gate),
84. MS: [illegible deletion] <Or> shall
85. MS: scene—
    1904: scene,—

86. MS: between—
87. MS: me whilst I <> queen?—
    1863: the Queen?
88. 1863: my Father's voice
89. MS: "Charge"—a <> the ruffians stand:
    1863: "Charge,"—a <> steel:—
    "Charge <> stand:
    1875, 1904: "Charge" a
90. MS: Smite and spare not hand <> hand, smite <> not hand <> hand."—
91. MS: There [*grew*] <swelled> a <> higher: [The revision is in pencil in Christina's handwriting.]
92. MS: the Cathedral spire:
    1863: the Cathedral spire;
94. MS: [*"You shall*] <"Sit &> roast <> meat, [*you shall*] <sit &> bake [The revisions are in pencil in Christina's handwriting.]
95. MS: [*You*] <Sit> who sat and saw us [The revision is in pencil in Christina's handwriting.]
    1863: sat and saw us
96. MS: head."—
96. MS: [After line 96 is the following stanza:]
    O queen my mother, come in haste; yet
        is your haste too slack;
    I have set my face towards where there
        is no looking back;
    I have set my foot upon the unreturning
        track.

    1863: [The MS stanza given above is also in the 1863 text, with the following variations:] 1. O Queen my Mother, come <> slack; 2. back,
97. MS: This thing <> do whilst my <> tarrieth:
    1863: This thing <> do whilst my Mother tarrieth:
98. MS, 1863: therewith;
99. MS: gems and rainbow-fan and
101. MS: to these people
    1863: to face; will
102. MS: queen and
    1863: curse King, Queen and Princess of
102. MS: [After line 102 is the following stanza, which is deleted with a vertical pencil line:]

[*Let them curse, yea curse, for we have*
earned no blessing, none:
If they strike I can but die, and death is
quickly done:
Yea, let them strike and let me die, a triumph
quickly won.]

105. 1863: goal, I
    1904: if I perish, perish—that's
105. MS: [After line 105 is the follow-
    ing stanza:]
    Once to stand up face to face with
        heart-pulse loud and hot
    —It may be in this latter day I stand
        thus in my lot—

And cry, "I love you, love you," to those
    who know me not;

1863: [The MS stanza given above
is also in the 1863 text, with the
following variations:] 1. hot—   2.
It   3. cry: "I
106. MS, 1904: heart, and
107. MS, 1863: This lesson <>
    learned which
    1866, 1866a: learned which
108. MS, 1863: if I perish, perish. In
    the Name of
    1904: if I perish, perish: in

SHALL I FORGET?

[Composed February 21, 1865. Editions: *1866*, 1866a, 1875, 1876a, 1904. The
notebook MS is in the British Library. In the MS, lines 3 and 7 are indented two
spaces.]

Title. MS: Shall I forget?
1. MS: grave?—
2. MS: nothing; you
    1866a only, 1904: see,
4. MS: soul watch
    1904: him, and

5. MS: of Paradise?—
6. MS: nothing; follow,
    Am. eds., 1904: see,
8. MS: soul lead

VANITY OF VANITIES.

[Date of composition unknown. Editions: *1866*, 1866a, 1875, 1876a, 1904. No MS
known. The poem was printed in *Verses: Dedicated to Her Mother* (London: privately
printed at G. Polidori's 1847), 62–63. In the 1847 text, lines 1, 4, 9, and 12 are
indented two spaces.]

Title. 1847: "VANITY OF
    VANITIES./ SONNET.
    1866, Am. eds., 1875: VANITY
    OF VANITIES. / SONNET.
1. 1847: "Ah <> vain!
    1866, Am. eds., 1875: Ah, woe
2. 1847: "Ah <> past!
    1866, Am. eds.: Ah, woe
    1875: Ah, woe <> past;
    1904: past!
3. 1847: "Pleasure <> last;

4. 1847: "Glory <> gain!"
    1904: gain.
7. 1847: Soundeth, making <>
    aghast
    1866, 1866a: aghast
9. Am. eds., 1904: fearfully,
12. 1904: weariness:
13. 1866: sighingly
    1904: Yea even
14. 1847: another: "How vain it is!"
    1904: another 'How <> is!'

L. E. L.

[Composed February 15, 1859. Editions: *1866*, 1866a, 1875, 1876a, 1904. The notebook MS is in the British Library. The poem was published in *The Victoria Magazine,* I (May, 1863), 40–41.]

Title. MS: Spring* [Note at bottom of page:] *L.E.L. by E.B.B.
Inscription. 1863: love."—E. B. BROWNING.
    1866, 1866a: love." / E. B. BROWNING.
  1. MS: Downstairs with friends I laugh I sport and jest;
    1863: Downstairs with friends I laugh, I sport and jest:
    Am. eds.: Down-stairs I
    1904: all;
  3. MS: wall:
  5. MS: done
  6. MS: birds mate one by one
    1863: birds mate one by one,
  7. MS: out for
  8. MS: no spring while <> is bursting forth,
    1863: is bursting forth;
    1875, 1904: is well-nigh blown,
  9. MS: no nest while
  12. MS, 1863: Whilst golden
  14. MS: Whilst lilies bud for
    1863: Whilst lilies
  17. MS: guess whose hearts are filled indeed
    1863: guess, whose hearts are filled indeed,
  19. MS: Whilst beehives <> whirr
    1863: Whilst beehives
    1875, 1904: While bee-hives wake

  20. MS: fur
  23. MS: myself as any <> dove;
    1863: myself as any
  24. MS: my goodly show, <> never think
    1863: never think
  27. MS: myrrh
  29. MS, 1863: some Saints in
  30. MS, 1863: some Angels read
  31. MS, 1863: another piteously:
  32. MS: Her <> [*love;*] <love.>
    1863: Her <> love.
  33. MS: birth
  34. MS: They leap <> mirth
    1863: They leap
  35. Am. eds., 1875: When spring-time wakes
  36. MS: a Saint: Take <> thy hurt:—
    1863: a Saint: Take <> thy hurt;
    Am. eds.: scathe";
    1904: saint, "Take <> scathe";
  37. MS: an Angel: Wait for
    1863: an Angel: Wait,
    1904: 'Wait, and thou
  39. MS: thou heart broken for
    1863: thou heart, broken for
    1876a: love!
  40. MS: Love only shall be worth,
  41. MS: Hate only shall have dearth,
  42. MS, 1863: earth.

LIFE AND DEATH.

[Composed April 24, 1863. Editions: *1866*, 1866a, 1875, 1876a, 1904. The notebook MS (MS1) is in the British Library; a fair copy (MS2) is in the Princeton University Library. In MS1 and MS2 no lines are indented. In the 1875 text, lines 2, 4, 8, 11, and 16 are indented two spaces.]

Title. MS2: An Escape.
  2. 1904: die;
  3. MS1: the [*daisies*] <wild flowers> blow; nor [The revision is in pencil in Christina's handwriting.]

    MS2: the daisies blow,
    Am. eds.: the wild-flowers blow,
  6. MS1, 1904: soars sky-high,
  7. MS1, MS2: that Spring is <> and Summer fleet,

12. MS1: the [*rain,*] <wane> [The re-
vision is in pencil in Christina's
handwriting.]
MS2: the rain,
1904: meanwhile; so, not
13. MS1: [*Nor count the*] <Of> sere
leaves [The revision is in pencil in
Christina's handwriting.]

MS2: Nor count the sere leaves
1904: [line indented four spaces]
15. MS2: blackened bean fields, nor
1904: bean-fields, nor, where
16. Am. eds., 1904: grain,
18. 1904: [line indented four spaces]

BIRD OR BEAST?

[Composed August 15, 1864. Editions: *1866*, 1866a, 1875, 1876a, 1904. The notebook MS is in the British Library. In the MS, the only stanza break is that preceding line 9.]

2. MS: and Eve
5. MS: not [*a*] <Eve's> peacock
7. MS: not [*an*] <Adam's> eagle;—
8. MS: be:
8. MS: [After line 8 are the following lines:]

To teach Adam how to build
    Simply at the first,
To teach Eve that hope and love
    Remain at the worst.

11. Am. eds.: thorny, thistly
1875, 1904: world,
13. Am. eds., 1875, 1904: lion,
14. MS: such,—
15. 1866a: lamb,
17. 1875, 1904: bough,
18. 1875: sod;

EVE.

[Composed January 20, 1865. Editions: *1866*, 1866a, 1875, 1876a, 1904. The notebook MS is in the British Library. In the MS, lines 2, 4, and 25 are indented two spaces, and all of the revisions are in pencil in Christina's handwriting. In the 1904 text, lines 19 and 21 are indented two spaces.]

1. Am. eds., 1875, 1904: door,
2. Am. eds., 1875, 1904: within,
4. MS: sin
8. MS: [*How will Eden bowers grow*] <How have Eden bowers grown>
9. MS: bend [*them?*] <them!> 1904: them?
10. MS: [*How will Eden flowers blow*] <How have Eden flowers blown> Am. eds., 1875, 1904: blown,
11. Am. eds., 1875, 1904: breath,
12. MS: tend [*them?*] <them!> 1904: them?
14. MS: Tree twelvefold fruited,
17. 1875, 1876a, 1904: the Tree of Death.
18. MS: nay

19. MS, 1904: Adam my
20. 1904: away—
26. MS: "I Eve,
27. MS: "Of [The line is at the top of a new page.]
28. 1866: another
30. 1866: lover—
1866a: lover,—
1875, 1876a, 1904: lover.
31. 1866, 1866a, 1875: eyes run 1876a: eyes run over! 1904: over!
32. 1904: grieve?
34. MS: die, mother,
37. Am. eds.: Thus Eve, our
41. MS: Each [*pitiful*] <piteous> beast
46. MS: his wheaten-stalk;

50. 1875, 1904: station:
59. MS: The mocking bird left
60. MS: [*The camel*] <Huge camels>
    knelt
65. Am. eds., 1904: desolation,
66. 1866a: [No stanza break follows
    line 66.]

67. Am. eds., 1875, 1904: dust,
68. 1866: crawling
69. 1866a only: an awful grin, and
    (1872a), 1876a: grin, and

GROWN AND FLOWN.

[Composed December 21, 1864. Editions: *1866*, 1866a, 1875, 1876a, 1904. The
notebook MS is in the British Library.]

Title. MS: Alas for me!
 1. MS: of spring
 2. MS: sere autumn's fall;
 5. MS: [*My*] <One> heart's [The re-
    vision is in pencil in Christina's
    handwriting.]

 8. MS: late summer's wane;
13. MS: alas [*for me*] <to see>
    Am. eds.: love,—alas
15. MS: be
16. MS: pass.

A FARM WALK.

[Lines 1–40 composed July 11, 1864; date of composition of lines 41–68 unknown.
Editions: *1866,* 1866a, 1875, 1876a, 1904. The notebook MS, comprising lines
1–40, is in the British Library.]

 4. MS: growing,
13. MS, 1904: tale
18. MS: as Church-bell ringers,
19. MS: feet
24. 1904: minute,
25. MS: pail and
27. 1904: maid,
28. 1904: creamy.
31. MS: head,
    Am. eds.: said, with
32. 1904: dreamy.
34. 1904: heavy-laden.
35. MS: ladies [*feathered,*] <plumed
    and> silked,

36. MS: not <a> sweeter
37. Am. eds.: sweeter, fresher
38. Am. eds., 1875, 1904: cotton,
54. 1904: bristle;
58. 1904: mothers.—
59. 1904: Alas one
65. Am. eds.: in farm-house of
66. Am. eds.: her cosey,
67. 1904: unknown.—
68. 1875, 1904: Good-bye, my
    Am. eds.: Good by, my

SOMEWHERE OR OTHER.

[Composed October, 1863. Editions: *1866*, 1866a, 1875, 1876a, 1904. The last two
lines of the notebook MS (MS1) are in the British Library; a fair copy (MS2) is in
the Princeton University Library.]

Title. MS2: A prospective Meeting.
 3. MS2: not yet, never yet, ah me,
 4. MS2: Thrilled to
 5. MS2: other: may

 6. MS2: Beyond the land, the sea,
 9. MS2: other: may
11. MS1, MS2: the sere leaves

A CHILL.

[Composed probably between October, 1863, and January 15, 1864. Editions: *1866*, 1866a, 1876a, 1904. The notebook MS is in the British Library. In the MS, the part of the page containing the last stanza and the date of composition has been removed from the notebook.]

3. Am. eds.: mother,
4. MS: The [*warm soft*] <careful>
   ewe.

CHILD'S TALK IN APRIL.

[Composed March 8, 1855. Editions: *1866*, 1866a, 1875, 1876a, 1904. The notebook MS is in the Bodleian Library.]

Title. MS: [*Spring wishing.*] [<*Child-love.*>] <Child's-talk in April.> [The revisions are in pencil in Christina's handwriting.]
1. MS: wren
3. MS: men:
4. MS: eight,
8. Am. eds.: rough, perhaps,
9. 1875: down; ah,
   1904: down; ah you
10. Am. eds.: The cosey nest
14. 1875, 1904: feet,
20. MS: [*A life of days all marked with white.*] <And we'll make merry while we may.> [The revision is in pencil in Christina's handwriting.] 1866, Am. eds., 1875, 1904: [line not indented] (1890), (1891): may,

21. MS: Perhaps one day
27. MS: Thro' pleasant sunny days of spring; 1866, Am. eds.: spring:
28. MS: Till if <> task
29. MS: sit, and <> should stretch your
30. MS: to bough, I'd
33. MS: swell,
34. MS: with housewife [illegible erasure] <matron> air
41. MS: last [*a springtide*] <an April> thro' [The revision is in pencil in Christina's handwriting.]
42. 1875: dew, 1904: dew,—
43. MS: Then tho' we 1875, 1904: twain:
44. 1904: you,

GONE FOR EVER.

[Composed October 14, 1846. Editions: *1866*, 1866a, 1875, 1876a, 1904. The notebook MS, which is in the Bodleian Library, is in the handwriting of Christina's sister, Maria Francesca Rossetti. The poem was printed in *Verses: Dedicated to Her Mother* (London: privately printed at G. Polidori's, 1847), 35–36.]

Title. MS: Gone for ever.
1. 1847: happy rose bud blooming 1875, 1904: happy rosebud blooming
2. Am. eds.: tree,—

7. MS: happy sky-lark springing
14. 1904: pain:
15. 1904: bower
16. 1904: hour

"THE INIQUITY OF THE FATHERS UPON THE CHILDREN."

[Composed March, 1865. Editions: *1866*, 1866a, 1875, 1876a, 1904. No MS known.]

Title. 1866, Am. eds.: UNDER THE ROSE./ "The iniquity of the fathers upon the children."
1. Am. eds.: O the
6. 1904: forlorn;
21. Am. eds.: that cost so
37. Am. eds.: curls,
38. 1866: eyes
39. 1875: pearls:
    1904: pearls.
41. 1875, 1904: me,
66. 1904: good,
75. 1904: poor,—
81. Am. eds.: [no stanza break after line 81]
89. 1875, 1904: The fisher folk would
103. 1876a: to nurse and
127. 1904: bed,
134. 1904: curiously,—
137. 1904: me.
145. 1875, 1876a, 1904: corpse I
146. 1904: stone.
155. 1904: undone:
161. Am. eds.: much,)
164. Am. eds.: days, day <> day,
165. Am. eds.: lay,
167. Am. eds.: O, so
     1904: Oh so
181. 1904: fall;
183. Am. eds., 1904: cheek,
194. 1904: lay.
196. 1904: know:
199. 1904: to-day.'—
206. 1904: word,
211. 1876a: hour
234. 1875, 1876a, 1904: deep:
239. Am. eds.: spare hand,
245. (1890), (1891): find,
246. 1904: mind,
248. 1876a: [no stanza break after line 248]
251. 1866, 1866a: "I never knew that she was worse
252. 1866, 1866a: [line not in text]
254. 1875: fast);
     1904: fast).
256. 1866, 1866a: [line not in text]

260. Am. eds.: Never, never
274. 1904: wine
275. 1904: flowers;
281. Am. eds.: drinking,
283. 1904: long,
284. 1904: home,
287. 1876a: primroses
289. 1876a: birds
298. 1904: long,
304. 1875, 1876a, 1904: smiled,
306. Am. eds.: flush,
315. 1875, 1876a, 1904: stay
323. 1904: history;
331. 1866a: who....
     1876a: who—
364. 1875, 1904: ears,
365. 1904: wit.
366. 1866, Am. eds.: my lady's child;"
368. 1904: together.
370. 1904: improbable;
372. 1904: thing.—
373. Am. eds.: O keep
     1904: Oh keep <> close:
376. 1904: blossoming
377. 1904: thorn—
379. 1875, 1904: glass,
380. 1876a, 1904: forlorn;
382. 1904: Oh I
     Am. eds.: O, I
400. 1876a: tale
401. 1876a: child)
419. Am. eds.: tangled clew
421. 1904: child—
424. 1904: in Paradise
451. 1904: patience.
463. Am. eds.: name,
465. 1875, 1904: workman Father;
469. 1904: grudge.
470. 1904: rather,
487. 1904: my Lady.
495. 1904: dead—
501. Am. eds.: before God,"—
503. 1904: nod.
508. Am. eds.: grave,"—
513. 1904: past, or
518. 1904: will.
521. Am. eds.: prayer,
522. Am. eds.: of Heaven,

526. 1904: youth,—
537. 1866a: any good man's name;
542. Am. eds.: grave,"—

544. Am. eds.: before God,"—
546. 1904: save.

DESPISED AND REJECTED.

[Composed October 10, 1864. Editions: *1866,* 1866a, 1875, 1876a, 1904. The notebook MS is in the British Library. In the MS every new line of a quotation begins with quotation marks.]

7. MS: That miscalled friends
8. MS: "Friend open
    1904: to Me.'—'Who
9. MS: Nay I
10. MS: hear.
11. MS: <Thy cry of hope or fear.>
    [The line is in pencil in Christina's handwriting.]
17. 1904: here?'
19. MS, 1904: comfort Me."—
20. 1904: 'I
22. 1904: thee.'
23. MS: see,

26. 1875, 1904: entreat my Face
29. MS: to Me."—
30. 1904: him: 'Cease,
34. MS: more
37. MS: yet?—
    1904: yet?'
38. 1904: urgently,
39. MS: to Me."—
41. MS: in."—
43. MS: thee."—
    1875, 1904: to Me, that
47. 1904: thee,—
48. MS: to Me."—

LONG BARREN.

[Composed February 21, 1865. Editions: *1866,* 1866a, 1875, 1876a, 1904. The notebook MS is in the British Library.]

Title. MS: Christ All in all.
1. MS: Thou Who didst <> tree
2. MS: My God for me,
3. MS: length

4. MS: Lord give
6. MS: Thou Who didst <> thorn
7. MS: scorn,
10. MS: be born.

IF ONLY.

[Composed February 20, 1865. Editions: *1866,* 1866a, 1875, 1876a, 1904. The notebook MS is in the British Library.]

Title. MS: If only!
1. 1875: If only I might love
    1904: If only I might love <> die!—
2. MS: live [illegible deletion] <on,>
3. MS: [*Although*] <Now when> the
    [The revision is in pencil in Christina's handwriting.]
5. MS, Am. eds.: high,
    1904: is lopt that
6. MS: how [*summer*] <Summer>
    glowed <> shone

1866, Am. eds., 1875, 1904: how summer glowed

7. MS: While [*autumn*] <Autumn> grips <> wan
    1866, Am. eds., 1904: While autumn grips
    1875: While autumn grips <> wan
9. 1866, Am. eds., 1875, 1904: When autumn passes <> must winter numb,

10. 1866, Am. eds., 1875: And winter
    may
    1904: And winter may <> while.
11. 1866, Am. eds., 1875, 1904: passes
    spring shall

12. 1866, Am. eds., 1875: that spring
    who
    1904: that spring who <> smile—
13. MS: Yea they
14. MS: Yea they

DOST THOU NOT CARE?

[Composed December 24, 1864. Editions: *1866*, 1866a, 1875, 1876a, 1904. The notebook MS is in the British Library. In the MS and 1904 text no words are italicized.]

Title. MS: Lord, dost Thou not care?
1. 1904: 'I
3. MS: Thou [*hidden in*] <veiled
   within> Thy [The revision is in
   pencil in Christina's handwriting.]
4. MS: Into Thy [*peace*] <shrine>
   which [The revision is in pencil in
   Christina's handwriting.]
   1875: [line indented four spaces]
   1904: shrine which
5. 1875: Dost thou not
6. 1904: ill?'—
7. 1904: 'I
8. MS: still.—
   1904: heart—lie still.'

9. 1904: 'Lord,
14. 1904: long?'—
15. 1904: 'I
16. MS: strong.—
    1904: heart—be strong.'
17. MS: 'Lie still' 'be strong' today: but,
    <> tomorrow;
    1904: 'Lie still, be strong, to-day:
    but,
20. 1904: sward,
22. 1904: sorrow?'—
23. 1904: 'Did
24. MS: thee? Leave Me tomorrow.—
    1904: thee? Leave Me to-morrow.'

WEARY IN WELL-DOING.

[Composed October 22, 1864. Editions: *1866*, 1866a, 1875, 1876a, 1904. The notebook MS is in the British Library. In the MS, only the second and fourth lines of each stanza are indented.]

Title. MS: "Weary in well-doing."
1. MS: have [*worked;*] <gone;> God
   <> me [*rest:*] <stay:>
2. MS: have [*gone;*] <worked;> God
   <> me [*stay.*] <rest.>
3. MS, 1904: to day;
4. Am. eds.: unexpressed,
   1904: yearnings unexprest,
6. MS: would [*rest;*] <stay;> God <>
   me [*work:*] <go:>

7. MS: would [*stay;*] <rest;> God <>
   me [*go.*] <work.>
8. MS: [illegible erasure] <He breaks
   my heart tossed to and fro;>
   1904: heart tost to <> fro;
9. MS: [illegible erasure] <My soul is
   wrung with doubts that lurk>
10. MS: [illegible erasure] <And vex
    it> so.
15. MS: with [*thee?*—] <Thee?—>

MARTYRS' SONG.

[Composed March 20, 1863. Editions: *1866,* 1866a, 1875, 1876a, 1904. The notebook MS is in the British Library. The poem was published in Orby Shipley (ed.), *Lyra Mystica: Hymns and Verses on Sacred Subjects, Ancient and Modern* (London: Longman, Green, Longman, Roberts, and Green, 1865), 427–29. In the MS and 1865 text the poem is written in two-line stanzas.]

1. MS: sorrow:
6. MS: us.—
12. MS, 1865: evermore:
14. MS: of heaven-content;
15. MS, 1865: or furnace fire,
    1904: flood or blood or
16. MS: desire.—
    1865: the Rest that
18. MS: bowed;
21. MS: Welcoming Angels these <> shine;
    1865: Welcoming Angels these
22. MS, 1865: own Angel, and
23. MS: night,
24. MS: right;
25. MS, 1865: day,
26. MS: slay.—
    1865, Am. eds.: the Devil keeps
28. 1865: lo! Who
    1904: lo Who
30. MS: upon His Hands:
    1865: upon His Hands;
    1904: hands:
31. MS: a Priest with God-uplifted Eyes,
    1865: with God-uplifted Eyes,
32. MS: us His Sacrifice:
34. MS: again:
35. MS, 1865: our own Champion, behold <> stand
36. MS: us at <> Hand.—
    1865: us at
37. 1865: us Grace
38. 1904: of Jesus' Face:
    1865: the Light of
40. MS, 1865: of Jesus' Heart.
41. 1875: up,
42. MS: cup.—
    1865: of Jesus' Cup.
43. MS: long:
    1865: and Life is
    1875, 1904: short, and
45. 1904: At His Word Who <> hither

46. MS: thither:
    1865: thither;
47. 1904: At His Word Who <> too
48. MS: [*The depth*] <Jordan> must <> us pass thro'. [The revision is in pencil in Christina's handwriting.]
    1865: us pass through.
49. Am. eds.: pang, searching
50. MS: then heaven for evermore.
    Am. eds.: then Heaven forevermore;
    1875, 1904: evermore:
52. MS: the Ark:
53. MS, 1865: by Christ His Grace,
54. MS: And then Christ <> to face.—
    1865: And then Christ <> ever Face to
55. MS: adore
56. MS: In Jesus' Name now <> evermore.
58. MS: the further bank.
    1865, 1866, 1866a: the further bank:
    1904: bank:
59. MS: the [*Spirit we all*] <Holy Ghost we> will praise [The revision is in pencil in Christina's handwriting.]
60. MS: In Jesus' Name unto endless days.—
    1865: In Jesus' Name, unto endless
    1875, 1904: In Jesus' name through
61–62. MS: <God Almighty, God Three & One,/God Almighty, God Alone.> [The lines are written in pencil in Christina's handwriting at the bottom of the page.]
62. 1865: God Almighty, God Alone.

AFTER THIS THE JUDGMENT.

[Composed December 12, 1856. Editions: *1866*, 1866a, 1875, 1876a, 1904. The notebook MS is in the British Library. The MS text follows a pattern of indentation in which, of every three lines, the second and third are indented.]

Title. MS: In Advent.

1. MS: [The following lines open the poem:]

> These roses are as perfect as of old,
>> Those lilies wear their selfsame
>>> sunny white,
>> I, only I, am changed and sad and
>>> cold;
> The morning star still glorifies the
>> night,
>> And musical that fountain in its swell
>> Casts as of old its waters to the light;
> Oh that I were a rose, so I might dwell
>> Contented in a garden on my thorn
>> Fulfilling mine appointed fragrance
>>> well;
> Or stainless lily in the summer morn
>> Tho' no man pluck it, yet the honey
>>> bee
>> Knows it for sweetness in its bosom
>>> born;
> Or that I were a star, from sea to sea
>> Guiding the seekers to their port of
>>> rest,
>> Guiding them till night's shuffling
>>> shadows flee;
> Or that I were a spring, to which
>> opprest
>> With desert drought, some wearied
>>> wayfarer
>> Comes from the barren regions of
>>> the west;—
> Then should I stand at peace and
>> should not err,
>> Or lighten and make beautiful the
>>> sky,
>> Or make more glad than
>>> frankincense and myrrh:
> But now it is not so; I, only I,
>> Am changed and sad and cold, while
>>> in my soul
>> The very fountain of delight is dry.

1. Am. eds.: eager home-bound traveller
2. MS: steadfast sailor on a wind tossed main,
4. MS: My fellow pilgrims pass me and
5. MS: That blessed mansion
   Am. eds.: peace,
6. MS: Where strong desire
   1904: pain.
7. MS: of unsatiate ease;
10. MS: passing angel, speed
    Am. eds.: O, passing
12. MS: strong:
13. Am. eds.: part,
15. Am. eds.: tenfold, hundred-fold, with
17. Am. eds.: Thousand, ten-thousand-fold, innumerable,
18. MS: one, yet
22. MS: of God, Which Thine
    1875: which thine own Self
    1904: Ah Love <> which thine own Self
24. MS: Love [*that*] <That> dost <> seven,—
26. 1904: in Thee;
33. MS: And have no
    1904: moan.
34. 1866, 1875, 1904: But thou, O
35. MS: waterflood,
36. MS: Life—death—until
38. MS: Of past sweet sin
    Am. eds.: grace,
39. MS: And often strengthened
40. MS: before Thy Face
    Am. eds.: face,
41. MS: from Thine Eyes repentance
    Am. eds.: hid,
42. MS: utmost justice stand in mercy's place:—
    1904: place?
46. MS: me;—while
    1866a: after star,
49. MS: moment,—when
50. MS: no night to
51. 1866, 1875: gazing-stock
53. Laid trembling
54. MS: moment must
    1904: tried.—
55. Am. eds.: Ah, Love
57. MS: of love Thine Own Love is,—
    1875, 1904: of love Thine own Love

58. MS: end,
59. MS: past,
60. MS: defend:
61. MS: Yea, seek with pierced Feet,
    yea, hold
62. MS: With pierced Hands Whose
    Wounds were
    1904: love.

65. 1875: while thou didst
67. MS: man,—while
68. MS: rod
69. MS: love,—not
70. 1875, 1904: mine, my God, my
    God!

GOOD FRIDAY.

[Composed April 20, 1862. Editions: *1866*, 1866a, 1875, 1876a, 1904. The notebook MS is in the British Library. The poem was published in Orby Shipley (ed.), *Lyra Messianica: Hymns and Verses on the Life of Christ, Ancient and Modern; with Other Poems* (London: Longman, Green, Longman, Roberts, and Green, 1864), 236-37.]

1. 1864: a Sheep
   1875, 1904: stone, and <> sheep,
2. 1875, 1904: beneath Thy cross,
3. MS: by drop [*thy*] <Thy> blood's
   slow
   1864: number Drop by Drop Thy
4. MS: [line indented four spaces]
5. MS: [illegible deletion] <Not so>
   those
   1864: those Women loved
8. MS: [line indented four spaces]
   1864: the Thief was

9. MS: the sun and moon
11. MS: noon:—
    Am. eds.: noon,—
    1875: [line indented two spaces]
12. MS: [line indented four spaces]
    1875: [line not indented]
13. MS: [*But*] <Yet> give
14. 1864: seek Thy Sheep, true <>
    the Flock;
15. 1875: [line indented two spaces]
16. MS: [line indented four spaces]
    1875: [line not indented]

THE LOWEST PLACE.

[Composed July 25, 1863. Editions: *1866*, 1866a, 1875, 1876a, 1904. The notebook MS is in the British Library.]

Title. MS: The lowest place.
1. 1904: place; not
3. MS: [line indented four spaces]

4. MS: [line indented six spaces]
7. MS: [line indented four spaces]
8. MS: [line indented six spaces]

BY THE SEA.

[Composed November 11, 1858. Editions: *1875*, 1876a, 1904. The notebook MS is in the British Library. The poem was published in *A Round of Days Described in Original Poems by Some of Our Most Celebrated Poets, and in Pictures by Eminent Artists*, engraved by the Dalziel Brothers (London: George Routledge and Sons, 1866), 68. It was also published in *Picture Posies: Poems Chiefly by Living Authors and Drawings by F. Walker et al.*, engraved by Brothers Dalziel (London and New York: George Routledge and Sons, 1874), 59. In the 1904 text, only the second line of each stanza is indented.]

Title. MS: A Yawn.
1. MS: [The following lines begin the poem:]

> I grow so weary: is it death
> This awful woful weariness?
> It is a weight to heave my breath,
> A weight to wake, a weight to sleep;
> I have no heart to work or weep.
>
> The sunshine teazes and the dark;
> Only the twilight dulls my grief:
> Is this the Ark, the strong safe Ark,
> Or the tempestuous drowning sea
> Whose crested coursers foam for me?

2. MS, 1866: from Heaven it (1882a), (1888a): moan.
3. MS, 1904: shore:
7. 1874: hid on its
8. MS: Salt passionless anemones
9. 1904: flower-like—just
10. MS: blow and propagate and thrive.
   1866, 1874: blow, and propagate, and
11. MS, 1904: curve or spot or
12. 1866, 1874: things Argus-eyed,
13. MS, 1904: alike yet
14. MS: pang and
15. MS: pang and
   1876a: pang,—and
15. MS: [The following lines close the poem:]

> I would I lived without a pang:
> Oh happy they who day by day
> Quiescent neither sobbed nor sang;
> Unburdened with a what or why
> They live and die and so pass by.

FROM SUNSET TO STAR RISE.

[Composed February 23, 1865. Editions: *1875*, 1876a, 1904. The notebook MS is in the British Library.]

Title. MS: Friends
   1904: FROM SUNSET TO RISE STAR
2. MS: friend but
   1904: cold;
6. MS: places, [illegible erasure] <hoard> your gold:
7. MS: wold
8. MS: and hungry on
10. MS: live alone and look
   1904: alone.
11. MS: sighs in the
   1876a: sedge,
12. MS: [line not indented] <> my [*buried*] <perished> years <> friends [*come*] <look> back, [The revisions are in pencil in Christina's handwriting.]
   1904: [line not indented]
13. MS, 1904: [line indented two spaces]
14. MS: [line not indented] [*Upon sweet*] <On sometime> summer's [The revision is in pencil in Christina's handwriting.]
   1904: [line not indented]

DAYS OF VANITY.

[Date of composition unknown. Editions: *1875*, 1876a, 1904. No MS known. The poem was published in *Scribner's Monthly*, V (November, 1872), 21.]

10. 1872: Summer-time brief,
   1904: brief,—
16. 1872: A sudden blast,
17. 1872: Lengthening shadow cast,—
   1904: cast,
21. 1872: that naught buyeth,
29. 1872: We pass out
   (1890), (1891), 1904: sight.—

ONCE FOR ALL./ (MARGARET.)

[Composed January 8, 1866. Editions: *1875*, 1876a, 1904. The notebook MS is in the British Library. The poem was published in *The Golden Sheaf: Poems Contributed by Living Authors*, ed. Charles Rogers (London: Houlston and Rogers, 1868), 192. In the MS every new line of a quotation begins with quotation marks.]

Title. MS: Once for all.
1. MS: said: "This <> rose."
   1868: said, "This <> rose."
2. MS: said: "I <> scent,
   1868: said, "I
   (1890), (1891), 1904: scent,
3. 1868: languishment;
4. MS, 1868: heart unclose."
5. MS: said: ["*The world*] <Old earth> has <> away [*its*] <her> snows, [The revisions are in pencil in Christina's handwriting.]
   1868: said, "Old <> snows;
   1876a: Old Earth has
8. MS: "In Autumn, the <> blows."
   1868: autumn; the <> blows."
   1876a: autumn; the
9. 1868: So, walking <> delight,
10. MS: upon [*a*] <one> sheltered

[The revision is in pencil in Christina's handwriting.]
   1868: sheltered, shadowed nook,
11. 1868: night;
12. MS: [line indented four spaces]
   1868: [line indented four spaces]
   <> sun.
13. MS: [line indented two spaces] <> answered: "Take <> took:
   1868: [line indented two spaces] <> answered, "Take <> took;
14. MS: [line indented four spaces] [*Death smites but*] <Winter nips> once <> all, for love is one." [The revision is in pencil in Christina's handwriting.]
   1868: [line indented four spaces] <> all, for love is one."

ENRICA, 1865.

[Composed July 1, 1865. Editions: *1875*, 1876a, 1904. The notebook MS is in the British Library. The poem was published in *A Round of Days Described in Original Poems by Some of Our Most Celebrated Poets, and in Pictures by Eminent Artists*, engraved by the Brothers Dalziel (London: George Routledge and Sons, 1866), 6. It was also published in *Picture Posies: Poems Chiefly by Living Authors and Drawings by F. Walker et al.*, engraved by Dalziel Brothers (London and New York: George Routledge and Sons, 1874), 50.]

Title. MS: E. F.
   1866, 1874: AN ENGLISH DRAWING-ROOM./ 1865.
1. MS, 1866: came amongst us
   1874: came amongst us <> South,
   1904: the South,
7. 1904: pale—
8. MS: She summer like and
   1874, 1904: She Summer-like and
9. MS: We Englishwomen trim,
10. 1875, 1876a: the self-same mould,
11. MS: of aspect cold,
   1874: Warm-hearted, but
12. MS: of self respect:

   1866: self-respect:
   1874: self-respect;
13. 1904: She, woman
14. MS, 1866: Less trammeled she
15. 1874: nature, not
16. MS: Warm hearted and
17. MS: for a while she
18. MS, 1866, 1874: Amongst us
19. 1874: forth,
20. MS, 1866: foam:
21. MS, 1866: sea
   1904: But, if
23. 1874: it, she
   1904: Rock-girt,—like

AUTUMN VIOLETS.

[Date of composition unknown. Editions: *1875*, 1876a, 1904. No MS known. The poem was published in *Macmillan's Magazine*, XIX (November, 1868), 84.]

2. (1890), (1891), 1904: grieves   7. 1868: with the stubble
4. 1904: and others' dropped

A DIRGE.

[Composed November 21, 1865. Editions: *1875*, 1876a, 1904. A fair copy (MS1) is in the Pierpont Morgan Library, and the notebook MS (MS2) is in the British Library. The poem was published in *The Argosy*, XVII (January, 1874), 25. In MS2 no lines are indented.]

1. MS1, MS2: falling?—   9. MS1, MS2: And the
3. MS1: are sweet in   10. MS1, MS2: the wheatfields are
4. MS1, MS2, 1904: Or at least when   turned to stubble,
7. MS1, MS2: cropping?—   1874: the wheat fields are
8. MS1, MS2: died when the leaves   11. MS1: And [illegible deletion] all
    are dropping,   12. MS1: For [*summer*] sweet

"THEY DESIRE A BETTER COUNTRY."

[Date of composition unknown. Editions: *1875*, 1876a, 1904. No MS known. The poem was published in *Macmillan's Magazine*, XIX (March, 1869), 422-23.]

Title. 1904: THEY <> COUNTRY   24. 1904: Lo this
3. 1869: past, for <> thank   30. 1904: remote;
15. 1869: thou far   32. 1869: near,
16. 1869: before,   36. 1869: fear,
21. 1869: sore
22. 1869: For the long journey that
    must make no

A GREEN CORNFIELD.

[Date of composition unknown. Editions: *1875*, 1876a, 1904. No MS known.]

Subtitle. 1876a: soar, and   8. 1876a: sank, and
7. 1904: soared,   12. 1904: stalks.

A BRIDE SONG.

[Date of composition unknown. Editions: *1875*, 1876a, 1904. No MS known. The poem was published in *The Argosy*, XIX (January, 1875), 25. In the 1904 text, lines 6, 8, 9, 11-21, 24, 25, 27-30, 34-36, 39, and 42 are indented two spaces; line 43 is indented four spaces; and the remaining lines are not indented.]

2. Jan. 1875: home,
3. Jan. 1875: roof,
15. Jan. 1875: tender,
17. 1904: opulent June

23. Jan. 1875, 1876a: feet,
33. 1876a: sand,
42-43. Jan. 1875: [written as one line]
43. 1876a: love!

CONFLUENTS.

[Date of composition unknown. Editions: *1875*, 1876a, 1904. No MS known.]

4. 1875, 1876a: [line indented four spaces]
12. 1876a: length:

18. 1904: free
20. 1904: thee.

THE LOWEST ROOM.

[Composed September 30, 1856. Editions: *1875*, 1876a, 1904. The notebook MS is in the British Library. The poem was published in *Macmillan's Magazine*, IX (March, 1864), 436-39. In the MS, single quotation marks are used throughout, and they appear only at the beginning and end of each quotation. All of the word revisions in the MS are written in pencil in Christina's handwriting.]

Title. MS: A fight over the body of Homer.
1864: SIT DOWN IN THE LOWEST ROOM.
1. MS: [The following lines open the poem; the stanzas are deleted with pencil lines:]

['*Amen: the sting of fear is past,*
Cast out and no more burdensome;
There can be no such pang as this
In all the years to come.]

[*No more such wrestlings in my soul,*
No more such heart-break out of sight,
From dawning of my longdrawn day
Until it draw to night.']

1-8. MS: [lines not in text]
5. 1876a: "Oh, what
9. MS: your [*grief? now*] [<*sorrow*>] <grief? now> tell me sweet,
10. MS: [*What is your grief?*'] <That I may grieve> my <> said,
12. MS: [*head;*] <head:>
14. MS: looked larger than
1904: own;
16. MS: a [*softer*] <tenderer> tone.
17. MS: ['*I may be second, but not first;*'] <Some must be second & not first>

18. MS: [*I*] <All?> cannot
19. MS: [*This weighs on me, this wearies me,*] [<*This is not*>] <Is not this too but vanity>
1904: this too but
21. MS: [*Just now too I have*] <So yesterday I> read
22. MS: each [*clashing*] <clangorous> king
23. MS: wrathful [*strong*] <great> Aeacides;—
25. MS: The [*happy*] <comely> face
26. MS: The [*white*] [<*swift*>] <deft> hand
1904: thread.
28. MS, 1904: sting,' she
29. MS: ['*He awes me like a* [*rushing*] <*snow swollen*> flood,] [<*He stirs my pulse like fiery wine*>] <He stirs my [illegible erasure] <sluggish> pulse like wine>
30. MS: spice;
31. MS: hand
32. MS: And [*grand*] [<*grave*>] <grand> like
34. MS: and tempest toss:—
35. MS: golden days
36. MS: [*But*] <Whilst> these

37. MS: laugh
38. MS: [*But*] <Yet> did <> her
    dextrous hand:
42. MS: might at least and
    1904: swords:
43. 1864: men, in <> fire,
44. MS: words.
    1876a: words,—
    1904: words—
45. MS: [*They fought with* [*arrow sword
    or spear,*] [*<weapons forged of
    men>*] *<weapons toughly forged>*]
    <Crest-rearing kings with [*goodly
    swords*] <whistling spears> >
47. MS: up hundred rooted trees
50. MS: the death grip grappling
51. MS: Whoever thought
56. MS: [After line 56 is the following
    stanza, deleted with pencil lines:]
    [*In famine, plague, disastrous war,—
    Oh shame to us in Christian lands—
    They poured libations to the Gods
        With faith and purest hands.*]
62. MS: strife,
65. 1864: sister laughed,
66. 1904: cloth,
68. MS: wife or slave or
70. MS: away;
71. MS: of night
74. MS: [*The mistress with her slave*]
    <Mistress & handmaiden> alike;
75. MS: [*Till purple fields of battle grew*]
    [*<The field grew purple to their
    hand>*] <Beneath their needles
    grew the field>
76. 1864: strike;
77. MS: Or look again: dim
78. MS: [*Dawned*] <Gleamed>
    perfect <> night:—
    1876a: night:
79. MS: [*Was this*] [*<Were these>*]
    <Were such> not
80. MS: [After line 80 is the following
    stanza, deleted with pencil lines:]
    [*They armed their hero for the war,
    They sent him forth to lose or gain,
    They met him in his triumph hour,
        Or sought him on the plain.*]
81. MS: shame [*is this,*] <it is,> our
    1875, 1876a, 1904: life;
84. MS: steed:
    1904: steed,

88.–111. MS: [The notebook page
    containing these lines is missing
    from the notebook.]
98. 1904: glass;
109. 1876a: said;
114. MS, 1904: length;
115. 1876a, 1904: not I,
119. MS: dooms [*you, you shall*] [*<me I
    should>*] <me I shall> only
120. MS: second not
121. MS: old Homer if <> will
122. 1864: his Books have
126. MS: life till death effulge their
    1864: life till death enlarge
    1904: span;
130. MS: man, who half <> god
131. MS: rest
132. MS: [After line 132 are the fol-
    lowing stanzas, deleted with pen-
    cil lines:]
    [*When he withdrew his wrath was just
        By the coarse tyrant richly earned:
    But tenfold, tender, self-devote
        His love when he returned.*]

    [*Of heavenly stature, crowned with strength
        With beauty like the heavenly host,
    He thundered on the astonished war
        Down hurling ghost to ghost.*]
135. MS: [*Beasts,*] [*<Steeds,>*]
    <Beasts,> Trojans, adverse
    Gods, himself,
136. MS: [*Filled*] <Heaped> up
139. MS: man the
    1864: men,
141. MS: acorns tusky
144. MS: [After line 144 are the fol-
    lowing stanzas, deleted with pen-
    cil lines:]
    [*His love just balances his hate;
        His strength remains not good nor sin:
    Shall we revere mere strength? as well
        Revere a steam-engine.*]
    [*That grim ally of brittle faith:
        We tolerate its lines and posts
    In doubt if it will serve our turn
        Or turn us too to ghosts.'*]
145. MS: met
146. MS: jeer:
147. 1875, 1904: rose; "I
148. 1875, 1904: low; "Forgive
149. MS: me these days seem [*happy*]
    <pleasant> days,

150. MS: This home
153. MS: Homer tho' <> his Gods
156. MS: [After line 156 are the following stanzas, deleted with pencil lines:]

[*Glutted with glory, lapped in love,*
  Achilles died, the story saith;
Christ thro' long hours for mocking foes
  Died a dishonoured death:]

[*Achilles perished for his friend,*
  He slaughtered foes and built a name;
Oh what is glory such as his
  To Christ's most glorious shame?' —]

157. MS: much-moved [*passion*] <pathos> of
159. MS: [*All flushed,*] <Grown pale,> confessed
160. 1876a: speak.
163. 1876a: spoke,
164. MS, 1876a: said:
166. MS: glad or wise or
171. MS: selfish souring
     1904: discontent,
173. MS: smiled half bitter half
175. MS: for [*a motto to the world,*] <his summary of life>
176. MS: *Vanity of vanities.*
177–178. MS: [*Lo the race is not to the swift* —/ *There's nothing new beneath the sun* —] < Beneath the sun there's nothing new—/ Men flow men ebb mankind flows on>
179. MS: If I am [*weary of my life*] [<*wearied of the world*>] <wearied of my life>
180. 1876a: Why, so
181. MS: vanities, he [*said*] <preached>
182. MS: sought;
188. MS: [After line 188 is the following stanza, deleted with pencil lines:]

[*Vanity and emptiness, the curse*
  Of ours and every other age;
Vanity of vanities, the text
  Of prophet, poet, sage.]

193. MS: this:
194. MS: die:—
197. MS: [*This time she scarcely answered me,*] < She scarcely answered when I paused>
     1875, 1904: paused

199. MS: here,'—lowvoiced and loving—'yea
     1904: loving, 'yea,
200. MS: than Solomon.'—
203. MS: [*Like Spring into the garden walks*] <Into the garden walks like Spring>
     1904: like Spring,
204. MS: All [*rosy*] <gracious> with content:
     1864: content,
     1876a: content:
205. MS: wont
207. MS: Not [*singing*] <warbling> quite
210. MS: Yet [*now and then*] <all the while> with
     1864: Yet all the
211. MS: flowers,
212. MS: wise;
214. MS: teach:
215. MS: [*Sweet*] <Fresh> rose
216. MS: Than [*blossoms*] <blossom> of
217. MS: myself
218. 1864, 1875, 1876a, 1904: the self-same nest:
220. MS: digest.—
223. MS: [*Mine eyes were dry, but cheek and lip*] < Till all the opulent summer world>
224. MS: [*Were paler*] <Seemed poorer> than
225. MS: busy hands [*were stilled,*] <fell slack>
226. MS: came;—
     1875, 1876a, 1904: came:
227. MS: the [*walk*] [<*turf*>] <walk>
229. MS: Well twenty
230. MS: now a
232. MS: life.
233. MS: of [*happy*] <prosperous> life
234. MS: grief or fear or fret;
235. MS: [*Beloved*] <She loved> and
     1864: She loved, and, loving
236. MS: [*Beloved*] <Is loved> and
237. MS: husband, honourable,
238. MS: world;
240. MS, 1876a: golden-curled:
244. MS: love [*had*] <has> been.
245. MS: Yet tho' <> charity

246. MS: And [*in her home*] <to her own> most
248. MS: the [*true*] <home> land of
     1876a: love.
250. MS: She like [*the*] <a> vine is full <> fruit;
     1864: She like <> vine is full <> fruit;
251. MS: Her passion flower climbs up toward
     1864: Her passion-flower climbs up toward
     1875, 1876a: heaven,
252. MS: Tho' earth <> binds [*the*] <its> root.
255. MS: she a kind [*lighthearted*] <light-hearted> girl
     1904: kind light-hearted
256. MS: [*Sorted*] <Gathered> our garden flowers,
     1876a: flowers:
     1904: flowers,
257. MS: Her [*look just shadowed*] [<*brightness shadowed*>] <song just mellowed> by
258. MS: having teazed me
259. MS: Then all forgetful, as She heard
260. MS: [*The*] <One> step
261. MS: [*While*] <Whilst> I? <> watched:
     1864: watched
262. MS: life to <> alone;
     1864: alone,
263. MS: interests

264. 1876a: felt, but
265. MS: first—how
267. MS: Line [*laid*] <graven> on <> on stroke,
     1876a: on stroke:
     1904: on stroke,
268. MS: But thank God learned
268. MS: [After line 268 are the following stanzas, deleted with pencil lines:]

     [*Still worn indeed I am and pale,*
     Yet lightened of a clog of care;
     Contented with my goodly lot,
     * For God has placed me there:*]

     [*Rejoicing at my sister's joy,*
     In sympathy with young and old,
     Feeding and trimming mine own fire
     * Tho' all the world wax cold:*]

     [*No longer bitter with my friend*
     Who cannot guess what I conceal,
     Who cannot bind the secret sore
     * I never own to feel:*]

269. MS: [*Learning*] [<*I strive*>] <So now> in patience [*to*] <I> possess
270. MS: after [*long drawn*] <tedious> year;
271. MS: [*Learning*] [<*I bend*>] <Content> to <> place
273. MS: sometimes when
274. MS: weak and
277. MS: Yea sometimes
278. MS: Toward the Archangelic trumpet burst,
279. MS: shown

DEAD HOPE.

[Composed March 15, 1865. Editions: *1875*, 1876a, 1904. The notebook MS is in the British Library. The poem was published in *Macmillan's Magazine*, XVIII (May, 1868), 86.]

Title. MS: An End.
 1. 1904: Hope newborn one
 2. MS, 1904: even:
 4. MS: in Heaven.
    1904: No not
 6. MS: away!
    1904: away—
 7. MS: buried [*in his grave*] <[*in the earth*]> <underground> [The re-

visions are in pencil in Christina's handwriting.]
 9. MS, 1904: is dead and gone,
10. MS: [line not indented]
14. 1904: [stanza break after line 14]
15–18. 1876a: [lines not in text]
16. MS: even:
18. MS: in Heaven.
    1904: No not

A DAUGHTER OF EVE.

[Composed September 30, 1865. Editions: *1875,* 1876a, 1904. The notebook MS is in the British Library.]

Title. MS: An Awakening.
  1. MS: noon
  3. MS: moon,
  6. MS: My garden plot I

   7. MS: all-forsaken
 11. MS, 1876a: future spring
 13. 1876a: and every thing,

SONG. ["Oh what comes over the sea"]

[Composed June 11, 1866. Editions: *1875,* 1876a, 1896, 1904. The notebook MS is in the British Library. In the 1896 version, lines 1, 3, 5, 7, and 9 are indented two spaces; lines 2, 6, 10, and 12 are indented four spaces; and lines 4, 8, and 11 are not indented.]

Title. MS, 1896: WHAT COMES?
  1. MS: sea
  2. 1896: past:
  3. MS: me

  6. 1896: blast:
  7. MS: me
 11. MS: me

VENUS'S LOOKING-GLASS.

[Composed October, 1872. Editions: *1875,* 1876a, 1904. No MS known. The poem was published in *The Argosy,* XV (January, 1873), 31.]

Title. 1873: TWO SONNETS./ I./
    VENUS'S LOOKING-GLASS.
    1876a: VENUS' LOOKING-GLASS.
  4. 1904: ground, and
  5. 1873: snort
  9. 1876a: in spring. Through summer
    heat
    1904: in Spring. Through summer
    heat

 11. 1875: [line indented two spaces]
    1876a: [line indented two spaces]
    <> flushed autumn through
 14. 1875, 1876a: [line indented two spaces]
    1904: toil, and laught and

LOVE LIES BLEEDING.

[Date of composition unknown. Editions: *1875,* 1876a, 1904. No MS known. The poem was published in *The Argosy,* XV (January, 1873), 31.]

Title. 1873: TWO SONNETS./ II./
    LOVE LIES BLEEDING.
  1. 1904: Love, that
  4. 1904: grey;
  7. 1875, 1876a: afterglow thrown <>
    from long set days,
    1904: afterglow thrown

  8. 1904: music past away.
 10. 1873: [line not indented]
 11. 1873: [line indented two spaces]
    1904: dead but
 12. 1873: [line not indented]
    1875, 1876a: then heart sick,
 13. 1873: [line indented two spaces]

BIRD RAPTURES.

[Date of composition unknown. Editions: *1875*, 1876a, 1904. No MS known.]

  3. 1876a: moonrise, every thing   4. 1876a: pale:

MY FRIEND.

[Composed December 8, 1857. Editions: *1875*, 1876a, 1904. The notebook MS is in the British Library. The poem was published in *Macmillan's Magazine*, XI (December, 1864), 155.]

  1. MS: hair
  2. 1875, 1904: eyes;
  3. MS: pale deaf blind she lies
  4. MS: pale but still
  5. MS: her yet not <> alone:
  9. MS: Weep not O friends, <> not weep,

11. MS: breast
14. 1875, 1876a: above;
    1904: above.
15. MS: Today as <> walked let <> love,
    (1890), (1891), 1904: love:

TWILIGHT NIGHT.

[Part I composed August 26, 1864. Part II composed June 25, 1863. Editions: *1875*, 1876a, 1904. Part II is in the 1896 edition. The notebook MS of Part I (MS1) and the notebook MS of Part II (MS2) are in the British Library. Part I originally comprised lines 71–85 of the notebook version of "Songs in a Cornfield." "Twilight Night" was published in *The Argosy*, V (January 1, 1868), 103. In MS1, only the first and third lines of each stanza are indented. In MS2 Christina wrote the revisions in pencil, and William Michael Rossetti later went over them in pencil to make them more legible. In the 1896 text the second and fifth lines of each stanza in Part II are indented five spaces, and the fourth line of each stanza is indented two spaces. In Part I of the 1904 text, only the second and fourth lines of each stanza are indented.]

Title. MS1: Songs in a Cornfield.
    MS2: Tomorrow?
    1896: TO-MORROW
  1. MS1, 1904: met hand
  2. MS1: Clasped hands together close and fast,
  3. MS1, 1904: stand:
  4. MS1: past.
    1904: past;
  5. MS1: Come day, come night, night comes
  7. MS1: from face,
    1904: from face:
  9. 1876a: pace:
12. MS1: If both by chance should not forget,

13. MS1: We should shake hands <> way
14. 1875, 1904: met,
18. MS2, 1896: over lane and lea
20. MS2: O care-less swallow,
    1876a: swallow!
22. MS2, 1896, 1904: Alas that
23. 1896, 1904: asunder!
24. MS2: to days, and days and days [*drone*] <creep> by;
    1896: by:
25. MS2: with [*wearied*] <wistful> eye,
27. MS2: will [*the*] <that> day <> nigh, [*the*] <that> hour
    1896: day draw nigh, that
28. MS2: yesterday; and

1875, 1876a, 1904: and not I think
to-day;
1896: and not I think to-day:
30. 1875, 1876a: "to-morrow," thus
1904: after day 'To-morrow' thus

32. 1896: sorrow;
33. MS2: the [*selfsame*] <accustomed>
way.

A BIRD SONG.

[Date of composition unknown. Editions: *1875,* 1876a, 1904. A fair copy MS is in
the Yale University Library. The poem was published in *Scribner's Monthly,* V
(January, 1873), 336.]

Title. MS: A [*bird*] <Bird> Song.
1873: A BIRD-SONG.
1. MS: Its a
2. 1873: Oh! last summer, green
1876a: Oh, last
3. 1904: bluer!
4. MS: It's well nigh summer,
1873: It's well-nigh summer, for
<> swallow;

5. MS: swallow his
6. 1875, 1876a: The bird race
quicken
1904: quicken, and
7. 1873: Oh, happy swallow, whose
8. MS: hollow!—I'd
1875, 1876a, 1904: swallow,
9. 1873: build, this weather, one <>
together!

A SMILE AND A SIGH.

[Composed February 14, 1866. Editions: *1875,* 1876a, 1904. The notebook MS is
in the British Library. The poem was published in *Macmillan's Magazine,* XVIII
(May, 1868), 86.]

3. MS: sweet love making, harmless
sport,
4. MS: treasure,
1868: Love, that
5. MS: Love treasure

7. 1876a: Long, long
8. MS: song:—
1904: song.
9. MS: lags who should <> flying
1868: lags who should

AMOR MUNDI.

[Composed February 21, 1865. Editions: *1875,* 1876a, 1904. The notebook MS is
in the British Library. The poem was published in *The Shilling Magazine,* II (June,
1865), 193. In the MS no lines are indented and the revisions are in pencil in
Christina's handwriting.]

Title. 1865: "AMOR MUNDI."
1. 1865: "Oh, where
1875, 1876a: "O where <>
flowing,
1904: flowing,
2. MS: the [*spice-wind*] <west wind>
blowing <> track?"—
3. 1865: me an' it

4. MS: back."—
5. MS: weather
6. MS: The [*breezy sweet-breathed*]
<honey breathing> heather <>
right:
9. MS: where [*thin*] <grey>
cloud-flakes <> seven
1865, 1875, 1876a: "Oh, what

10. MS: skirt?"—
11. MS: dumb portentous,
    1865: "Oh, that's <> portentous,—
    1875, 1876a: "Oh, that's
12. MS: An undecyphered solemn <>
    hurt."—
    1865: An undecipher'd solemn
13. 1865, 1875, 1876a: "Oh, what
14. MS: sickly?"—"A scale-clad
    hooded worm."—
    1875, 1904: sickly." "A
15. MS: hollow so <> follow?"—
    1865, 1875, 1876a: "Oh, what's
16. MS: "Oh there's a <> term."—
    1865: "Oh, that's <> th' eternal
    term."
    1875, 1876a: "Oh, that's

17. MS: "Turn again O <> sweetest,
    turn again false <> fleetest,
18. MS: This way whereof thou
    weetest I <> track."—
    1865: This way whereof thou
    weetest I
    1875: beatest, I
    1904: beatest, I fear, is
19. MS: "Nay too steep [*thy*] <for>
    hill-mounting, nay too late [*thy*]
    1865: hill-mounting,—nay,
    1875, 1876a, 1904: for hill
    mounting; nay, <> for cost
    counting:
20. MS: easy but <> back."—

THE GERMAN-FRENCH CAMPAIGN.

[Date of composition unknown. Editions: *1875*, 1876a, 1904. No MS known.]

Title. Part I. 1904: THY <> CRIETH
19. 1876a: weeping,
    1904: dust and weeping,
21. 1904: measure
35. 1904: the Lord:
40. 1876a: fair France!

44. 1876a: Sister France!
52. 1876a, 1904: "France, France,
    France!"
54. 1904: blood;
58. 1904: chain:

A CHRISTMAS CAROL.

[Date of composition unknown. Editions: *1875*, 1876a, 1904. No MS known. The
poem was published in *Scribner's Monthly*, III (January, 1872), 278. In the 1872
text the stanzas are numbered 1-5.]

2. 1872: moan;
9. 1872: Our God, heaven cannot
   1875: hold Him,
10. 1872: sustain,
15. 1872: The Lord God Almighty—
17. 1872: whom Cherubim
    1904: for Him, whom
21. 1872: whom Angels
    1904: for Him, whom
25. 1872: and Archangels

27. 1872: and Seraphim
28. 1872, 1904: Thronged the air;
29. 1872: only His Mother
31. 1872: Worshiped the
    1876a: Worshipped her Beloved
34. 1872: am?—
35. 1872: a Shepherd
36. 1872: lamb;
37. 1872, 1904: a Wise Man
39. 1872: give Him,—

CONSIDER.

[Composed May 7, 1863. Editions: *1875*, 1876a, 1904. The notebook MS is in the
British Library. The poem was published in *Macmillan's Magazine*, XIII (January,

1866), 232. In the MS, lines 1, 3, 4, 6, 8, 10, 11, 13, 14, 16, 18, and 20 are indented
two spaces. In the 1866 text, lines 1, 6, 11, and 16 are indented eight spaces and
lines 3, 4, 8, 10, 13, 14, 18, and 20 are indented four spaces.]

2. MS, 1904: brief:
   1875: brief;—
4. MS: we drop away,
   1904: away
5. MS: We fade as doth a leaf.
7. 1904: account;
8. MS: Yet God
9. MS: mount;

10. MS: guards them too.
14. MS: all our care
15. MS: all our coil?—
17. MS: harvest-weeks,
18. MS: food:
19. MS: Sure then He seeks
20. MS: To do us also good.

BY THE WATERS OF BABYLON. / B.C. 570.

[Composed June 29, 1864. Editions: *1875,* 1876a, 1904. The notebook MS is in
the British Library. The poem was published in *Macmillan's Magazine,* XIV (Oc-
tober, 1866), 424–26.]

Title. MS: In Captivity.
1. MS: Here where <> dwell I <>
   [*bone,*] <bone;>
   1866: Here where <> dwell I
4. MS: me which
6. MS: man, and
8. MS: me as
9. MS: dumb-struck sore-bested and
   1866: dumb-struck, sore-bested
   and
14. MS: toward Jerusalem;
15. MS: His Heart is
16. MS: His Ears against
17. MS: His Hand He
18. MS: His Law is
19. MS: we as
20. MS: dark
21. MS: Are [illegible erasure]
   <outcast> from His Presence which
25. MS: manifest,
27. MS: we oppressed
29. MS: hissing, and
34. MS: Here [*while*] <where> I [The
   revision is in pencil in Christina's
   handwriting.]
   1876a: sit, my
35. MS: home-land I must see <>
   more
   1866: home-land I must see
38. MS: my figtree and <> vine
41. MS: my harvest field
42. (1890), (1891): wine
   1904: wine.
47. 1876a: dogs; whom
48. MS: clean

49. MS: land [*that*] <which> spewed
   [The revision is in pencil in Chris-
   tina's handwriting.]
51. 1876a: fathers dote:
52. MS: away,
53. MS: wives,
55. MS: live remote <> help
   dishonoured lives
56. MS: song
57. 1876a: gyves—
59. MS, 1904: twice accurst
60. MS: the accursed throng:
61. MS: heart [illegible erasure]
   <that> is
62. MS: plain
66. MS: but once again.
   1866: again.
   1876a: find him once
68. 1876a: wrath.
69. MS: Yet [*this*] <This> is
75. MS, 1904: Stablished for
76. MS: O Lord remember David and
77. MS: The [*glory*] <Glory> hath
78. MS: now before
81. MS: good, [*o*] <O> God our
   [*god:*—] <God:—>
   1904: good, O God our
82. MS: it
83. MS: hide Thy Face
84. MS: from Thy Book <> writ,
   1904: writ,
85. 1866: praise,
87. MS: [line indented two spaces]
   1866: days,
88. MS: [line not indented]

PARADISE.

[Composed February 28, 1854. Editions: *1875*, 1876a, 1904. The notebook MS (MS1) is in the Bodleian Library and a fair copy (MS2) is in the Yale University Library.]

Title. MS1, MS2: Easter Even.
  3. MS1, MS2: than any eyes
  4. MS1, MS2: of our's.
  5. MS1: the perfume bearing rose
     MS2: the perfume bearing rose,
  6. MS1, MS2: stem
  7. 1904: violet,
  9. MS1, MS2: of Paradise;
10. MS1: bird was singing <> place,
     MS2: bird was singing
12. MS1, MS2: It rose like
14. MS1, MS2: trees;
     1876a: Soft-cooing notes
17. MS1, MS2: fourfold river flow
18. MS1, MS2: And fair it was with
20. MS1, MS2: music sweet and slow.

25. MS1, MS2: The tree of life was budding there
30. MS1, MS2: feed;
31. 1876a: taste,
33. MS1, MS2: called Beautiful,
     1904: the Gate called
35. MS1, MS2: begin
37. MS1, MS2: harps—oh <> stars—
38. MS1, MS2: branches many leaved—
     1876a: O green
40. 1876a: conceived!
45. MS1, MS2: feet,
     1904: all heaven beneath
47. MS1, MS2: the Saints

MOTHER COUNTRY.

[Composed February 7, 1866. Editions: *1875*, 1876a, 1904. The notebook MS is in the British Library. The MS revisions are in pencil in Christina's handwriting. The poem was published in *Macmillan's Magazine*, XVIII (March, 1868), 403–404.]

Title. MS: Mother country.
  3. MS: country
  5. MS: country
  7. MS: Its [*peacocks*] <spices> and cedars
  9. 1904: dreaming,
10. MS: land,
     1868: land:
12. MS: strand
13. MS, 1868: With its bowing
14. MS, 1868: And its shining
19. MS: plumage,
20. MS: song
23. MS: I [*see*] <mark> the
25. MS: here
26. MS: [*And*] <Or> what
29. MS: Here death's hand
33. MS: handmaid

34. MS: [*And*] <Or> what
36. MS: the [*grass*] <turf> is
38. MS: seen,
39. 1875: never,
44. 1876a: clod;
54. 1875, 1904: strong:
55. 1875, 1876a, 1904: of,
57. 1904: of,—
58. 1875, 1876a, 1904: begun;
59. MS: yesterday
60. MS: run,
61. MS: Life new born with <> morrow
63. MS: ever,
64. MS: [*Or undone undone.*] <Undone, undone.>
66. MS: breath
71. MS: vanities

"I WILL LIFT UP MINE EYES UNTO THE HILLS."

[Composed February 1, 1856. Editions: *1875*, 1876a, 1896, 1904. The notebook MS is in the Bodleian Library. The poem was published in Orby Shipley (ed.), *Lyra Eucharista: Hymns and Verses on the Holy Communion, Ancient and Modern; with Other Poems* (London: Longman, Green, Longman, Roberts, and Green, 1863), 167–68; 2nd ed. (1864), 206–8. In the MS the even-numbered lines are indented two spaces and the odd-numbered lines are not indented. In the 1896 text, lines 9, 21, 33, 34, 41, 43, 45, and 47 are not indented; lines, 1, 3, 5, 7, 10, 12, 13, 15, 17, 19, 22, 24, 25, 27, 29, 31, 35–37, 39, 46, and 48 are indented two spaces; and the remaining lines are indented four spaces. In the 1896 and 1904 texts the words of the saints and Jesus are enclosed in quotation marks.]

Title. MS: "Now [*we*] <they> desire a better country."
1863: Conference between Christ, the Saints, and the Soul./ *Come up hither, and I will shew thee things which must be hereafter.*
1864, 1896: Conference between Christ, the Saints, and the Soul.
1904: I <> HILLS

1. MS: desire
4. MS: day.
1863: day:
8. MS, 1896: hills.
1863, 1864: On th' everlasting hills.
9. 1863, 1864, 1896: the Saints—There <> us,
11. MS: in Jesus
1863, 1864, 1896: say—We
12. 1875, 1876a, 1904: day or night.
13. 1863, 1864, 1896: My Soul saith—I
14. 1863, 1896: gained;
15. 1863: spent, yet <> bought;
16. MS: attained.
1863: laboured, but <> attained:
17. MS: to rise and grow
1863, 1864: to rise and
19. MS, 1896: lo
1863: lo,
20. MS, 1863, 1864, 1896: crown.
21. 1863, 1864: the Saints—Fresh Souls increase
1896: the Saints—"Fresh
22. 1864, 1896: languish nor recede.
23. MS: our Jesus
1863, 1864, 1896: say—We
27. MS: love
1864: out Love,

28. MS: death.
1863: death:
1864: Nor escape from Death;
1896: Nor escape
30. MS: Yet mock <> name,
1863: name,
31. 1863, 1864: best belovèd die
1875, 1904: die,
1876a: best belovèd die,
1896: My best-beloved die
32. MS, 1863, 1864, 1896: them.
33. MS, 1904: us
1863, 1864, 1896: the Saints—No
35. MS, 1904: in Jesus
1863, 1864, 1896: say—We
36. 1863, 1864: once dièd for
37. MS, 1904: Oh my
1863, 1864: Oh, my Soul, she
1896: Oh my Soul she <> wings,
39. 1864: immortal Things
40. MS, 1896: day.
1863, 1864: the Heavenly day:
41. 1904: faints:
42. MS, 1863, 1864, 1896: me?
43. MS: see; say the Saints:
1863, 1864, 1896: see—say
1904: the Saints;
44. 1863, 1864, 1896: Saith Jesus—Come
45. 1863, 1864: the Saints—His Pleasures please
1896: the Saints—"His
47. MS: taste [*my*] <My> sweets; saith
1863, 1896: sweets—saith Jesus—
1864: taste My Sweets—saith Jesus—

"THE MASTER IS COME, AND CALLETH FOR THEE."

[Date of composition unknown. Editions: *1875*, 1876a, 1904. No MS known.]

Title. 1904: THE <> THEE   19. 1904: loveth

WHO SHALL DELIVER ME?

[Composed March 1, 1864. Editions: *1875*, 1876a, 1904. The notebook MS is in the British Library. The poem was published in *The Argosy,* I (February, 1866), 288. In the MS the first line of each stanza is indented two spaces.]

Title. MS: Who shall deliver me?
4. MS: myself:
7. MS: myself
8. MS: out: but
16. MS: myself;
18. MS, 1876a: ease and rest and
24. MS: [After line 24 are the following lines; the revision in the fourth line is in pencil in Christina's handwriting:]

Lord, I had chosen another lot;
But then I had not chosen well,
Only [*thy*] <Thy> choice for me is
     good:
No [*different*] <diverse> lot in
     Heaven or Hell
Had blessed me, rightly understood;
None other, which Thou orderest not.

"WHEN MY HEART IS VEXED, I WILL COMPLAIN."

[Date of composition unknown. Editions: *1875*, 1876a, 1904. No MS known.]

Title. 1904: VEXED I
1. 1904: me—
2. 1875, 1876a, 1904: whom thou settest
15. 1904: love who,
19. 1876a: died
    1904: Alas thou
21. 1904: I, blessèd, for <> counted curst,
23. 1904: [line indented two spaces]

26. 1876a, 1904: am Thine;
27. 1904: lo Thy
29. 1904: me? Speak and
31. 1904: breath,
32. 1876a, 1904: own—deep
33. 1875, 1876a: to my beloved
    1904: sleep—
34. 1904: death.
35. 1904: patience: sweet <> be:
36. 1904: Yea thou

AFTER COMMUNION.

[Composed February 23, 1866. Editions: *1875*, 1876a, 1904. The notebook MS is in the British Library. The poem was published in Robert H. Baynes (ed.), *The Illustrated Book of Sacred Poems* (London and New York: Cassell, Petter, and Galpin, [1867], 8.]

1. MS, 1867: call Thee Lord Who
2. MS, 1867: call Thee Friend Who
3. MS: Or King Who art mine only Spouse above,
    1867: art mine only Spouse above,

4. MS, 1867: call Thy sceptre in my
5. 1904: Lo now
6. MS: nod;
    1867: nod,
7. MS: lit Thy Flame in

9. MS: in [*our*] <Our> home above
    1867: above
11. 1867: [line indented two spaces]
13. MS: upon Thy Breast:

1867: [line indented two spaces]
    <> breast—
14. 1867: [line not indented]

SAINTS AND ANGELS.

[Date of composition unknown. Editions: *1875*, 1876a, 1904. No MS known.]

18. 1876a: over;
22. 1876a: Solomon, wrote
30. 1904: sure;

31. 1904: sun,
38. 1876a, 1904: gate appall?

A ROSE PLANT IN JERICHO.

[Date of composition unknown. Editions: *1875*, 1876a, 1904. No MS known. The poem was published in F. G. Lee (ed.), *Lyrics of Light and Life* (London: Basil Montagu Pickering, 1875), 11–12.]

7. (1890), (1891): to Thee
    1904: to Thee,

11. 1876a: Wilt thou not

Appendixes to Volume I

A. Table of Editions and Reprints

In order to be certain that the absence of end-of-line punctuation was not the result of imperfect inking in each printed text recorded in the notes, I collated several copies of each text. A complete list including anthologies, journals, newspapers, and other works containing authoritative texts that are used in this volume would be very long; the list below is therefore limited to the editions and reprints of collections of Christina Rossetti's poems. An *a* after the date of publication indicates an American edition and parentheses enclose the dates of reprints. Reprints are cited in the textual notes only where they show a new variant; the variants designated 1862p and 1896s are recorded only if they differ from the first editions published in those years (p = page proof, s = special edition).

1862   *Goblin Market and Other Poems.* London: Macmillan, 1862.
        Yale University Library, Zeta Ip R734 862
        Princeton University Library, Ex 3913.1.339
        University of Texas Library, STARK 7229

1862p   *Goblin Market and Other Poems.* London: Macmillan, 1862. Christina's page proofs, bound, with her pencil corrections.
        University of Texas Library, HANLEY R734g

1865   *Goblin Market and Other Poems,* 2nd ed. London: Macmillan, 1865.
        Harvard University Library, Typ 805.65.7520
        University of Texas Library, 61-226
        Princeton University Library, 3913.1.339

1866   *The Prince's Progress and Other Poems.* London: Macmillan, 1866.
        Louisiana State University Library, 828 R734pr
        Princeton University Library, Ex 3913.1.373
        University of Texas Library, Wp R734 866p and Sitwell 758 AC

1866a   *Poems.* Boston: Roberts Brothers, 1866.
        Harvard University Library, 23473.26.18A and 23473.26.18B
        Stanford University Library, 821.6 R831ro
        Princeton University Library, 3913.1.1866

(1872a)   *Poems*. Boston: Roberts Brothers, 1872.
          Library of Congress, PR5237.A1.1872
          Princeton University Library, Ex 3913.1.1872

1875   *Goblin Market, The Prince's Progress, and Other Poems*. London:
          Macmillan, 1875.
          British Library, 11647.ff.28
          Princeton University Library 3913.1.339.12

(1879)   *Goblin Market, The Prince's Progress, and Other Poems*. London:
          Macmillan, 1879.
          Harvard University Library, 23473.24

(1888)   *Goblin Market, The Prince's Progress, and Other Poems*. London:
          Macmillan, 1888.
          Princeton University Library, Ex 3913.1.339.1888

1876a   *Poems*. Boston: Roberts Brothers, 1876.
          Harvard University Library, 23473.26.19

(1882a)   *Poems*. Boston: Roberts Brothers, 1882.
          British Library, 11609.dd.18.

(1888a)   *Poems*. Boston: Roberts Brothers, 1888.
          Harvard University Library, 23473.26.20A
          Library of Congress, PR5237.A1.1888

(1890)   *Poems, New and Enlarged Edition*. London and New York: Mac-
          millan, 1890.
          Harvard University Library, KD 5818 Hilles Library
          Princeton University Library, 3913.1.1890

(1891)   *Poems, New and Enlarged Edition*. London and New York: Mac-
          millan, 1891.
          Harvard University Library, KPD 5493

(1892)   *Poems, New and Enlarged Edition*. London and New York: Mac-
          millan, 1892.
          Princeton University Library, Ex 3913.1.1892

1893   *Goblin Market*. Illustrated by Laurence Housman. London:
          Macmillan, 1893.
          Harvard University Library, Lowell 1753.4.3 and
             WKR 22.1.10
          University of Texas Library, Wp R734 862 gc
          Princeton University Library, NE 910.G7H76.1893 (SAP)

1896   *New Poems, Hitherto Unpublished or Uncollected*. Edited by William
          Michael Rossetti. London: Macmillan, 1896.
          Harvard University Library, Keats *EC8 K2262 Za895rb
          Princeton University Library, 3913.1.367
          University of Texas Library, ApR 734 896nba

1896s   *New Poems, Hitherto Unpublished or Uncollected.* Edited by William
Michael Rossetti. London: Macmillan, 1896. Special edition of
one hundred large paper copies printed in January, 1896.
      Princeton University Library, 3913.1.367.11 (#35)
      University of Texas Library, HANLEY R734n (# 76)

1904   *The Poetical Works of Christina Georgina Rossetti, with Memoir and
Notes by William Michael Rossetti.* London: Macmillan, 1904.
      Louisiana State University Library, 828 R734pXr
      The editor's own copy

B. Tables of Contents from the English and American Editions

Goblin Market and Other Poems
(London: Macmillan, 1862, 1865)

The Prince's Progress and Other Poems
(London: Macmillan, 1866)

Poems
(Boston: Roberts Brothers, 1866, 1872)

Goblin Market, etc.

Goblin Market, The Prince's Progress, and Other
(London: Macmillan, 1875)
and *Poems, New and Enlarged Edition*
(London and New York: Macmillan, 1890)

Poems
(Boston: Roberts Brothers, 1876)

Indexes

INDEX OF TITLES

INDEX OF FIRST LINES